For the Love of
Dolls and Roses
A story of the author, her life, her successes and failures.

by Mildred Seeley

Vernon and I receiving an "in appreciation" award. I am wearing a 100-year-old gown.

Dedication

I would like to dedicate this book to

and the other doll collectors and dollmakers worldwide.
Each and every dollmaker and doll collector should put their
name above and know the book is for them personally.

This story has been written as I remember it. If others remember it
differently, blame it on my age. Then too, if there weren't some errors, there
would be nothing to talk about or criticize.

SCOTT PUBLICATIONS
30595 EIGHT MILE
LIVONIA, MI 48152-1798

Copyright ©1994
ISBN# 0-916809-75-7
Library of Congress# 94-65258
NO. 3532-1-94
PRINTED IN USA

The talents of many people are
needed to make a good book.
Since we believe that this book
surpasses being just good, we
want to acknowledge the staff at
Scott Publications who helped
fulfill our vision.

Editor: Anna Galli
Art Director: Connie Carley
Proofing: Annette Malis,
   Carmen Gurizzian, Sandy
   Williams, Lyn Sims
Typesetting: Mary Grayson
Publisher: Robert Keessen

Contents

Foreword

It was about ten years ago. One of those irritating instances had just happened again, and I was angry. A "competitor" had copied a piece of our advertising almost word for word. I happened to be speaking to Millie Seeley that same day, and I started grumbling about it. I was certain Millie would commiserate with me because wasn't that just the sort of thing that's always happened to her?

Instead, her words surprised me. "Florence," she said, "forget about it. You can sue them, but all you'll do is waste time and pour money into lawyers. Use that same energy and do something *new*. If you keep one step ahead of the pack, then all they're really doing is copying your old ideas—and meanwhile you've moved on!"

And that is Millie Seeley. A curious mixture of visionary and pragmatist. Bursting with new ideas and plans and programs—but with both feet firmly planted on the ground. It is, in fact, no coincidence that Millie loves her roses so much for she is a bit like them—firmly planted, beautifully bloomed, and fortified with just a bit of thorn if you do her wrong. Just ask the architect who didn't build her house! This sweet lady is nobody's fool.

Which is exactly why her autobiography is sure to be a page-turner. This first-ever account of one woman's adventures in the doll world is nostalgic but never sentimental. It's funny, wry, touching, kind and very wise.

Learning the "inside story" of doll collecting from Millie Seeley is no small treasure. This woman occupies a unique position in the world of doll collecting. Her collection of antique dolls is, arguably, one of the very finest in the world. For like all great art collectors, she has learned to select, then to "deselect," to build, then to eliminate, then to choose again, always upgrading, always improving.

A doll artist of consummate talent herself, she also has that oh-so-rare art of a natural teacher—imbuing her students with a sense of "can-do" as well as "what to do." An innovative organizer, she founded the Doll Artisan Guild; an accomplished writer, she has authored a number of very readable and purposeful books; an inveterate "sharer," she has started many, many would-be collectors on the path of successful doll knowledge. It is not an exaggeration to say that Millie Seeley has contributed in a very dramatic way to the rebirth of the entire doll movement in the late 20th century.

Finally, it is the way in which Millie Seeley lives with her dolls that is her great gift. She has built a home to house her dolls as well as herself. They surround her, they line her walls. But they are not static. This splendid house/museum is alive with space, with the shared enthusiasm of the hundreds of doll-lover friends who've come to visit. To watch Millie in her home is to know the best side of collecting—honest joy in the beauty of an object and absolute desire to share that joy and knowledge with all who come into range.

—*Florence Theriault*

Introduction

There was a sizable crowd around the table Scott Publications had set up for me to autograph books. I had just signed a book—"For the Love of Dolls, Mil"—the way I usually sign both letters and books.

All around me was a group of young ladies from Australia. One, original doll artist Rose-Mary Cheney, was on her knees by my chair! Everyone was laughing and Rose-Mary was saying, "You are the one, you did it for me. You got me involved in dollmaking." The girls were showing me Rose-Mary's original doll *Fawn*—one of her Flamboyant Fantasies—a winner among winners. One of the girls handed me a rose wrapped in plastic.

Vernon and I were at the 1991 world's largest doll show in Anaheim, California. I was there to autograph my newest book, my 19th, *Judging Dolls*. This was just one of the many conventions and shows Vernon and I have attended over the years since we started the hobby of dollmaking.

The gratitude, the well wishes, the hugs, the photographs—the hundreds of wonderful letters that I receive—are all my reward for having started

Fawn is an original porcelain doll by Australian doll artist Rosemary Cheney.

the dollmaking hobby. These happy people are like the roses in my garden, or a galaxy of sparkling stars. These are the happy people that hold my world together.

The making of dolls for the pure joy and love of dolls was what I had in mind when I envisioned sharing my know-how of dollmaking thru my books and molds. I really meant it to be just a simple thing that would make many people happy.

PART 1

The Beginning

My folks had my picture taken when I was
about three months old.

Mildred Dean
Van Valkenburgh Seeley

Sometimes the stage is set and awaits an actor or actress to bring the scene to life. Perhaps life is like that, at least mine was. Maybe some playwright turned my life into dolls and roses.

My mother Carrie Bell Van Valkenburgh lived on Rose Avenue in Oneonta, New York. Her best friend was Mildred Whitney whose father owned the Whitney Greenhouses. (At that time, roses were started from cuttings in the greenhouse where they were kept until their first bloom.)

It must have been that in the womb I smelled the roses, for if I had had a choice in the matter, I would have been born in the greenhouse. I tried. A carriage with horses whisked my mother off to the Oneonta Hospital, just a half-block away. I arrived March 27, 1918 about ten in the morning.

The next day mother and I were surrounded with roses from the first-in-bloom bushes. Mildred Whitney came with a gift for the new baby. The package contained Mildred's play doll, a Heubach Koppelsdorf.

Here I was on life's stage, set with roses and a doll. This doll was the nucleus of my collection. She sits in a rocking chair in our home today.

My mother, Carrie Bell Dean, and father, Albert Van Valkenburgh, had grown up in Masonville, New York. At this time they lived up the street from the greenhouse with my two older sisters, Dorothy and Phoebe. My father worked as an electrician for the city of Oneonta. He actually turned on the city's lights at dusk.

My big sister had already named me Rose, but mother made the decision on Mildred, for her friend, and her maiden name, Dean, for my middle name. To be the third in a family of girls is like a fairy godmother's wish come true. Mine was a pampered place with lots of care and attention. They even had my picture taken on a white bear skin. Up to this point in my life, I was told everything regarding my childhood. Beginning at age three, I remember.

My father was working as a farmhand for J.I. Roberts in East Merideth, New York. We lived in a little house down the road from the farm where he worked.

About this time, my memory buttons were pressed, pressed and impressed with unusual and unrelated things.

I remember the floor plan of the house—how you had to go thru mother and dad's room to get to the children's room.

Once I went with my mother to fill my mattress with clean straw. I was still sleeping in a crib.

Susy was my first doll. She was made from a sock. Mother had to repaint the eyes whenever she washed her.

My new red slippers were a special gift. I cried and wouldn't let anyone take them off when I went to bed. During the night, one came off and fell in the pot by the bed. I was devastated. Mother washed it, but it was felt and shrunk; it would never fit again.

My older sister Phoebe with her big doll marked "Special" made by Armand Marseille. My other sister Dorothy is being held by Mildred Whitney, who I was to be named for. I had not yet arrived.

My sisters wheeled me in this carriage.

At three, I was pudgy, happy and healthy. Note the galoshes or arctics with buckles.

I have never returned to the house, but I remember the screen door where larva crawled up part of the way and fell off. They were crawling everywhere. These were from a row of locust trees on the right side of the house. I loved the locust blossoms. I can still smell them.

The round wooden tub where water flowed continually in the back of the house was our water supply. There was an outside toilet that everyone used but me. I used a pot.

My father would walk home on the crosscut from the farm. I was allowed, with my mother watching from the house, to go meet him. He carried me back to the house on his shoulders. I remember once riding down to the edge of the creek where he picked blue flag (iris). These delighted my mother.

I remember my mother had sweet peas growing beside the house and geraniums on the stoop. I love the smell of sweet peas even today.

When my sister Dot, who was four years older than I, would see the doctor go up the road with his carriage and matched team of black horses, she would say, "I am going to marry a doctor or be a doctor. I want a carriage and horse just like his." She always played doctor. She attempted to give me a spoonful of ink, among other things. I was always her patient. Mother saw the ink spots on my dress. Boy, did Dot get it!

Maude Roberts, the girl next door, had a big wedding. My mother was the matron of honor. We kids were not allowed to attend. Phoebe was in charge. Mother strung a clothesline between two trees and put a sheet over it to make a tent. We played in this while she was gone. While playing, we heard this big humming. We saw bees flying and lighting above our heads. They were honey bees swarming—but we didn't realize the danger.

Mother was on her way down the path. She saw the bees and scooped us into the house. Someone came and cut off the whole branch with the swarm attached. We watched from inside the screen door. I have only seen bees swarm once since.

My father left the farm for a good paying job as a foreman of the Milking Machine Division of the Meridale Dairy Farms. This was a large dairy corporation with numerous barns, houses, offices, and homes for the employees.

At about this same time, father got an inheritance from his family. He bought a black Model T. When he bought the car, the salesman gave him a small red windup tin car which my father gave to me. I cherished the gift and kept it, finally entrusting it to my son Jay.

I remember riding in the car over the bumpy dirt road to Meridale to see our new house. On the way back, the car stalled on the railroad tracks.

It was cold and getting dark. Mother knew there was a train due. The expression of fear on my mother's and sisters' faces are still indelibly engraved in my mind. I could feel Mother's heart beating as she took me out of the car, wrapped me in the paisley shawl, and held me close.

We could hear the train in the far distance. A man appeared from nowhere and helped my father get the car off the tracks just in time. The train had long since passed when the men, after cranking and cranking, finally got it started.

Today, I think of this whenever I pass thru our hallway and see that same paisley shawl hanging on my wall. This was a gift that Grandfather Dean brought Grandmother from New York City for Christmas in 1899.

We moved into our new little house. We were a happy family.

Family

To present my family I hunted thru dust and rumor-filled closets in search of somebody to write a wild story about. I thought a pirate, one of the master Dutch painters, a multimillionaire, or a horse thief would make a good story. I found none of these.

By the time I was born, most of my relatives were dead. Then, too, I was never one to dote on relatives or times past. I was always looking to tomorrow or the day after. To look back was not exciting.

By hunting thru a few of the old pictures saved by my cousin Emma Carpenter (who was some 20 years older than I), I have pieced together my family. But I was unable to find a picture of my father.

Right: The Dean clan in front of the homestead which burned. My mother is on the right. That is probably my father next to her.

Grandmother Phoebe Ann Scott Dean at 17.

Great-Grandmother Matilda Carissa Hill Dean.

Great-Great Grandmother Abigail Gould Dean. (The name of the girl and her relationship is unknown.)

My mother, Carrie Bell Dean, Uncle Wesley Dean and Aunt Lottie Dean on August 27, 1904.

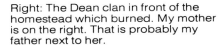

3

Left: Both Grandfather Milton Page Dean and (above) Grandmother Phoebe Ann Scott Dean died before I was born.

A distant cousin, John Rogers.

"Old pictures saved by Cousin Emma Carpenter"

Left: Great Uncle Reuben Dean was called Nubby.

Left: Grandfather Milton Page Dean at one year of age.

From left is Great-Uncle Tracy, Allis Scott and Great-Aunt Amelia Scott in front of a house I remember well. It still stands.

Charlotte Carpenter, 20 years older than my mother, was the first in a family of ten. She was my "Dear Aunt Lottie."

I first remember Aunt Lottie, or perhaps just Aunt Lottie's house, when I was four. My father had driven Mother, Phoebe, Dot and me to Oneonta from Meridale in our new Model T. My mother and her sister Charlotte were close. I suspect for my father, this visit was an ego trip to show off his new car to a member of my mother's family.

Aunt Lottie lived alone on Normal Avenue in Oneonta in her two-story yellow house that was pinched between two other houses. When she came out of the house, she was nearly covered with a full apron.

She carefully inspected the car, then took us all inside. Aunt Lottie was a generation older than my mother. Her three children, Dr. Charles Carpenter, Dr. Clifford Carpenter and Emily Carpenter were all grown. Her husband Tom had been killed long ago on the D & H railroad tracks where he worked. Aunt Lottie was making it on her own. Pensions and Social Security had not come into being.

Dear Aunt Lottie was a frail little thing, just a hair taller than my five-foot mother. Her soft white hair made wide waves up to the swirled knot almost directly on top of her head. Wispy curls of escaping locks came down in front of her ears. More of these curls softened her forehead. Her eyes were green, a beautiful color

that had gone with her once-red hair. Her face, neck and hands were etched with deep wrinkles, echoing the hard work and the stress of educating three children.

She was that soft lovable grandma type that any child would want to hug. She was the nearest thing I ever had to a grandma.

Aunt Lottie had a passion for antiques and a love of bargaining. She collected antique furniture, dishes and almost anything she could make a nickel on. A small sign by her front doorbell read "Antiques."

Dishes were piled on top of dishes, under the table, on the chairs, and up one side of the stairs that went to the second floor. There was no place to sit, but there was a narrow path thru and around the piled high furniture.

Aunt Lottie loved to bargain, loved to sell. My mother often said she could tell when things were going Lottie's way, because a good bargain was always accompanied by a soft whistle.

I started to tell you about the visit. I had barely gotten in the front door when I desperately needed to make a call. My sister Dot took me by the hand and carefully guided me up the carpeted stairs, being careful that I didn't touch or knock anything.

The fairly large room at the top of the stairs was something entirely unfamiliar to me. "This is just like a pot, only fancy. Sit here," she said pointing to the wood-colored seat. A large white bathtub was on the side of the room. It stood on four lion's feet. A white pedestal

Aunt Charlotte (Lottie) Carpenter, at 17, was the mother of Clifford, Charles and Emily. Aunt Lottie taught school in Walton.

Cousin Clifford Carpenter, M.D., went into veterinarian medicine. He developed the rock cornish game hen for big-time food production.

Cousin Charles Carpenter, M.D., spent years studying venereal diseases and their cures. He worked on the sterilization of the moon shot. He died of a heart attack following a lecture.

5

Cousin Emily (Emma) Carpenter looked after her two younger brothers and bailed them out when necessary. She had infantile paralysis at 19 and had to use crutches, braces and a wheelchair.

Dear Aunt Lottie holding a grand nephew.

Me, Phoebe and Dorothy. My older sisters had red hair. Mother made all our dresses.

held the wash basin. My sister explained the use of each bathroom device as she washed my hands, putting a little plug that hung by a chain into the hole in the basin's bottom.

Then she showed me the wood-colored box that was ceiling-high above the toilet. From this came pipes and a chain with a wooden handle. Dot said, "We pull on this chain and water comes down to clean the toilet." At this moment, she pulled and water came rushing and there was a big gurgle. The water kept rushing down, it didn't stop. Dot couldn't get it to stop. I was scared that water was going to run all over. I was scared we had broken the thing.

Dot ran down and got Aunt Lottie who said that she had been having some trouble with it. She stopped the water in a minute.

As I visited Aunt Lottie for the next 30 years, I never went into that bathroom without thinking of my first experience. She never changed the fixtures, nor did she ever change the piles of antique dishes. If one were sold, two more took its place.

Years later when I was in college just down the street, I would run in for a few minutes to see Aunt Lottie. She had a little girl giggle that sprinkled my day with sunshine. She was always giving me something—an antique spoon or dish. One of my favorite things that she gave me was a ceramic water pitcher with Dutch figures in relief on it. I loved it.

I used it thru the years for lemonade. I use it even today. My son Jay looks at it and immediately thinks lemonade. I must give it to him.

Moving

We attended the Baptist church in Meridale where the enthusiastic congregation sang loud and with spirit. My mother taught me to sing Baptist hymns, of course. She played the piano with Baptist gusto. Once at church I watched with horror as adults and children were dunked into the reservoir of water to be baptized.

I still didn't have a regular bed. The sides had been taken off the crib to make me a little bed. Mother and Dad went to Oneonta to buy me a bed for my fourth birthday. Phoebe was left in charge. When it began to get dark, Phoebe tried to light the lamp. The flames ran up and caught the hand towel hanging above. Dot began to yell. Phoebe said, "Open the door." She grabbed the towel and threw it into the snow. When Mother and Dad came home, the towel was still smoldering. They were so proud of Phoebe and her quick action. She had probably saved our lives.

The first Christmas I remember was when I was four years old in this same house. On Christmas Eve we were taken into the parlor. The whole room had been magically transformed. A big hemlock tree stood sparkling with ornaments and tinsel. As we stood awed by its beauty, father lit and placed real candles all over the tree. The twinkling lights made dancing shadows. For a moment it was fairyland.

I was suddenly aware of my mother's fear of fire. The candles were only lighted a minute or so when father lifted me up to blow out the upper ones, and my sisters blew out the lower ones. Mother breathed a sigh of relief.

Mother brought in the candle-covered Christmas cake, served us all a piece, and we went to bed. The Christmas cake, an angel food cake, was a tradition in Mother's family. She said it was the birthday cake of the Christ Child. I followed in my mother's footsteps and make a Christmas cake for Christmas Eve. My children also keep the tradition alive.

Not all of life can be roses, or rose-laced reminiscences. Within two weeks after Christmas, my father was seriously ill with pneumonia and died. For the family and my mother, the world fell apart. I only remember the casket in the spot where the Christmas tree once stood.

There was no money. My mother was not prepared to support three girls. I came down with a terrible cough, and she was sure I was dying of pneumonia too. I had caught whooping cough.

Mother was up all night with me coughing and vomiting. It went on for six weeks. I was nothing but bones. My mother got a job cooking for Mr. Dutton, the manager of the Meridale Farms. His home and office was just across the road.

Mr. Dutton gave me two of his childhood toys, a wooden stick with two little wheels and a dingle bell inside, and a pull toy with two small ducks in front and a big one behind, all flapping their wings and squawking.

Things got worse. Mother let the car go back to the dealer when she found it was only partially paid for. She couldn't make the payments on the house. Phoebe at 14 went to work at Merideth Inn setting tables and making beds. We had to move. Mother put her furniture in storage in Otego and took a job in New Kingston working for Elmer Faulkner. He had the house and farm next to the store. He was no relation to M.J. Faulkner who owned the store.

I made friends with M.J. I walked with him to and from the store at noon. He often brought a little sack of candy which I was to share with Mother and my sister. I made friends with Jeanne whose parents rented the house next door.

When Jeanne didn't like what was happening, she bit people, including her mother. One day, M.J. was drawing Jeanne and me in a cart to the store, and Jeanne decided she didn't like the back seat.

She bit me on the upper arm until it bled. For days I would have nothing to do with her. She would come to the door and say, "I want to play. I won't bite Mildrum any more."

After we were settled in, my mother found out what a mean and demanding man she had come to work for. Also, she found out he was sick; he had tuberculosis, and Mother didn't want her children exposed to this.

She started looking for a better place for us. M.J. Faulkner found Mother a place to work after nearly a year.

We moved to a farm four miles from Lake Delaware. It belonged to Frank Graham. We lived in a large new house that had not yet been painted. Mr. Graham had never been married, and he had built the house for his mother. She died before it was finished.

The house had electricity, a bathroom and frescoed walls. There was a beautiful wood stairway that came down from the bedroom we used. There was a tiny back stairway that led to the hired hand's room. There was no connection from that room and the rest of the upstairs.

There was a rose garden of old sweet-smelling-moss roses in the front of the house. The garden had been Mr. Graham's mother's. My mother and I loved the garden and the house. I liked the big barn and dairy cows. I liked the screech owl that lived in the barn.

It came time for me to go to school. The one-room school was about two miles away across the lots and woodlands. Mr. Graham walked us the first day until we could see the school. We walked back the same way. My sister would yell at me when I dragged behind. She told my mother she wasn't going to take me. It got harder and harder for me to walk the distance as it grew colder and the snow came. Mother took me out of school when I developed a cough.

Mother and me. She had wavy auburn hair. I got plain, brownish, straight hair.

Me and Touser in front of the barn in Mill Creek.

Things change. Here I am a bedraggled child of 6 or so. Note the high-topped lace-up shoes.

Mother made our clothes. We wore long underwear that had legs that went down under our long brown stockings. Our underwear had a trapdoor with three buttons on the back. Over this, we wore a garter waist with long pieces of elastic going down to hook our stockings on. Over this bottom part we wore bloomers. These were puffy things made to match or go with our dresses. They had elastic in the waist and in the legs. We wore wool slips and wool dresses. We were still cold. I went back to school in the spring after the eclipse of the sun which we looked at thru smoked glass. The rooster crowed.

Mr. Graham had a hound puppy that came in the house. Everyone had a big button jar to replace lost buttons. I played with the buttons, making necklaces and bracelets. I found that if I tossed the puppy a button, he could catch it. I had fun throwing him buttons which he swallowed. In the days that followed Mr. Graham found buttons in the yard. Boy, did I get it!

I forgot to tell you about Christmas in this new house. It's not that I remember much except the dolls. Aunt Lillian in Staten Island sent Dot and I each a bisque Armand Marseille walking doll. Colleen, my daughter, owns the Armand Marseille now.

One had brown hair and one had bright red hair like my sister Dot. The redhead was for Dot, but my mother knew Dot would hate the doll as she did her own red hair. She switched dolls, and I got the redheaded one. I didn't like the red hair that much either. I don't remember how or when my mother got the wig changed. At the same Christmas there was a big party at the Lake Delaware Church. I played the messenger boy in the church pageant. Anna Grace was supposed to play it, but her folks wouldn't let her play a boy. I really wanted to be an angel.

After the pageant, all the girls were given dolls. These were fat mama dolls with composition heads. Dot hated hers, she was too big for this kind of doll. They were dressed in pink and blue rompers and had bonnets over their painted hair. I ended up playing with both dolls.

My mother liked working for Mr. Graham in the new house, but it was short lived. Graham's sister's husband died and she had no place to go, and no money. My mother was replaced by the sister. Mother had to find a new place. Jobs of this type were scarce and paid very poorly. Mother took the only thing available.

This time it was back to a home with oil lamps, pots, a watering trough and an outhouse. Mother went to the barn to help milk the cows. Her new boss, a widower named Mr. Jack, had one child. Her name was Alice and she was the same age as I. Mother worked hard. She had to heat water on the stove to do laundry or dishes. We took baths in a metal tub in the kitchen.

We washed our hair in an earthenware wash bowl. Alice was spoiled and had to have her own way about everything. I never saw her after we left the farm. This farm was in Mill Creek, a side road out of Otego, New York.

We girls were all allowed to choose a kitten at the Miller farm down the road. Mine turned into a big tiger cat that I loved dearly and took with me when we moved.

We walked to a one-room school with eight grades. Dot was in the seventh grade and wanted to pass her Regents. This was the first time I had attended school regularly.

It seems when we are young, we measure time by Christmases. That was the Christmas I had eczema all over my arms, legs and neck. I was already timid, but this made me not want to see anybody. My mother made me special clothes with silk sleeves under my heavy dresses, both to cover up and keep from irritating my sore arms. Mother finally got enough money to take me to the doctor. He gave her a black tarry salve which did no good, and only made me look worse.

All three of us girls got doll carriages and dolls for Christmas. Jay now has my doll from that Christmas. The little blue carriage is in my living room.

Spring came. I had never heard whip-poor-wills before. The woods up the hillside were filled with pink lady slippers. The creek was lined with yellow cowslips and then the delicate blue of forget-me-nots. I was born to love spring, flowers, birds—all of nature. We went down to the creek often. One evening at supper I was telling everyone what I had seen. I saw a frog sitting on and squeezing another frog until her innards

My little blue doll carriage and the doll I received when I was born.

Pink Lady Slippers grew in abundance in the woods behind the farm in Mill Creek.

Me, at 7, and Tiger Tim on the steps of the old farmhouse in Mill Creek. I'm wearing black patent leather Mary Janes, my church shoes. Note the garters holding up my socks.

Here I am with Touser again. I'm still wearing long brown stockings, but I have sandals now.

were coming out the back. My mother tried to change the conversation. But I was feeling so sorry for the pinched frog, I kept talking.

I got a new khaki suit (my first store-bought clothes). This was what little girls played in. It was a blouse with a wide back collar and a V-neck. The bloomer bottoms had bands around the legs. I got a new pair of black Mary Jane patent leather shoes for church.

We rode to church in the two seated surrey (yes, with fringe). We went to West Oneonta. We only went when my mother could persuade Mr. Jack to take us. My mother was quite capable of driving a team, but he wouldn't let her. We drove the surrey all the way to Oneonta to shop once in a while.

Mr. Jack was an ill-tempered man with heart problems. He didn't like to pay my mother, but he would buy something for all three of us girls. My mother again felt she should find a more stable place for us.

Phoebe was now working for the Dunns of Oneonta. She worked for her room and board throughout high school and Oneonta State Normal School, a local college. She cooked, cleaned, and took care of the Dunn's son, John.

Phoebe found a place for my mother to work in Oneonta on Morgan Avenue. My tiger cat went with me when we moved. There were two girls in this family with no mother. Mother took care of all of us for the summer. It was a new kind of life for me.

New Kingston, N.Y.
Sunday Morning

Dear Carrie Bell,
As you know Sarah died of cancer almost a year ago. I have made do with local women help which has, in no way, been satisfactory. I need some one who can take over my home, the cooking and the cleaning.
I have tried in numerous occasions in the last month to locate you. Finally I remembered your sister Charlotte and telephoned her. She was kind enough to give me your present address.
As for your children, I understand Phoebe is attending Normal School. Your two younger children will be welcome in my home. You may remember I was very fond of Mildred when you worked in New Kingston before.
I remember you as a hard working and very pleasant lady, just what I would like in my home as a house keeper.
I will be making a trip to Oneonta this comming Thursday. I will stop to see you. Hope you will have an affirmative answer for me.
Yours truly
M. J. Faulkner

This is the letter that would change my life.

I learned to roller skate on the sidewalk. We hunted pieces of flint and arrowheads which we used as "money" to buy books and toys from each other. My eczema disappeared. I loved school with only one grade per classroom. I found I could run faster and jump farther than anyone in my grade. I could go hand over hand the length of the bars.

Dot was now ready for high school. Mother got her a place to work for her room and board with the Shermans. She took care of their two children.

It was obvious to me that my mother was not happy. I slept with her because there was no place else to sleep. She cried at night.

The Letter

One day M.J. Faulkner from New Kingston sent the following letter.

My mother worked a few more weeks and then M.J. came for us. This arrangement was apparently heaven sent. My mother had been thru enough. She loved New Kingston and the house we lived in.

In two years, M.J. and she were married. M.J. told me he had always wanted a little girl. He became Dad, a wonderful Dad. Now Dad, the store, and my little friend Jeanne who now lived above the parsonage, took over my life.

The Skimmelton

Dad told it this way:

"You _____ fools get the _____ out of here," Dr. Holcomb shouted from the railing of the upper veranda. He was standing barefoot in a below-the-knee white nightshirt. "We want to get some sleep." He banged the door and disappeared in the darkness. The merriment from the noise-makers went on.

No one had explained to the doctor, a newcomer to the Catskill Mountains, that it was an honor to be welcomed home after your honeymoon by a rousing friendly skimmelton. After another blood curdling session of screeching, howling and horn blowing, they all went home.

My new stepbrother, Curtis, Tiger Tim and me.

Mother and Dad on their wedding day November 24, 1928. Right: Note that Phoebe and Lyman signed as witnesses on the marriage certificate.

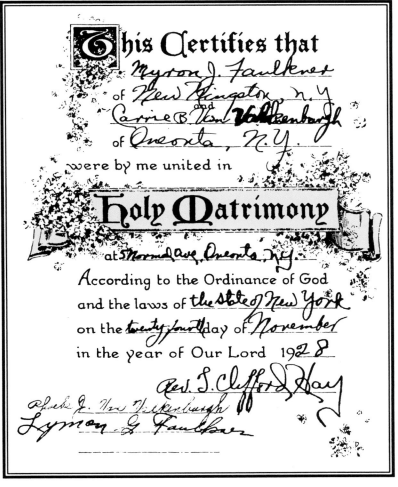

This Certifies that
Myron J. Faulkner
of *New Kingston, N.Y*
and *Carrie B. Van Valkenburgh*
of *Oneonta, N.Y.*
were by me united in

Holy Matrimony

at *Normal Ave, Oneonta, N.Y.*
According to the Ordinance of God
and the laws of *the State of New York*
on the *twenty fourth* day of *November*
in the year of Our Lord 19*28*

Rev. S. Clifford Hay

Phoebe J. Van Valkenburgh
Lyman L. Faulkner

The Minister's Welcome

After two weeks of ministering in our little church, the young preacher went back to Ohio and returned married. He and his wife were temporarily to live in Uncle John's house, two doors up from us. The young people of the village and hollers quickly planned a welcome skimelton for the couple on their first night in New Kingston. The noise began about midnight.

Dad heard a knock on the back door. There was the preacher and his bride in their night clothes wrapped in blankets, white with fright.

"Gabriel is coming—is coming," the preacher was finally able to blurt out. They had sneaked out of their back door and come across the backyard to our house.

Mother & Dad's Skimmelton

My stepfather and mother were on their honeymoon in New York City. I was left with the house and a nice old Mrs. Ingles to care for us both. I found cartons of fat Hershey bars and wood boxes of White Owl cigars piled in the hallway. I asked her why they were there. "It is customary to pass out candy and cigars at a skimelton," she said.

Mother and my new Dad came into Margaretville by train about 9 p.m. Lyman, my new stepbrother, went to Martgaretville to meet them. A mile below the village he was stopped, and Mother and Dad were taken out and put in a carriage and driven the rest of the way home with music and noise.

I heard the noise before they arrived. Mrs. Ingles explained what was happening so I wouldn't be scared. The noise making began in earnest as Mother and Dad came into the house. The house was opened, people swarmed in.

They brought sandwiches, cakes and a milk can of sweet cider. We used every cup, every plate in the house. Everyone ate his fill. They passed out candy and cigars. I had never seen so many people in our house and on both porches. In the corners, on the dining room table, in the kitchen, on every surface—these wonderful farmers and villagers had left gifts—an antique plate, a pair of hand-knit mittens, a bushel of apples, two Mother Hubbard aprons, a doily, jars of fruit and jam, a bowl of headcheese, and on and on. All the gifts were products of their farms, or things they had loved or hoarded. This was my first and only experience with a skimmelton.

One large milk glass plate stands in my china cabinet today, a special gift to Mother at that skimmelton. This is an extra large plate, and Colleen will love having it to put special cakes on.

PART

The Country Store and New Kingston

The country store, M.J. Faulkner Company, New Kingston, New York, from left to right (1st window) is the Post Office, (3rd window) the candy counter and the string of bananas, (4th window) the feed room, (5th window) a drum of cod liver oil and a drum of car oil.

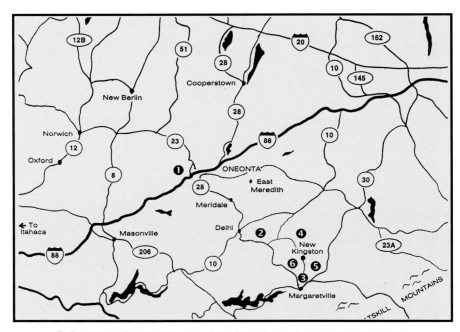

SOUTH CENTRAL SECTION OF N.Y. STATE

Oxford — taught 4th grade

To Ithaca — taught 5th & 6th grade

Masonville — mother's birthplace and home

East Meredith — very early childhood here

Meridale — father died here

New Kingston — village home and Faulkner store

Margaretville — attended 8th grade and high school here

Oneonta — born here, went to college here and raised our children here

1. Jack Farm

2. Graham Farm

3. Dunraven — my first job

4. Our Winter Hollow Farm

5. Johnny Cake Lane

6. Winter Hollow

The Country Store

The store was like a patch of brilliant primroses in the center of a soft pastel watercolor. The store was like a short story edited with a focus on the entire village. The store was like a bright, directed light sending a beguiling interplay of light and shadow over my life for many years.

The store was a major part of my formative years. I worked there, played there, and was given love there. The store, like our home, was a part of every day. My life, merry-go-round style, circled around it. Most of the time music played.

The town's activities revolved around it—the whole valley of scattered farms revolved around it. It was the focal point of everyone's life.

I will relate how the store influenced my simple upbringing. Perhaps it was the key to my contented, happy adult life.

The store, a beige clapboard covered box with a peak, stood close to the road in the middle of a huddle of assorted modest gingerbread Victorian homes in the hamlet of New Kingston, New York.

From under the extended peak, like a hangman's rope, came a large hook. There was an opening at the peak where the hook and rope went over a large wheel. The set-up was for hoisting heavy things like oyster shells (used for feeding chickens in order to harden their eggshells), blocks of dairy salt (which the dairy cows craved), and items that came packed in large wooden boxes, such as pick axes, crow bars and shovels. It was fun to see things go twirling up high into the air and then be hauled in at the opening. We were always warned to stay well away should any of these things fall. Other times, a team of horses with a wooden wagon would drive up under the hanging hook, and bags of whatever would be lowered into the wagon bottom along with feed for cows, chickens, horses or pigs from the other parts of the store.

As you pushed thru the self-closing door on the store front, there on the left was a post office with 32 little boxes and two drawers. Protruding from the little boxes were all the keys (no one ever took them out). The two drawers were meant for people whose mail was too cumbersome to be stuffed into the little square box. I remember Andrew Van Benscoten had a drawer; the other drawer remained empty as long as I can remember.

In the center of the mail boxes was the little grilled window with a shelf. Under the shelf was a wooden drawer with change for people buying stamps. On the right of the boxes and high on the wall was a clock that ticked softly, told the day of the week, the month, and the moon's phases.

It was a wonderful old thing with gold on its glass and a large pendulum. I watched Dad wind the clock each Sunday morning before breakfast. He put the key in one hole, then another, and turned it just the right amount, never over-winding the clock.

The post office counter was

My friend Jeanne Robertson (Palen) and I (right) starting 8th grade. This was when taking school pictures began.

battered due to the years of bearing heavy canvas bags with ropes and locks on the top, heavy boxes, metal egg crates and maple syrup cans.

The post office corner was a tiny corner of my childhood. I helped to sort mail, pushed post office rent receipts into each box as reminders to pay the 25 cent mailbox rent. I tied up bundles of letters, weighed packages and at a very early age, had to figure postage.

The Sunday paper, *The Herald Tribune*, came on Saturday. I put the sections together. There were only four copies—two were for customers and Dad's copy. One went to a former New York senator, George Owens, who lived on the righthand end of the village going north. The other went to Andrew Van Benscoten, a Cornell graduate, chicken and dairy farmer. The extra copy we hoped to sell.

When I was in high school, there were two copies of the *Daily News* that came into the post office. My friend Jeanne

and I used to sneak this out of a box and read Dick Tracy and sometimes follow the scandals.

I read all the postcards as I stuffed them into the boxes. There were numerous rubber stamps in the drawer below the desk, that read "Fragile," "Special Delivery," "Eggs," "Rush" and so on. My older sister Dot had a letter going out to her boyfriend. Jeanne and I decided to fix the letter. We got out the stamps and stamped, "Eggs" and "Fragile" in red on both sides. I put the letter in the middle of the bundle to go out.

Weeks later Dad got a letter reprimanding him for using special stamps where not necessary. It didn't take Dad long to figure out how it could have happened. Having a sense of humor, he just said we should not do it again, even on love letters.

I liked the smell of the ink and enjoyed sitting on the wooden stool behind the post office. The store itself smelled differently in each of its areas. The close-together shelves behind Dad's desk formed the drugstore with Lydia Pinkham's Little Liver Pills, castor oil, quinine, Castoria, epsom salts, adhesive tape, cotton, Vaseline, clover salve, Vicks Vapor Rub, Musterole, peroxide, peppermint, and other large and small tubes, bottles and tins. These were so near Dad's little office corner that the area had a medicinal smell. I liked the smell. I thought of it as clean or perhaps it was the peppermint that reminded me of candy. It was in this corner that Dad, sitting in his swivel office chair with his battered old adding machine on one side and his typewriter on the other, solved all my childhood problems and granted all my wishes as I grew up.

I would sit on Dad's lap and eat a chocolate candy taken from his stash and tell him what I wanted. As I grew older, I pulled a chair to his desk and we had a talk. Even after I came home from college, the office corner was the place I discussed my finances and sometimes my boyfriends.

Most of all, I remember Dad telling me how proud he was of me if I'd painted a picture, made a basket during a game, gotten a first prize for my 4-H muffins, or written a story that I received a bad grade on (because I couldn't spell). The squeaking of Dad's swivel chair, the one long and four short rings on the telephone's party line, and the smell of peppermint were the smells and sounds of the office corner.

To get from the post office to the office corner, one must pass thru the dry goods section where the counter was smooth and polished from having nothing on it but fabric, lace, bindings, thread and elastic. But sometimes Dad needed this flat surface to cut a piece of glass for a window pane. Other times, someone needed a pair of rubber boots, arctics, rubbers, work shoes, red or blue printed men's handkerchiefs or Oshkosh overalls. These went over the counter, too. Along the back edge of the counter was a measuring device for fabrics that Uncle John had inlaid.

I liked this department. Under the counter was a big Butler Bros. Catalog. I was allowed to fold down pages—my wish list. Behind the counter were shelves with printed and plain cotton, and sometimes a bolt of something finer that my mother had ordered. With discretion I was allowed to take pieces from the cotton bolts to dress dolls or teddy bears while I was watching the store. Jeanne was allowed equal amounts.

We made flare skirts by cutting circles and putting a hole in the center for teddy bears. As I got older, I was allowed to help myself to fabrics to sew 4-H projects for as much as I could treadle on the old Singer. Jeanne sewed on mother's machine too. This was an in-between part of my life that lasted from seven to 17.

It led to dressing dolls, to 4-H prizes for my sewing, to my bedroom where I made curtains and covered cushions, to helping my mother design hooked rugs to match fabrics.

Parts of this department are still in my life today. There are three spool cabinets that read "Clark's O.N.T. Spool Cotton" in my study and living room, and Dad's needle cabinet sits in my kitchen.

Over the cellar door were three high shelves where medicines for horses and cows were kept. Below these were heavy snaps with rings, hanging halters, boxes of fancy buttons for the side of horse halters, other bits of harness repair parts. The smell of new leather made me think of horses. A horse was always on my wish list. On the end of these shelves the lamp chimneys stood in a row—by size—coated with dust. Next stood the kerosene lanterns, coated by dust too.

In the back corner, there was a special kerosene pump that was supplied by a tank in the store's cellar that was filled from a pipe that went outside. The pump consisted of a small stem that came up thru the floor with a smooth round wooden cross-bar handle. A pipe came thru the floor with a turned down spout. Under the spout was a circle of tin with a wire over it to keep the kerosene from splashing. Any leakage or overflow from the pump went back down to the cellar tank.

I learned to prime the pump and fill the customers' kerosene cans without too much spillage. The whole corner smelled like kerosene. The only place to wash was in the little sink with a pail of water brought from the house each morning. The water was cold. The FelsNaptha soap smelled worse than the kerosene on my hands. I liked this pump that Uncle John had built to fill the kerosene cans without having to leave the main part of the store. Since we seldom had more than one storekeeper, this system worked very well.

I remember when electricity was brought to the village and the kerosene pump was idle, except for people who had no electricity or used it to start their kitchen stove fires in the morning.

Most of all, I remember the pile of electrical poles that were heaped beside the dirt road just below the one-room school. We had electricity for a long time in our house and store by using our own little Delco generator in the store cellar, so the coming of electricity meant little change in my life.

Back to the pile of poles. We never swam, because there was no place deep enough to swim. But the creek was clean and sparkling, and we enjoyed putting stones and sod in it to make it deeper. I had the idea if we could get one of those poles across the creek, it would be heavy enough to hold enough boards, sod and rocks to make a spot deep enough for swimming.

All the summer-visiting boys and girls, the Owens kids, Jeanne and I rolled the top pole off the pile. We then rolled and coaxed the pole inch by inch to the creek. It took us days be-fore we got it moved across the stream. It worked. It was the first time I had been in water up to my waist.

We had several weeks of fun. Then Dad called me into his office corner. It didn't smell like peppermint or chocolate, more like the castor oil on the shelf. He said he couldn't be-lieve that we kids could move one of those big poles, but he had gone up and looked for himself. Not only did he see the pole, but he was sure I was the planner.

The electric company had been in to see him. They were only reporting a pole missing. They hadn't observed the trail leading to the swimming hole. Dad said I had really stolen the pole from the electric com-pany! I really hadn't thought of it that way and wondered if I should try to put it back.

He, always coming to my rescue, said he had paid for the pole and it was mine now, but that I should never do anything like that again. The castor oil smell went away with a nice diamond-shaped chocolate-covered maple candy.

Back to the store. Across from the horse harness and cellar door was the register that opened from the furnace in the cellar. The furnace burned both wood and coal. Near the regis-ter stood the cookie rack. I liked the cookie rack. I could smell the chocolate of the Oreos, and the sweetness of Fig Newtons, Ginger Snaps and Nabiscos. We usually carried six kinds, all set in their square boxes with glass covers on top to entice customers, or more often, the men sitting around the furnace register telling stories.

Around the corner, a wheel of cheese sat on a paper-covered board with a wooden cheese box over it. There were always bits of cheese, the big cheese knife on the counter, and the smell of cheese. An open brown square box of soda crackers was nearby. My Dad was always giving out samples of cheese with a cracker. I'm sure he used the sample for bait, because one taste of that cheese, and every-one had to have a pound or two. Dad could cut a wedge of cheese almost to the exact ounce the customer wanted. I learned to cut cheese, but told the customer that I could only come within a quarter of a pound of the desired amount. The cheese cutting always made me hungry.

The coffee grinder on the other side with its huge wheel was always a temptation to give it a few turns. Coffee from the last grinding sent up the won-derful aroma of freshly ground coffee.

Nearly all the groceries and money passed over a case filled with cigars. The case had ten cigar boxes when full. Also in-side, there was a little glass with a wet sponge in it to keep the cigars just right. White Owls, Dutch Masters and Premiums had little gold and red bands that I hoped the buyer of the cigars would give to me.

I also loved the cigar boxes, even with their strong odor, to put my rock collection in and my wished-for butterfly

Miniature 1895 child's toy store stands in my kitchen as a reminder.

collection that never happened. Behind the cigar case were the Camel and Lucky Strike cigarettes. There, too, was the chewing tobacco which had to be taken to the ugly, sticky cutter in the cellar-way to be cut into chunks for ten cents per cud. I remember disgusting men sitting on the store porch in the summer evenings —chewing and spitting. I never liked the smell of tobacco.

My favorite spot was the candy counter. I always felt I owned this all by myself. I shined the glass and washed the glass candy dishes. These were oblong and fitted five across the front and five across the back. I ate candy and filled the dishes. Each were one cent. There were chocolate drops that came in a wooden tub; chocolate-covered

diamonds with maple cream; caramels; Tootsie Rolls that came wrapped; round chocolate mints, both pink- and green-filled; Butter Fingers; horrible shoestring licorices; tiny jelly beans or red cinnamon candies that you got a little glass scoop of for a penny; assorted colored gumdrops; and always the lollipops.

My candy counter—there was nothing like it. I filled it, cleaned it, I smelled it, I ate it. As I got a little older, I made fudge of several kinds and sold it in the counter. This was some of my first earned money as all the money was for me. No one was concerned that the sugar, cocoa, butter and other ingredients came from the store. Dad, Uncle John, and all the men who came into the store could

hardly wait for me to make another batch. Can you believe I was a skinny kid?!

"Don't eat the black ones," Dad said as he rounded the counter where I was refilling the gumdrop dish in the candy counter. "Why not?" I asked. Someday I will take you to Oswego, New York, where the candy company is located and let you see for yourself. Look on the boxes and on that big tub of Oxheart chocolates, and you will see they are made in Oswego.

"Now the candies like all those bright colored gumdrops are molded and lined up on big turning belts where they are dried and sugared. Often the belts get stuck and gumdrops get squashed and gummed up in the rollers. The machines are stopped, and the men scrape the belts and rollers. The scraped-off gooey mess is dropped back into the boiling pots. Black coloring and anise flavoring are added. This is the only color and flavor that will cover all the other colors and flavors. "Aik," I yelled. "I won't eat any black ones ever."

You could not get around the counter without passing the string of bananas that hung in the window. The string—half gone, full, or with only a few stragglers at the top—was always there, and with it, the smell of over-ripe bananas, and the awful banana knife. The banana knife had a special hook on the end of the blade with a very sharp place at the curve.

It was supposed to reach up into the stem and easily cut down four or five bananas.

Twice it got me. I hated the smell of over-ripe bananas and the banana knife.

There was the usual kaleidoscope of canned vegetables, canned fruits, baking powder, corn flakes, cornstarch, tapioca, Old Dutch Cleanser, Bon Ami, soap, and bluing. Flour, salt and sugar came in cloth bags. Stock on the shelves had to be moved and filled. I was supposed to see the need and either fill the shelves, or pull what there was out to fill the shelf.

I started out as a helper, getting butter from the unheated feed room, soap, oatmeal, or a box to put the groceries in.

About nine every morning, except Sundays, the wagons and the trucks stopped at the store on their way to the creamery to deliver their milk. They stopped with their grocery lists. We packed the groceries while the farmer delivered his cans of milk to the creamery just down the unpaved street.

We packed the groceries, listed them, and put the slip in the big charge file. Along with any big box of groceries, Dad had me pack a little sack with candy—a lollipop for each child and some chocolates for the adults. Along with groceries, lamp chimneys or drugs, the list might call for nails, staples or a length of rope.

The rope came down from the attic and thru a hole near the cubby holes for each bristly nail keg. The rope came on huge spools and these were rigged by Uncle John on a bar so they unwound as you pulled

from below. There were three holes for the three sizes of rope.

One size was large enough to tie up a dog, the second for general use, such as making a rope halter for a calf, the other was large enough to hold a rearing horse. The rope ends laid coiled in the bottom of their narrow stalls like rattlers in various sizes ready to strike at a passerby. Jeanne and I used to be very careful, especially when we tied our imaginary horses to the kerosene pump.

I hated to weigh out nails. I hated the kegs infested with vicious slivers and the black stuff that got all over my hands. The prices were on a little chart above the kegs. Ten penny nails took just ten to the pound. Fencing staples had razor sharp points. I never had to get these from the keg unless I was alone in the store. Without gloves I could end up bleeding.

The feed room, which opened with a metal latch over a metal nick fastened to the door frame, had two windows. The large double doors opened on the store porch where the boards were splintery from contact with the feed handtruck.

There were 100 pound bags of feed for chickens, cows and horses piled in rows. There was bran, cotton seed meal, scratch grain, oats, ground corn, and about ten others, including a special egg mash. This was a special Cornell formula that Andrew Van Benscoten and Dad made in the old creamery butter churn.

It contained cod liver oil

which had to be mixed with a small amount of meal so that it would mix evenly with the whole 20 bag batch. I can still smell the cod liver oil, and I wanted no part of the hand mixing. The other feed in the feed room had an aroma almost as sweet as a cake baking. This was the scent that followed me. As I grew older and returned from being away, just opening the feed room door gave me a happy feeling. I can still smell that sweet odor after 60 years.

The sweet odor of ground grains was not just in the feed room. When Jeanne and I were little we went to her grandfather's farm—a nice dairy farm on the left, just before you entered the village. On the farm we helped to feed the cows, each got her measure of grain before milking time. Then Dad bought a farm a mile above the village—300 acres of hillside named "Winter Hollow."

We went to the farm each day. I sometimes fed the cows, but usually I took care of the team of horses. Then my wish for a horse, my secret birthday candle wish, my wish on the first evening star, the wish I shared with Jeanne came true. My Dad bought me a horse, a white dappled horse with the gentlest nature a four-legged creature was ever endowed with. I rode both bareback and with a saddle.

The summer I was a junior and senior in high school my Dad gave me the job of taking care of a tiny railroad station and his feed business in Dunraven. I was capable of billing the cauliflower that was to be

Dad and Mother were a happy pair.
Above right: Winter Hollow Farm—our
farm—where I kept my horse.

Me, Dad and Aunt Lottie.
Left: Dot, me and Phoebe on a
trip to Niagara Falls.

A view of the village of New Kingston.

Me, my flapper hat and my first camera.

shipped on the train. I kept track of the feed bills, answered the phone and waited on feed customers.

The smell of grain and molasses was with me for two wonderful summers. My German Shepherd dog went with me on a daily basis. I moved my cat and her two kittens into the feed building. For several weeks during the summer I even had my horse stabled in an outside shed.

This was my first salaried job. I worked hard, kept Dad's books, and in my spare time, wrote poetry and short stories, cleaned and polished my horse. I was paid $50 per month. At the end of the first month, I told my Dad I needed and wanted a watch. Would it be all right if I bought one? He said, "I'll buy you a watch. Put your money in the bank for college." He did order me a fine watch which lasted far into my adult life.

The store's porch was held up by four fat posts. Half of the front of the porch had steps as did both ends of the porch. The other half was in front of the feed room where wagons and trucks were loaded. On the right of the door was a blackboard, not a slate, just boards painted black. On this, notices of all kinds were written—the times for funeral services, prayer meetings, and special things for sale inside the store.

One of the main things Dad used it for was to get his loaned-out tools and equipment returned. I remember once Uncle John wanted Dad's big house jack. The notice for it to be returned was on the board

This postcard was sold in Dad's store. It is of a bridge that was in sight from the Dunraven feed store and railroad station where I worked. We swam under the covered bridge. I made many sketches and paintings of it.

for weeks. Finally a man from Dunraven said his neighbor had it. It came back.

One Halloween, the whole board was taken by boys playing pranks. We never found it. On the community Christmas Tree—there it was.

The country store is still with me in a way. I have an antique minature store with little items similar to ones we sold.

Sunday

Sunday was different. The store was only opened for the winding of the post office clock, and a check to be sure everything was all right. Any produce that was spoiling was taken to the house for us to use or mother to can. Nothing was wasted.

This is me around the time of my first paying job which was taking care of the Dunraven feed store and railroad station.

A postcard of the Presbyterian Church.

Sunday was different in the village too. All 23 houses smothered in giant maples that lined the gritty street were sleeping. The village was like a scenic postcard with its stone-arched bridge, its brick-a-brack houses, and on the knoll at the left end, the Presbyterian church with steeple and bell.

In front of the church were two wide flagstone walks coming from the two church doors to the main walk. At the end of the walk from the church door was a huge square flagstone, half suspended in mid air, with a hand wrought iron post with a round smooth hand-size ball on the top. Another of Uncle John's works of art—this was the unloading place for carriages on Sunday morning. (There were three more of these horse mounting, horse tying, or carriage mountings in the village. Uncle John had made them

all. Most had two or three steps. I always wondered how he got the holes in the flagstone to put the iron rods thru.)

Above the houses the dirt road turned again and crossed the creek on a little iron-railed bridge. Only then, as you came thru the "balm of Gilliad trees" (what the Scotch called the Sycamore trees), could you see the box with a roof and five windows and a chimney. Two tiny buildings stood one on each side of the stone walled yard. This was our one-room schoolhouse.

Our hamlet was ten miles east to Margaretville, unless you went over the mountain, and 15 miles west to Bovina Center. That was all there was to it—that was New Kingston. This was the spot where people who were burned out in Kingston during the Revolutionary War were given a tract of land to live on. These peo-

ple never came, but they sold their acreage to Scotch and Dutch farmers who have populated the area ever since. Scotch live on the steep hillsides, and Dutch live in the valley—all dairy and cauliflower farms.

Sunday morning the village street was empty. There were no sounds except the swallows chattering, a robin chirping and the far off call of the rain crow (coo coo). The air smelled only of newly cut hay. Summer was like that.

My older brother Lyman and I would climb up into the church tower's tiny floor with all the spiderwebs and dust and pull the big rope to ring the church bell. There were two ropes. The small one just pulled the clapper (this was to toll the bell for funerals). I often went with him to ring the bell. I always wanted to do it but he said it was too hard.

But I did ring it. I rang it twice, once when World War II ended, and once when my friend Jeanne got married. I was all grown up then, so it really didn't count.

Dad seldom missed going to church. Sometimes after a six-day week he would be so tired he would doze off. I was supposed to keep him awake. Sometimes a fly on his bald head or nose would do it. Other times from the choir, Mother would raise her hymnal as a little sign to me to wake Dad.

Preachers never stayed long in New Kingston. We had a succession of students and preachers that couldn't get a job anywhere else. One over-ambitious new preacher decided to get all the members to tithe—so there would be more money for the preacher. He talked to my Dad about it. Dad said he would be glad to do just that.

Next week Dad figured out his income and put his tithe in his usual envelope. Monday morning the preacher was in the store bright and early to talk to Dad. You see, Dad had always put the same amount in the envelope each week, a good bit more than the ten percent tithe.

There are lots of stories about New Kingston preachers I could tell. My older sister Phoebe had a date with one. This preacher, just out of the seminary, was always fooling around and playing jokes on Jeanne and me. So we decided to fix him once and for all. We got a pail of water perched up on the edge of the veranda roof. When he came all dressed up, we let him have it. My mother was horrified, and Phoebe couldn't believe we would do such a thing. I explained we had good cause.

The church was big and always smelled dusty or moldy. I sat with my Dad and counted squares on the ceiling; traced patterns on the edge of my Sunday School paper from the stained glass windows; and saw faraway roads and strange birds in the water-stained wall behind the preacher.

I loved the music with my mother singing in the choir. I studied the ladies' hats. I redesigned them. I redesigned everything including the preacher and the service. The only thing

My parade. I am behind the wagon.

that was right was my mother's large and lovely bouquet of delphiniums and peonies in front of the altar.

I didn't like church, except the music. I didn't like the preacher. He picked on me. We were all supposed to memorize 51 Bible verses. Jeanne did. The other farm girls did. I did reluctantly. All the girls got their Bible Storybook for memorization but me. I had improvised in a couple of places, so I didn't get mine.

I said to Jeanne, "The verses are in the Bible, why do we have to remember them?" I was slow to memorize anything. Sometimes I was sure I was slow at everything. Jeanne could paint better than I. She could sing better. Everything I could do, she could do better. Maybe there was one exception: I could plan. I could plan

to get us into trouble and plan to get us out. I could figure how to get this done and how not to have to do that. I organized and unorganized everything.

When I was eight, I planned a children's parade. Jeanne and I dressed all the children in crepe paper and antique dresses. We gathered all the carts and wheelbarrows and went from one end of the village to the other. Dad, Mother and George Owens surprised us all with homemade ice cream when the parade was over. The next summer I planned a wedding. Sammy Beardsley was the groom and Betty Scott the bride. They were both six or seven. I planned a secret club. I planned Halloween parties and games in the old creamery. Dad had bought the old creamery and made it over into a place to mix and bag cow and chicken feed. It had a big engine that turned the old butter churn. One large room was sealed in and a floor put in for a full size basketball court for Lyman.

Mail Call as I Remember

Mail came in to the post office about one each afternoon except Sunday. Usually, the mail carrier brought bread from the Muller Bakery in Margaretville with him too. As the mail was sorted, people in the village came in to open and peek into the little cubes to see what had come. Everything came by mail—the farmer's milk checks, the creamery men's checks, orders from Sears Roebuck, seeds, and lots of letters.

Annie Hunt came. She lived alone in the rain-washed yellow house, the one with the peaks, turrets and lightning rods, an apple tree away from the church. Was it a one-black shawl day or a two-black shawl day? Jeanne and I always tried to guess. She wore a hat, shawls and high shoes regardless of the weather. No one else in New Kingston wore shawls or high shoes.

Warren Archibald strolled in. He was the only person in New Kingston who didn't work for a living. His father had been a wealthy writer and preacher in Boston. He lived with his wife Iris and son Andrew in a "modern" house just below the Robertson farm. He had a nice green lawn, flower beds and a house full of animal skins and trophies which made me shudder.

He also had a mountain lion cub which I loved dearly. I would go down with Jeanne to see the lion. I was allowed to walk it on a leash. She was called Patchie. Warren sometimes walked the lion to the store to get his mail. Patchie and I were friends. She would sound much like the coffee grinder when I patted or rubbed her neck—she was purring.

Warren never had enough to do. He dipped his white pigeons in pink and blue dye and let them loose to startle people. His wife Iris had a beautiful singing voice and often sang solo in church. Iris had grown up in New Kingston across from the store. She was married to Warren at 15 or 16. He was a lot older.

The carpenter's wife Mrs. Chism lived across the street. She came in for her mail and a loaf of bread. One day as she bent to get a loaf of bread from the big basket, her hair fell forward. She was bald. Jeanne and I both saw it and looked away. She looked to see if anyone was looking as she pushed it back. Jeanne and I talked about it and laughed often. We had never seen a bald woman. We decided not to reveal her secret to anyone.

Three houses in the village didn't have permanent residents. Across the street and up one home was where Mr. Rohdemyer summered for a few years. He was famous (as far as we were concerned) for putting together the Rohdemyer Hymnal. He gave Mother a signed red leather bound copy. I was more impressed with the tiny wild flowers he gathered, pressed, and arranged in little frames. (I pressed flowers and ferns too—mine molded.)

Jeanne's maternal grandmother and grandfather lived in the next house with her Uncle Bob. When Grandfather Russell died (he was the church treasurer), the box was full of IOU's. This house had no electricity, bathroom or water. All the water was carried from the pump across the street or the creek. The next house belonged to Jeanne's Uncle Frank who lived with his Uncle Jimmie Winters.

That house had no improvements either. The living room was not used—it had never had heat in it. Everything was just as his wife had left it. Pictures of ancestors hung on the wall. There were carpet-covered platform rockers and a Victorian side table with a basket full of double pictures and a stereoscope. The rug was flowered, the curtains were lace, and dark green shades that pulled down from rollers with springs were behind the curtains. The shades only knew the down position.

Frank was a school teacher in the red schoolhouse at the end of Johnny Cake Lane. My father had taught there before him. Jimmy Winters always came for the mail for his sister, Frank and himself. He bought bread, cigarettes and candy.

The next house was one of those that sold, rented, and sold again. No one ever stayed

Left: Jeanne, Patchie (the mountain lion) and me. Right: Me and Spunkie.

Left: Me and Patchie.

Left: Dot cut my hair in the newest style—I hated it. Right: Me, Dad and June Kretzel, a summer friend.

in it long, mostly it was empty. Behind this house was a small cement and rock smoke house. Uncle John had built it. Everyone put their hams and bacon in it while Uncle John supervised the smoking and the adding on of hickory chips. This house should have belonged to the farm and barn behind it, but it didn't.

The farm belonged to Elmer Adee who lived on our side of the street in the house next to ours. He had a succession of housekeepers. I only remember Needa, a black woman with a little boy. She was there when Elmer had a heart attack in the barn and died. Elmer never came for his mail until four o'clock, just before he went to the barn to milk the cows.

Uncle John, who apparently was no one's uncle that I was aware of, lived in a large white house with a veranda on the front that ran around to the side. The gingerbread on each side of the posts had flowers, as did the upstair's veranda. The same pattern was in the roof peak. Uncle John had made it as he had much of the gingerbread on the other houses.

He made the squirrels that I dearly loved on our back porch. All the houses but three had some cut-out work or gingerbread, two were too old, and one, too new. Behind Uncle John's house was a horse barn with a second floor. The second floor was a wood shop. A ways behind the house was the "hoop hole," a small pond used for soaking wood to make it pliable so Uncle John could

bend it and make wood hoops for barrels.

He no longer made hoops, but the shop was intriguing. He had no electricity, so he concocted wheels and gears to speed up drilling. He had tools for shaving, planing, and things my wildest imagination could not figure out. Uncle John built buildings. He once made a chicken coop for me. He made gadgets, fancy latches, wood stools—almost anything anyone needed. He showed me how the stone arch bridge was built.

He even moved houses. He moved our house so we would have a lawn in front and be in a row with the other houses on the street. He made beautiful stone walls. He planted trees. He had one suit which he called his church and funeral suit, two hats (one for Sunday), a leather vest that never wore out, and overalls. He ate at our house for dinner at noon and supper at night. He lived alone. I don't remember his wife.

Uncle John never came to get his mail. If there was anything important like a letter from one of his daughters, I chased him up with the letter.

Mrs. Dowie seldom got any mail, but I took her whatever there was. I often brought her a bouquet of flowers or something to cheer her up. The Dowies had owned a large successful dairy farm just below the village. They became too old to run it, sold the farm, and had moved next to us. I must have been eight or nine when Mr. Dowie died. It was the first

funeral that I remember attending. After he died, part of my duties were running errands and taking care of Mrs. Dowie. She was very fat and had a bad leg with ulcers on it that smelled throughout the whole house. The ulcers never healed. She was a sad woman. She had one daughter who had died on her wedding night. The hate for the daughter's husband never eased. She gave me her daughter's wedding dress. When she died, they had an auction in her yard of her lovely furniture. I was sad.

From then on I never believed in funerals. They are too difficult for family and friends and do no good for those who are gone

The blacksmith shop was across and down from the store. It no longer functioned. All the equipment stood idle, the big doors closed. Most people were driving cars. Al Scott's wife lived up the stairs, over the smithy shop. Al was there on weekends and in Dunraven during the week. He drove his matched team of bay draft horses back and forth until one of his horses was hit by a car, right in front of the creamery.

They shot the horse with all of us looking. I never passed the spot in the road that I didn't smell the blood and feel badly for the beautiful draft horse. How could anyone hit a horse on a straight stretch of road? Well, Mr. Archibald took his eyes off the road to watch a tiny circus pony colt that the Bearsleys had bought for their two small children and hit the horse.

Bearsley managed the creamery, that is until they found out there was a discrepancy in the butterfat percentages. I babysat their children. I loved the two of them.

Al's wife had lots of henna-colored hair. She looked down from her second-story windows. She surveyed the street from the church down to the creamery. She saw every house and every person in the street and yards. When the mail rush was over, she came down for her mail. She was the kind of woman that should have had a canary, but she didn't. It would have been something to tell her troubles to.

Family Routine and Happenings

Time away from the store was almost nonexistent. The store opened at eight in the morning and closed at eight at night. When I was in high school, Dad decided to close the store at six p.m. My sister sometimes worked in the store, my brother Lyman worked mostly in the feed business but sometimes he worked in the store. My mother only worked in the store in emergencies. We had lots of hired help but only in the feed business.

Everything was organized. There was so much work in so many places with so many people, that Dad had to know exactly where everyone was and what they were doing. Breakfast was at 6:30 a.m. Dad built the fire in the kitchen wood-burn-

ing stove each morning when he got up at 5:30. He ran the teakettle full of cold water and put it on the front of the stove to heat.

Dad gave three raps on the stove pipe that went from the kitchen stove, thru the ceiling and the floor of my bedroom, and into the chimney. I was the type who popped out of bed always eager to meet the next day. I could smell the wood fire.

Much of breakfast preparation was done the night before. The table was set when we did the supper dishes, the oatmeal was partially cooked, and the grapefruit were cut. In the morning, the eggs and meat were cooked and toast was made. Sometimes we had pancakes. How many appeared for breakfast depended on all kinds of things. If Uncle John was working for us, he came. My brother, even after he was married and had breakfast at home, came for coffee and a second round of pancakes. (He had a bottomless pit for a stomach.) Any extra feed helpers might come. The kitchen table and the big country kitchen were never crowded.

Mother always had a cloth on the table because the table was old and the expansion leaves didn't match. Lyman made the rule that the one to get the first spot on the clean tablecloth had to wash the dishes. This served to make us all very careful. My sister Dot usually washed and I dried.

The breakfast was a working breakfast as all the plans for the day were made. Dad knew just

what had to be done, and now was the time for others to be assigned. There were three loads of dairy feed to be delivered. Lyman would do this. Someone had to pick up a shipment of groceries in Margaretville and that person could do the banking. My sister would do that. Mother would make and pack three lunches for men going to the Dunraven feed store to unload a car of hominy and cottonseed meal that had just come in. I would put new straw in the chickens' nest and fill their mash hopper and help mother with the cooking and baking. It was not all work, I had time to play.

Jeanne stayed all night with me often. She often ate at our house. One morning she had gone with me to feed the chickens before breakfast. Jeanne sat very quietly and Dad asked her if there something the matter. Jeanne looked up and asked, "Do hens pee?" The table was full of workers and family. Another time, Jeanne was having breakfast with us and the box of all-bran was on the table. She was just beginning to read. She was studying the box. "This relieves constipson, what is that?"

Mother canned. It was a way for us to have wonderful meals all winter. She canned strawberries, blueberries, even black berries, bushels of peaches and pears. She canned string beans from the garden along with beets, carrots, corn and chicken. In the fall she canned meats, beef and pork. She had a four quart pressure cooker in which

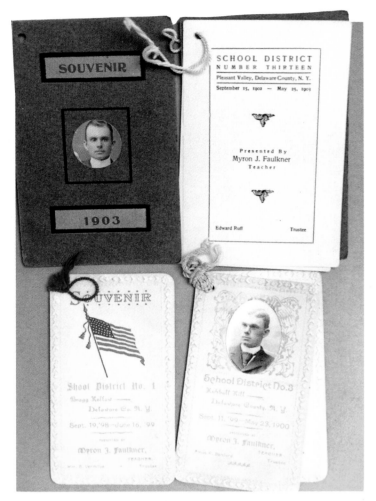

Left: A listing of Dad's students in his one room school.

Dad and his white cat.

she did meats and certain vegetables. Fruits were done in a small washtub. She cured meats as dried beef and corn beef and rubbed hams with maple syrup and salt and probably other things before they were smoked.

We had a cool part of the cellar where we kept barrels of apples, potatoes, dried onions, carrots and beets covered with soil. We had cupboards with row after row of canned goods. We had crocks of sweet pickles. We butchered beef and hogs in the fall. We killed chickens regularly.

My mother had a special hand-written, hand-bound recipe book. In this were hand-me-down recipes for cakes, puddings, pickles, curing meats, and making dried beef. There were recipes that one would not run across anywhere else. There were two recipes for making soap, one hand soap and one washing soap. I helped make soap many times.

We had no Clorox in those days, so we boiled our white clothes in a copper boiler on the stove to kill the germs and whiten the clothes with a cup of mother's washing fluid. Another recipe was for hand lotion made of rose water and glycerin. She made a salve of lanolin too.

One of her specialties was maple cream. It was a way to keep maple sugar soft for use on pancakes. She made sparkling jellies, jams and sauces.

I expected to have and to save this wonderful book all done in my mother's beautiful handwriting.

At Christmastime we packed sacks of candy for all the children in the valleys—usually about 50 sacks. We used half-pound brown paper bags because this was what we had in the store. We brought the big boxes and tubs of candy from the store and put them around the kitchen table. There could be as many as 15 kinds, including special kinds that came in at Christmas. We had peanut brittle, ribbon candy, old fashioned chocolate drops, hard candy in numerous varieties, peppermint balls, chocolates formed like little Santas, candy canes, and on and on.

Candy packing was a fun family project. We did it after supper the night before the community Christmas tree. We marched around the table singing Christmas songs. We put in an orange first, then candy to fill the bag. Every bag got some of everything. Lyman was always Santa Claus, probably because he had a Santa suit. Once my sister Phoebe played Mrs. Santa with him. Lyman loved giving out the presents and especially the candy.

Dad

Dad had come from Virginia to Margaretville when his mother died. His father had died earlier. He worked and finished high school, then went to Teacher Training Institute to become a teacher. He taught school in Bull Run, then in New Kingston. He bought the store in New Kingston. I think Uncle John owned a part of the store, then Dad bought him out.

Dad had a big camera which took pictures on glass plates. He took pictures of New Kingston and had them made into postcards. These we sold in the store. At ten I was given a camera, a little pink-colored pullout. I was not much of a photographer.

Rock Coal Story

At both feed stores we were a little careless, leavings bags of feed or coal on the porch all night for the next day's delivery. Off and on we lost a bag or two of coal. Finally, we decided that all must be locked inside at night. Railroad cars going thru carried many things. One day a car carrying crushed stone was bumped enough for a good bit of it to come down on the tracks.

Uncle John went out to clean the tracks. Being Scotch and conservative, he bagged the crushed stone to use in mud ruts. He put the bagged stone on the feed store porch tied up like coal. The next morning the bags were gone. Someone was sure surprised when they opened the bags to feed their furnace fire!

Dolls

It was not often, but once in a great while, Jeanne and I would get out my dolls and play with them. Dad put a floor in the attic of the garage to be a playhouse. I had it "furnished" with doll-sized high chairs, doll chairs, table and two beds. I used orange crates as cupboards

Postcard of New Kingston, note grass and steps to the second floor, and no gas pumps.

This is about all of the village—23 houses. The Dodge truck was ours and the Buick Sedan. Dad's store is on the right. This was one of the many photos taken by Dad that he made into postcards.

for my dishes that I still have. We used wood boxes for chairs. I had cooking utensils and an iron stove. I had two composition baby dolls that we played with most. My three bisque dolls, two A.M.'s, and my Heubach Koppelsdorf only came to the playhouse on special occasions. These were usually guests.

We sometimes played with my little all-bisque dolls on the back porch—a rainy day game. Mostly I put clothes on my cat and put her in the little blue doll carriage.

These dolls are in more or less perfect condition today. One belongs to Jay, one to Colleen, and I still have the one given to me by Mildred Whitney of Oneonta, New York, on the day I was born.

Me and Peaches,
my second cat.
Right: My sister Dot.

Jeanne on Pet.

Pet and Pal.

Me and Pal. Note Amelia Earhart cap!

Growing and Learning

The chickens, their care, and their profit were mine. Dad furnished the mash, scratch grain and oyster shells. I furnished eggs for mother, all she could use, and the rest went to the store for which I got paid. My "setting hen" was a big Rhode Island red who hatched all the eggs.

For several years I raised pheasants for the state. After the eggs hatched I took care of the birds for six weeks. A county 4-H agent came and counted the pheasants. I was paid $1.00 for each one. I saved the money for college. One year I raised 36, another 41. These projects were supervised by both Dad and Mother. In these small ways I was taught saving, banking and investing.

My mother seemed to know everything about raising animals or birds. One spring I asked Dad for some duck eggs. He brought me home four. Duck eggs take a week longer than chicken eggs to hatch, so mother started the hen sitting on the duck eggs a week before we put in the chicken eggs. Two ducks hatched. They swam in the hoop hole all summer. We didn't know what to do with them come winter, so Dad gave them to a farmer and came home with a turkey for Thanksgiving. He knew I would never eat a duck. I loved animals. I must tell you about our trained calves. Jeanne's paternal grandparents, Giddeon and Tillie Robertson, came from Scotland. They were wonderful to me, treating me like another grandchild. Tillie made bread

on Saturday morning. Jeanne and I were there for warm bread and jam. Once in a while we stayed all night on the farm.

It was here that our Jersey calves lived. Jeanne and I trained two calves each. We worked at it, off and on, all summer. The calves went with us up to the store. They went wherever we led them. When winter came, we hitched them up to a hand sleigh and drove them. The first two we trained were Opal and Sapphire; the next two were Pet and Pal. The village people became used to seeing two half-grown cows tied up here and there, usually at the back steps of our homes.

It seemed to me that it was always summer in that hamlet, and that the trees on the mountainsides, sloping right into the village, were always green. Spring was a short delightful time when such beauties as hepaticas, Dutchman's breeches, squirrel corn, adder's-tongues, trillium, and the wonder of ferns uncoiled their feathered fronds.

The brooks ran high over slippery rocks. Little waterfalls splashed. Jeanne and I walked thru the cow yards, squeezed between the wooden poles on the wooden gate, and ran over the cow-mowed pasture to the woods. The woods were made up of beech, maple, silver birch, ash, linden and a few hemlocks along the edge. Low branches of shinhopple (viburnum) had rings of white bloom. Pin cherry and choke cherry bloomed along the brook. We walked in the woods and up the mountain. No one ever worried

where we were or how far we went.

Yes, there were a few weeks called autumn with the brilliant red and orange of maples and the yellow of beeches. The beechnuts fell or were shaken out of their star-shaped prickly cups.

I push hard on the memory button, it was like I didn't want to remember winter. There was winter, a long, hard, cold time when I helped Mother bring in frozen clothes from the clothesline. I carried in wood for continually stuffing into the grey enamel stove.

When I rode on my Flexible Flyer down the little hill in front of the church, my hands and feet would be white with cold. Jeanne and I came home and sat in the kitchen with the oven door open to get warm. I hated the cold, but I loved the frost pictures etched on the window panes. I slept between flannel sheets.

I walked to school carrying my dinner pail with a thermos of hot cocoa. The schoolroom was cold. The teacher wore her coat and boots. The ink bottles were frozen. The teacher built a fire in the stove in the middle of the room. About two thirds of the children were present; the rest were sick with colds.

We sat two at a desk and went up and sat on a long bench in front of the teacher's desk for a class. All seven grades were in one room. I never felt I was learning anything. The books we had, our library, were three short shelves in a bookcase. They didn't interest me—*The Bobbsey Twins*, etc.

The bottom shelf had a portfolio of state birds and another of state flowers with beautiful color plates. These I desperately wanted to study, but the teacher said no. They were only for the teacher.

As an adult, I acquired a set of these flower plates after all the one-room schools were closed. I treasure it today. I happened on another set, and I bought it for my son Jay.

There were never any books with the things I wanted to learn. I wanted to know about rocks, insects, butterflies, trees, animals and art. The school had nothing, and there was nothing at home. There was no way for me to get the books I wanted. I didn't even know there were books about butterflies.

Always in the summer I watched the butterflies as they gathered on aster, milkweed and jo pieweed. I knew which butterfly I would see where. Once, I found a chrysalis of a black swallowtail on the carrots. I brought it in the house and pinned it on my mother's plant on the kitchen window shelf.

Every time I dried the dishes, I studied it. No one knew what it was. Dad said it might be a butterfly. On the second day, it emerged just as I was doing the breakfast dishes. It was one of the greatest things that happened to me. Mother thought it was beautiful. Dad said we had observed a miracle. Once the wings expanded fully, we all went out to see it fly away.

I told about this in school. The teacher didn't believe a word of it and stopped me before I could finish.

I wanted to make a butterfly collection. I was always going slowly, carefully, and catching one between my thumb and forefinger, looking at it, and letting it go. I do the same today. I caught a big black and yellow butterfly (a tiger swallowtail) and took it into the store. I asked Dad to kill it for me. He looked at all the drugs on the shelf and said he didn't think there was anything that would work. He said let's try kerosene.

We doused the poor thing with kerosene. The colors on his wings all went dark and greasy. I wished I hadn't asked. Dad said put it in the sun and perhaps the sun will evaporate the kerosene. I put it on the steps in the sun, forgot it for an hour or so. When I went back, the wings were all ragged. A bird had eaten the body.

I never tried again, until my own children wanted to collect butterflies.

The Dragons

In the peaceful village of New Kingston there were certain cellars and buildings that housed dragons. These were fierce, belching, and grumbling gasoline-eating iron dragons. I was scared to death of them from the time I can remember. I was cautioned not to go anywhere near, to stay away. I didn't need to be cautioned or told, instinct made me keep my distance from these scary monsters.

Most of these noisy monsters were housed in the little buildings attached to the big cow barns. They huffed and puffed and pounded the air twice each day at milking time. This was the creature that mechanically extracted the milk from the gentle Jersey cows.

There were others of these dragons. Some lay silent for months at a time, then were dragged to the log pile in autumn where, after much coaxing and a good meal of oil and gasoline, it sawed the logs to just the right length to be used in the country kitchen stoves.

There were other versions of these smelly dragons. Their gauges and heavy iron wheels turned with wide leather belts that were always attached to something. I was too afraid of the hissing and spitting to get close enough to see just how they functioned.

The indoor, or cellar-housed monsters, had a pipe leading to the outdoors. This was so he could cough his poisonous fumes into the clean mountain air and not contaminate the building.

We housed two of these noisy working monsters. I hated them, was scared of them, yet was in awe of what they accomplished. Our little dragon made electricity for the house, the store, and the three street lights. Even though I knew this huffing and puffing was for a good cause, I couldn't persuade myself to go into the store cellar when the dragon was having one of his spells.

There was also a huge one of these iron monsters at the old creamery building. This one had a foot-wide belt that rotated the old butter churn to compound Dad's special feed mixtures for cows and chickens. When this one huffed and puffed and blew exhaust, anyone could be convinced that it ate little girls. I stayed my distance and kept my friend Jeanne away from it.

One Friday night Jeanne and I were invited to go home with two sisters who lived on a farm seven miles above the village. We had done this before, and the sisters had also come to my house for a Friday and Saturday night. We were delivered back home on Sunday morning in time to go to church.

This time it was a special occasion. The parents were celebrating their tenth wedding anniversary with a square dance. The whole house was ready. Pies, cakes and sandwiches were made, and other food was brought in by the neighboring farmers all up and down the hollers.

The house was full, more than full, with men, women, and children of all ages. One upstairs bedroom was full of coats and hats, another had sleeping infants. The dining room table had been removed and chairs set along the sides of the room. Between the kitchen and the dining room, in the double doorway, a fiddler played and called the square dances. A woman hammered the piano.

We kids were allowed to do our dancing in the kitchen. We did the best we could. We were having a grand time.

The party was well underway, a real shindig. The walls were bouncing with the loud music and the voice of the caller. Two of the girls complained of a bad headache. They went to the upstairs bedroom and lay down. I had a headache too. Jeanne said she did too. (She always had everything I did.) We thought it was the noise and smoke and went outside to get a breath of fresh air.

Suddenly there was some excitement. The youngest son in the family had been standing on a chair near the fiddler. He fell off the chair, fainting dead away. At almost the same time an elderly woman, that I didn't remember having seen before, said she was faint and then fainted.

The little boy was rushed out the back door for some air and almost immediately came to. His father, as he carried the boy, noticed that someone had put a tin can over the exhaust pipe from the cellar engine. The little boy in his play had put the can on the exhaust earlier that day.

The house was opened and aired out. The engine, being directly under the kitchen, had belched most of its fumes in that area. The little boy told everyone what he had done. The girls with the headaches were better and the fainting woman revived. The party went on but not with the same gusto.

I don't know or remember whether it was from this instance that I became scared of engine dragons or whether my fear had always lurked in the darkness. I knew I was afraid of these barking, spewing cellar dragons. Even when I was big enough to know that they couldn't eat little girls, I still made wide circles around the beasts.

Spring Walk

One Sunday after talking about it to Dad we decided to walk straight over Pisga (our highest mountain) and down to the other side to Weaver Hallow. Dad said he would meet us at Laughman's house on the other side and give us a ride back. We took so long that my mother was sure we were lost. We made it. Laughman and all of us stirred off maple sugar before we drove back. This was the boiling down of maple syrup, then stirring it in a dish until it made sugar. Before it was stirred it could be drizzled on snow to make Jack wax.

Maple syrup time was the only time Dad ever missed church. When he bought the farm he got a "sap bush" at the same time. It was a good sap bush, about a mile straight up the mountain with no road. There was already a sap house and an evaporator inside it. We used horses and a sleigh with a gathering tank to collect the sap from the hundreds of buckets hanging from spiles on each maple tree.

A husky fire was built under the evaporating pan which was never allowed to go out. We kept pouring more sap in on one end and drawing off syrup on the other. Steam rose from the pans, and if there was a little wind you couldn't see your friend next to you. Someone tended the syrup night and day.

It was dangerous business as the boiling syrup could boil over or could burn the pans. We always had safety precautions. My job was driving the horses. I could guide them on the narrow paths between the trees while the men snatched the buckets from the dripping spiles.

A good amber maple syrup was a cash crop for farmers, but it was hard work. A gallon sold for $6 in 1930. We always had orders for gallons to be shipped, and the rest was sold in the store. It now may sell for $50 per gallon.

Summer Visitors

For a quiet little hamlet far back in the Catskills, summers held an awakening. I had mentioned before that the former New York senator Honorable George Owens had retired on the upper end of this little group of houses. He still went back to New York City for most of the winter, but the summers were something else! The senator had five sons, one named George of course. Each of the sons had a son named George along with a multitude of other children.

This village seemed like a wonderful place to summer grandchildren. They came in lots, some with parents, some without. They came from the streets of Brooklyn. They spoke with an accent foreign to us villagers. They used words which Jeanne and I did not know. My mother was horrified at our new companions' vocabularies.

They jumped rope on the sidewalk singing dirty rhymes. They played hopscotch on the walk and organized kick-the-can games. They were scared of cows and called the ducks—turkeys, chickens, birds. They ran thru lawns and gardens but were afraid to go into the fields or the woods. Jeanne and I got a short, intensive course on how the outside world lived and talked.

I think it was the wild ones that impressed us as some of the children were polite and well trained. One granddaughter became a good friend of mine. We corresponded for many years during the winter months.

I remember one summer when she came to New Kingston she brought her new birthday doll with her. It was a May Starr doll with records that played. She would show us the doll and play a record for us, but she never let us touch the doll. My bisque dolls seemed pretty ordinary compared to this talking doll.

These Owens kids enlightened the country kids about where babies came from, and how they got there. Not that you could tell country kids who have observed the birth of everything from kittens to calves much, it was just that they had whispered it like a secret.

I must say they awakened the village in the summer like nothing else could.

Parents as Teachers

My mother never pushed me. She would say in her gentle way, I hope you will help me bake this morning...pack men's lunches...or whatever was urgent for the day. These were extra tasks done after my chores of feeding the chickens, bringing in wood and making my bed.

Dad was different. He assigned tasks which he expected completed without supervision. I was the volunteer type and could often get myself into jobs too big for me. I would say to Dad, "I'll clean store shelves this morning." This always made him happy, and he would say, "Do you think you can clean to here?" He would measure off a distance about a third of what I thought I could do. I would offer to add up the customers' bills. He would say, "See if you can finish the top row." This would be about half of what I would think I could do. If I offered to rake the lawn, he would say, "Just do the back one." He would always thank me and praise me for finishing the job. It was not until I was older that I realized he had a hang-up concerning the finishing of a job. This was his way of making the end result within my reach, to give me the good feeling of finishing a task. Many times I would hear him say to my brothers, "Finish the job. Even if you are tired, finish it." He practiced what he preached.

Having grown up under this influence, I probably pushed the same teachings on my children. "Finish the job," I asked of them.

Dad had another way of teaching. When I was still in

grade school and again in high school, Dad would take time to read the little stories and essays I wrote. He would praise my efforts. Numerous times I remember him saying to me, "You love to paint. You paint so anybody can see the same wondrous view you do. You can do exactly the same with words. You paint the character with words so that anyone can see him. You paint the setting with adjectives, until others can see the colors as you do." He would diagram a sentence to show me how the adjectives worked.

I hope in my writings today I remember his teachings.

The store was located a village farm and a house away from our home just two light poles away. This was a joke among my friends and my first boyfriend. Dad turned on both street lights at dusk and turned them off when he went to bed!

Our home was a modest nine-room house that I thought was the greatest on earth. At that time our house was the only one with electricity, furnace, bathroom (we had two), washing machine and electric iron.

Most houses had hand pumps in the backyard for water and outhouses behind the big houses. Others did their laundry in tin tubs in the kitchen. They heated their homes and cooked their meals on wood burning stoves. I was in and out of every house in New Kingston. I delivered mail, groceries, sometimes a cake my mother had baked. I ran errands for everyone.

My Mother was the boss of the house. She worked hard, cleaned, washed, ironed and fed the ever-expanding dinner guests. When she sat down, she darned socks. She grew house plants and had an ever-blooming flower garden. She was an artist with no time to apply her talents. She did decorate birthday cakes for the family and anyone she knew having a birthday. She designed and dyed material for her own hooked rugs and refinished furniture.

She taught us to bake, cook, keep our rooms neat, and me to grow plants and love everything growing. She allowed me to have cats and kittens, a dog, ducks, pheasants, chickens, pollywogs, salamanders, turtles and rabbits. Both Mother and Dad were interested in birds. We fed them suet in the winter and always threw out grain for them. My parents taught me about the local birds.

I remember once that Dad and I delivered a few bags of grain in his small truck. As we drove thru the farm meadows far above the village, we stopped. The grass was full of bob-o-links. It was the first and last time I ever saw bob-o-links and heard their happy songs. I never had a bird identification book, but I did have some cards with birds that came in soda boxes.

Dad found a page out of something that had many of the breeds of chickens on it. I quickly learned the breeds of chickens, and he taught me the breeds of cows—Holstein, Guernsey, Jersey, Brown Swiss and Dutch Belted. Most herds

The house where I grew up as it looked in 1931.

of dairy cows in New Kingston, as was ours, were a mixture. The Holsteins gave lots of milk, the Jerseys had lots of butterfat.

As you can see, everything, everyday, all our activities circled around the store.

We did get away occasionally. Sometimes it was a trip to New York City to buy Christmas stock, Sunday picnics, the county fair, often to Margaretville. We once took a trip across New York State and back. It was my best geography and history lesson.

We went to Watkins Glenn, visited the lake shores and historical points. Phoebe, Dot and I rode in the back seat and Dad and Mother in the front. We read Burma Shave signs all the way. Another time we visited Canada. Once, we took Jeanne and rode the Hudson River Day Boat to New York City.

Another time we rode the ferry to Staten Island and visited the Lunns. We went to the state fair. Dad and I had our first airplane ride—in an open cockpit seaplane. I loved it, but it made Dad sick.

This life was a happy one, a very satisfactory one. I loved every day. I was never envious or jealous of anyone. I never knew you were supposed to have bad teenage years. I worked, wrote, painted and got satisfactory marks in school. I loved my family and my animals, especially my horse and dog.

Radio

It seemed to me like we were always the last family to get anything new that appeared on the market. This was not exactly true; we had electric appliances, such as irons and washers that no one else in the valley had. I guess it was the frivolous, not essential things, that we were the last to get.

I remember one summer when Miss Lucy Tracy, our hefty school teacher, was packing up to leave for the summer. She brought over her small, hand winding phonograph for us to use. Both mother and I enjoyed listening to the records while rolling pie crust and straining apple pulp for jelly during the summers.

Dear Miss Tracy was the teacher who rented part of the house across the street. She came into our kitchen almost every evening, perched her very large underside precariously on our wood box, and stayed until mother asked, "Like to have a little supper with us?"

The next summer when Miss Lucy Tracy left, she brought over her radio. Dad was not happy over the loan. "Suppose something happens to the radio," he said. "You children will be listening to that thing when you should be working."

Well you can guess who listened to that thing once he found out there was news on it.

Dad became addicted. He pounced upon the dials to hear every WGY news broadcast. Mother and I preferred to hear "When the Moon Comes Over the Mountain," introducing the young singer Kate Smith.

I do remember one time when we were all glued to the radio. Lucky Lindy was flying over the Atlantic in the Spirit of St. Louis. Nothing was being accomplished at our house. Mother, who knew everyone would want to eat, stayed more or less with the roast and potatoes baking in the oven. I was sent out occasionally to bring up an armful of seasoned wood to keep the fire burning.

We all hung on every word until Lindbergh landed in France. It was such a great adventure, and we were able to hear it all. There was a rhyme that went something like this "Lucky Lindy, Lucky Lindy flew to France, all the way by the seat of his pants."

By this time I knew what I wanted to be. I started by ordering a black leather-like aviator's cap with flaps that snapped under my chin and goggles on my forehead. I read everything on Amelia Earhart. I pictured myself a second Earhart and wore my cap in preparation.

March 16, 1992, Amelia Earhart again made the headlines. You will remember her Lockheed 10 E Electra ran out of gas July 2, 1937, and the coast guard lost radio contact. She and her plane were never located.

Now searchers have found a shoe in the size that Amelia

wore, a medicine bottle, a piece of aluminum of the type used on her plane with rivet holes, and an antennae on the island of Nikumoror 500 miles off her course.

The Amelia Earhart story has been one of the most tantalizing and enduring for me. Over the years, other stories have come out and many believed she was captured as a spy by the Japanese. Stories of my childhood heroine live on.

I said we were always the last in town to get something new. These things repeat themselves. I was grown and married when televisions were coming out. Our neighbors had one. I put off buying one partly because of the cost and partly because we liked reading to the children. I felt no need for one.

When we moved to Oneonta, my children would beg to go to the neighbors to watch television with their children. Finally, we gave in. I'm sure the Mouseketeers are embedded in Jay's memory as clearly as the little white mice in his Charlotte's Nursery, his mice-growing project.

The Depression, Barter and Cars

I was 11 in 1929 when the stock market crashed. It seemed that no one in New Kingston understood or cared. These people lived on their monthly milk checks from their dairies, which never quite covered their grocery and cow feed bills. There was always the store charge account. No one had money in the bank. They were not going to starve with gardens in their backyards and cellars filled with canned meat and fruit.

Dad had an immediate problem. When a carload of feed came in on the railroad, it had to be paid for before the railroad car could be opened for unloading. He had a car of hominy coming in and was desperate for enough money to pay for it. He borrowed bits of money from the whole family, a little here and a little there. Earlier, he would have scolded Mother for hoarding a little money, but this time she was his lifesaver.

The Depression moved in on long legs and completely straddled our village. If we hadn't had the newspaper with pictures of bread lines, we would not have known about the Depression. Everyone was still poor as far as money was concerned anyway. Only Dad was aware of the Depression and its overhanging clouds.

It was at this point that we began hiring less help that we paid in cash. I also became conscious of the barter system in the store and around home. A load of wood would be delivered behind our house, (we burned wood both in the kitchen stove and the cellar furnace), and the farmer would go home with bags of chicken feed. A villager would come and split and pile the wood, and three days of work would be taken from his charge account. Eggs were brought in dozen lots or cases. We sold eggs, but mostly we shipped them to New York City. Packing eggs was one of my jobs.

Farmers' wives would occasionally bring down a milk pail of wild strawberries, cherries or blueberries. These went to our house where mother and I canned them or made jelly. The lady went home with necessities for her kitchen. In the fall we got apples, half a pig, a side of beef, even a turkey, or a pail of sausage in trade for whatever was needed at the farm.

It was about this time that I started to learn to drive. We always had a car and two trucks. The Dodge truck had wire mesh on the sides. It was our first truck, or the first one I can remember. I recall that reverse was where first gear was on later trucks. This truck also had to be cranked to start.

One day Uncle John, who didn't do much driving, needed a load of gravel to make a cement foundation. He took the truck to the edge of the creek and hauled the gravel from about eight feet below and loaded it into the truck. He got in the truck and started it—in reverse instead of first. The truck went over the steep edge and stood on end in the creek. Uncle John got a little cut on his head, but nothing else. His feelings were hurt worse.

He climbed out and went to the store to get a bandage and some help. My brother Lyman and a few other men went quickly to the rescue. Jeanne and I watched from the sidelines. They were trying to figure out how a team of horses could pull the truck back up. Uncle John came back and sized up the situation. "Get a couple of poles and we can turn

the truck," he said. "Then I can drive it down the creek to a level spot."

Uncle John was the one who built a little box to put behind me to reach the pedals to drive the truck. I learned to drive on the pickup truck. I was not taught in the usual manner.

At breakfast Dad drew the dashboard and pedals on a piece of cardboard from an empty cornflake box. "This is the starter. The truck will not go ahead until you move this shift." He showed me where each thing should be. "Go now, see if you can start the truck, then turn it off and come back."

I went thru a long series of drawings and do-it-yourself instruction. Before long I was allowed to drive the truck down from the store to the old creamery where it was stored. I learned to drive the big Mack truck in the hayfield while the men loaded the hay. I was allowed to drive the pickup truck on the farm road, but never on the main road.

It was years before I was allowed to try for my license. Dad knew I would have to parallel park in the test, and I had never driven in town. Again, he drew the method on paper and sent me to practice by myself. I got my license. Now I wanted to take the car to town. I was a high school senior. Dad said that as soon as I could change a tire, I could take the car. I waited and hoped for a flat tire.

One day I went to the garage and there was a flat tire on the back of the Essex. I jumped

Brother Lyman, sister Dorothy and me on the left.

for joy. I thought: here is my chance. I rang a special little telephone line to the store and told Dad. I went out feeling great. I got the jack out of the car and looked at the spare. I adjusted the brake and was about to proceed when Lyman came. "I will change it for you," he said. Lyman was big and husky and never one to let a lady do something he felt a man should do.

He changed the tire and let me let down the jack so the Essex stood on all fours. We walked to the store together. To Dad's questions about the change, Lyman said, "Milly will never have to change a tire. All she will have to do is look helpless or shed a tear or two."

He convinced Dad. After that, I drove the car anywhere, and never in my life have I changed a tire.

Muskrat Farm

There are many things that my children cannot remember living without—jet planes, televisions, bathrooms, atomic bombs, microwaves, and even little things like an alcoholic beverage.

In New Kingston nearly every cellar had a barrel of apple cider. The farmers made wine from dandelion blossoms and another from elderberry blossoms. Once I was horrified when one of my farm friends showed me rows and rows of fermenting elderberry wine. She said don't tell anyone.

The drinking of alcohol was discussed at our breakfast table. None of my family drank but we had to be aware of villagers who came into the store under the influence of the cider barrel.

By the time I was in seventh grade and went to Margaretville on the bus, I was aware of the muskrat farm activities.

There was a small building, not much more than a shack with a chimney, on the edge of a small pond. We passed the shack each day in the bus. The man who lived in the shack had a small flagpole. Sometimes he had a white flag on the little pole, sometimes he didn't.

The boys on the bus joked about this bootlegger and his supply. Other people said he really did have muskrats in the pond and was raising them. They went out to see the musk-

rats, and this was a way to pick up a quart jar of moonshine.

One winter we had loggers with their teams of horses staying in the village. Jeanne and I enjoyed seeing the heavy draft horse drag a pile of logs from up on the mountain down thru the village. The rough speaking mountain men, with faded plaid wool jackets and whiskers, hitched their teams to a single bobsled and dragged the logs. This made a wonderful slippery place to ride down the hill.

Jeanne and I were told to avoid the lumberjacks. The village people could not wait for them to be gone.

One night, several of the men got hold of some bad moonshine from the muskrat farm. One, and perhaps more, of the men died from drinking it and the others were sick. The whole thing was kept very quiet as far as we kids were concerned. When I asked, Dad said that they had drunk something with wood alcohol in it.

The 1920s Flappers

I was ten when the flapper age broke into the Wall Street crash and the Great Depression. My sister Phoebe was already a schoolteacher and was never much for the latest fashions. But my sister Dot was something else. She had the right figure and long wavy red hair and everything else a "flapper" needed. She spent every cent she earned, or that Dad gave her, on clothes—flapper attire.

I should explain for my younger readers about flappers. During the winter, girls in the

1920s wore heavy, black, high galoshes or arctics with buckles. (This was before the zipper.) The girls left the galoshes unfastened, and they made a flapping sound as they walked. The girls who did this were called flappers.

As time went on, flapper was used to indicate the dress styles and even extended to women who wanted to be free from the conventions of the day. Flappers drank, smoked, danced the Charleston, and sang *Bye Bye Blackbird*. Wind-up phonographs (Victrolas) and the piano furnished the music.

As far as flappers in New Kingston were concerned, there were none. Everything was about ten years behind the rest of the world. Dot would have to run off to a larger town or city with her boyfriend for any kind of social life.

The social life in New Kingston consisted of church socials, missionary meetings, and Home Bureau or Farm Bureau meetings.

I watched my flapper sister but never had any desire either for her clothes or wild social life. I preferred nature study, horseback riding, learning to cook, and painting.

Dad's Stories and Other Stories

Dad was a storyteller. He saw the humor in everyday life. His stories were things that actually happened in and around New Kingston.

He was always very careful not to offend anyone or to tell something that was indiscreet.

He always warned me not to write anything concerning local people that could offend. His wonderful storytelling was building me to become a writer.

One frosty morning Dad was putting the last bag of feed on a wagon when he overheard a conversation between a grizzled old farmer and a villager.

"I see you're getting a new team, Ned," the villager commented. "Naw, I've had these horses for years, they still work. What made you think I was getting new horses?"

The smart-alec villager gave the horse a pat where his skin was barely covering his ribs. "I see you got the frame up."

When my brother Lyman was a little boy, he worked at the store and was often required to hold the reins of a horse or a team while the owner went into the store to make a few purchases. A Mr. Bellows, who taught school around the district's one-room schools, was known throughout the county for his extensive vocabulary.

It was a sunny afternoon and Mr. Bellows drove up to the store with his black mare and red carriage. He intended to stay a day or two in the village.

He said to the nine-year-old boy standing by, wishing to be of service, "If you will extricate this quadruped from this vehicle, I will award you with admirable compensation." Lyman stood, mouth open, as if trying to understand a message in a foreign language. "Unhitch the critter and put him in the barn, Lyman," a villager said.

Dad told that story many times after.

Another story that Dad told was when Mr. Bellows was explaining to a child the meaning of phenomenon. "If you see a thistle, that is not a phenomenon. If you see a mockingbird, that is not a phenomenon. But if you see a kangaroo sitting on a thistle and singing like a mocking bird, then that is a phenomenon."

A New Kingston young man had fallen into the habit of drinking far too much. His mother was concerned with his drunkenness and devised a plan to scare some sense into the young man's head. For years she had told him the devil would get him and give him his comeuppance—for drinking was the devil's work. Nothing seemed to impress the young man or help him correct his ways.

The worried mother figured she would scare him into not drinking. She got her neighbor to dress up like the devil. The mother spared no effort in designing the costume, complete with cow horns and long red underwear.

The devil, knowing the young man would pass the cemetery at midnight, hid behind one of the gravestones. As the drinker approached, he stepped out and in his best voice growled, "I'm the devil." The young man kept walking. "I'm the devil," he growled, flapping his arms. "I'm the devil," he said, following the young man.

Just then, the young man turned, "Who the hell is disputing you?" Some years later he was still drinking heavily.

⁂

In our small, poor church we got the dregs for preachers, they were either new and unpracticed or just unwanted. One Sunday morning before the main service, the preacher wanted to tell a pointed story to the children. He wanted to emphasize and impress on the children the value of prayer and the power of God, and how we should use it even though we were young.

The story he told went like this. Two little girls were walking to school, dawdling and playing as they went. They heard in the distance the teacher ringing the first bell. One little girl said to the other, "We are going to be late."

The other little girl said, "When we are in trouble the preacher said to pray." The little girls got down on their knees beside the road and prayed that they wouldn't be late for school. While they prayed, the last bell rang. They were late and had to stay after school. The preacher explained that God had heard their prayers but still had to punish them for dawdling.

When I got home from church, I had Jeanne and another girl with me. Dad said he would like to tell the story over.

"Two little girls were on their way to school, dawdling and playing a little as they went.

They heard the teacher ringing the first bell and they still had a ways to go. One little girl said, 'We had better pray.' The other little girl said, 'I think we can run and pray at the same time.' They got to the school just as the teacher was coming out to ring the last bell."

Dad explained, "It's okay to pray, but be sure you are running at the same time. This will always work in all the things you do no matter your age."

Anti-Rent Rebellion

The old Essex pulled up short on the side of the dusty Dingle Hill road at the old Moses Earl Farm. "Why are we stopping here?" I asked.

Then, looking to the side, I saw the historical plaque. Dad always stopped at all historical plaques and gave me a short, usually interesting, history lesson. "This is Decision Corner," he said.

There was a wordy plaque telling of the Anti-Rent Rebellion. This was the scene of the culmination of the bitter struggle on August 6, 1845. Osman Steele, the sheriff, was shot here by a group of masked and calico-outfitted farmers when he tried to hold a "distress" sale of cattle for unpaid rents.

This 1844-45 time period in my home county of Delaware and several adjacent counties was important to every farmer and villager.

Early land grants were vague because much of these counties were unexplored. These patents, the Bradt, Kortright,

Charlotte Valley, Walton, Livingston, Hardenburgh, and a few others were the largest sections. Some were as large as a million acres. Farms on these patents had to pay rent, not only in dollars, but in produce, cows, pigs and chickens. The owner had land agents who supervised the rent collecting. A farmer could never buy his farm but kept on paying, paying, forever.

In 1844-45 the farmers rose up and planned a rebellion. They donned sheepskin masks and calico clothing. They used tin and conk horns to notify their neighbors of the coming of the sheriff.

This was a case of feudal tyranny and unscrupulous practices against the tenant farmers. The land barons let their agents harass farmers with distress sales, eviction notices, ill treatment and abuse.

The farmers, finally taking the law into their own hands, rose up in rebellion. They hoped that these feudalistic laws could be changed by votes rather than by guns, but things got out of hand.

This seemed like a small obscure little war, but this was a battle for democracy. It was undeniably a part of America's freedom for which we must fight and fight again.

I feel that the decision of these men and women, these Anti-Renters, to rebel and fight to preserve the right to own land (one of democracy's concepts), in its small way affected us all. The Anti-Renters were successful in getting legislation passed.

This little war with its big meaning is not mentioned in history books, so I mention it here, so our children will know.

Cat Heads

Before Vernon and I were married, Dad wanted to take us to Summerset, Virginia. He wanted to show us the house where he was born and the state of Virginia.

Dad was quite a historian and we visited monuments and graveyards. The people living in the old Faulkner Farmhouse were the Roberts. They wanted us to stay with them. They took us thru every room, every corner of the old house.

For breakfast we had "cat heads" along with thick bacon and grits. A black woman was cooking. Dad visited with her. She was a daughter of Charity who had worked for his folks. Her family had always lived in the little cabin down the path. This same family had always worked for the Faulkners from back when they were slaves.

The cat heads that Charity's daughter made on the griddle on top of the stove were a flat, very flat biscuit. She put biscuit dough on the griddle, then put a hot iron cover over the top. I understood that these dipped in sorghum grew on you. It wasn't breakfast without them.

Neither Vernon or I were impressed with either cat heads or sorghum. But "cat heads" became an expression used over and over for the next 50 years. The whole family likes biscuits, nice fluffy oven biscuits. These have been made often over the years. Once in a while they do not rise. "Cat heads again," someone says.

Now my daughter-in-law and my son are skilled in making cat heads. We all plan to find the secret to making always-fluffy biscuits, but until then, we have a name for any bread or biscuit that is not quite perfect.

Making Tracks

Dad told the story of the little black boy just the way the boy could have told it.

"I wuz pickin' blackberrie. I looked up from my almost full pail and there was a bear, a black un. I run. I look over my shoulder. The bear was smellin' my tracks and comin' closer. You like my tracks, I make you plenty more."

The expression, "make tracks" in our house went back to the story. It meant to really hurry as if there was a bear behind you. I used the same old expression with my children, but probably forgot to tell them the story.

A Cat Tale

The lumberjack's chubby cook from the house next door came into the store lugging a battered straw suitcase, a worn shopping bag, and her pocketbook. Her green wool stocking cap was pulled over her ears. Her black arctics were flapping. Her face was red, very red. "I need a ride to Margaretville," she said breathing hard. "I'm going tomorrow," Dad replied. "I need to go now. I've quit my cooking job with them cussed loggers." "Taking your cats with you?" Dad asked. Then the story came out.

Dad had heard the men complain and complain about the cat hair in the food, and cats all over the furniture and on the table in the kitchen. That morning, one of the log men, still under the weather from drinks the night before, saw the cats on the back porch railing. Bang, bang, bang—three in a row, he had shot the cats. The cook was devastated, these were her only real friends. She immediately devised a plan to get even with the lumberjacks.

At supper time, the cook prepared an especially-good dinner with a stew and all the trimmings, just the way the men like it, with plenty of seasoning. After dinner, one of the men, hoping to tease the cook into a swearing rage, asked, "Where are the damn cats?"

"You just ate them, guts and all," she said, picking up her packed suitcase and slamming the door behind her.

There were many, many stories that came out during the time the loggers were in New Kingston, most of these were not for the ears of children. I just happened to be present for this one.

The cook went back to her old farm house halfway up the mountain road. The road from that time on was known as "Cat Hollow Road."

Hot Water Jane

"Hot water, Jane. Hot water, Jane," Bouton yelled as he

tottered down from his hillside garden with a can of striped, about-to-escape, "tater" bugs.

At the doorway Jane met him with the steaming teakettle and quickly scalded the six-legged crawlers.

Ike Bouton was a warm roly-poly little man with apple red cheeks and a shiny round head without a stitch of hair. He had long since lost his hearing which accounted for the whole village knowing when the can of potato bugs was coming to the back door.

The couple eked out their meager living in their last lean years with their garden and with Jane's sewing. They kept their lawn neat and everything trimmed. The inside of the house echoed the outside, immaculate and everything in its place. Even the woodshed with Ike's muddy boots and pile of split maple firewood was swept.

Now Jane was the antithesis of Ike. She was a huge, fiery woman who ordered Ike around, made sure he was presentable, and that he completed tasks she set out for him. She communicated with him with little more than a whisper.

When they went up the hill to church on Sunday mornings, they gave the appearance of a diligent tug protecting the course of a stately ship. She wore the same flowery hat with two green apples on it as long as I could remember. Her dull satin green dress hung nearly to the ground. It was undoubtedly in full fashion some 20 years earlier and had probably come

mail order from one of New York City's finest shops.

Ike's striped brown suit was neatly pressed, even though years had taken their toll on it. He wore the same green striped tie. His white shirt collar was starched board stiff.

He ushered Jane carefully like a faithful sheep dog into their regular wooden pew halfway down the sanctuary. Every Sunday was the same. Ike sat, stood and opened his song book on cue, yet everyone knew he never heard a thing.

The only indication that he was not soaking up the sermon was his left hand slipping out his fine gold watch from the watch pocket of his vest to view the time.

To the left of the Bouton house was a fine horse barn with two stalls, a loft for hay and bins for grain. A fine carriage had stood behind the big sliding barn door in better days, but no more. Now the barn was empty except for a child's express wagon, a few bottomless chairs that were waiting to be repaired, a pitchfork and a few garden tools.

When fall came, they used the child's wagon to carry the heavy squash, pumpkins and turnips down from the hillside garden.

Again, all thru the village, we could hear Ike, "Hold 'er Jane, hold 'er Jane," as Jane pulled back to keep the wagon from running away with Ike.

Long after Ike and Jane were gone, our whole family used, "Hot water, Jane" when we wanted something in a

hurry. We used, "Hold 'er, Jane" when we wanted the driver to slow up going down a hill, or to slow up anything we were doing. I still use both with Vernon and my grown children. Now everyone knows the origin.

Birdie

Birdie swished the flies away and scooped up a dipper of water from a pail. Birdie handed Dad the dipper. "Here, see how good our water is up here." By the time the dipper got to Dad, so many flies had settled on it, he couldn't decide on a place to drink.

Dad was visiting his sister-in-law with the idea of giving them a little financial aid. He was trying to be very tactful and figure out something Birdie really wanted. Birdie, washing the dishes with a rag in a blue enameled pan on one end of the table, pushed back her hair with her arm from her sweaty head.

Dad said, "I could have the water run in the house for you and a sink put right under that window." At that moment, the dishes finished, Birdie picked up the pan. In one big swoop the water flew out the open window. Only slight spatters hit the well-stained frame and upper half of the window. "Now what would anyone want a sink for, if they have a window." She was wiping the table with her apron.

Another time Birdie came to New Kingston and was looking at the names on the postal boxes. She was laughing and laughing—"Van Benscoten, Winter, McLaughlin—people have the funniest names here in New Kingston." Dad didn't say anything, but laughed to himself. Who could have a funnier name than Birdie Parasol?

Sunburned

On the way home Dad was reminiscing and telling us stories. "My colored mammy was a dear. She took care of me, and then my three brothers and sister as they came along.

"We called her Aunt Charity. I suppose she was part of the family. When I was little, I said to her, 'Aunt Charity, why are you black?' 'I ain't black, I's jus' sunburn.' I believed her. I don't remember when I realized she was neither a member of the family nor sunburned."

School

As I told you, all my early schooling was in one-room schools with eight grades in one room. That is until Dad realized how bad my education really was and decided to send me to Margaretville. He realized that 30 students in one room with one teacher was impossible. He had been a teacher himself and now was the school trustee. He decided that the whole eighth grade should be transported to Margaretville. He had a real community fight but was successful.

We eighth graders found Miss Jenks's class something different from anything we had ever been exposed to. She was a

Dad, Mother and I. We always seemed to have some cats and kittens.

strict disciplinarian and made sure every child learned. Coming in from a one-room school I was embarrassed at how little I knew. I couldn't get up, stand by my seat, and answer a question.

If I had to read a paper in front of the class, I stumbled and felt faint. The only thing that encouraged me were my good grades, and the teacher always choosing my papers to read to the class. Then too, in art, my pieces were always chosen to be hung.

I knew I had to get over this shyness, the self-consciousness. I talked to my Dad. The next school year, my high school freshman year, he said he would come to Margaretville and pick me up if I wanted to stay after school for drama club. I didn't really want to, but thought, as Dad did, it might help. I was poor, scared, and

really hated drama. I stayed thru the year and two plays. Next year Dad came to Margaretville to get me so I could take Prize Speaking. I worked and worked on my 20 minute recitation. I was scared, skinny, and stiff when I got up before that gymnasium filled with people. I threaded my way along, almost unconsciously, until I heard my Dad cough. He had been at a bank meeting and came in late. (I didn't know then that his cough was from his heart trouble.) For the moment I lost the thread of my recitation. I had to be prompted from the side. I came in third. I felt lucky that I had even gotten thru it.

I took two more years of drama. I never felt comfortable, never really wanted to do it. I guess it did do something for my confidence, but not much. It was not until I was in college

Me in college.

at Oneonta that I found I could do anything—make speeches, announcements, sing, run meetings, do anything with confidence.

As an adult I was able to teach, run seminars, give lectures, but I would rather not. These things raise my blood pressure.

Last year I was asked to give a lecture at the United Federation of Doll Clubs convention. I thought at first what fun it would be. Then I thought of the stress and said no. Even on my favorite subject, dolls, I must say no.

I expected all of life to be beautiful like the valley I lived in. I expected life to be stitched together with beauty, humor, love and work—like the old patchwork quilt in the chest in the hallway. As I have written, I felt it was best to leave some things, like town scandals, torn and out of focus as Dad said they should be.

College

I was sent off to Muskingum College in Ohio when the time came. My English teacher in high school wanted me to go to the Breadloaf School of English to study writing. Coming from a wee village to a big college campus was hard. I was too timid to really enjoy the opportunity.

In February my Dad got pneumonia, I wanted to come home, but I didn't. I spent Thanksgiving vacation on my roommate's father's farm, a pig farm in Ohio. They burned corncobs in their fireplace for heat. Easter I spent with a sorority sister in Pittsburgh. Their house was on a hill overlooking a steel mill. At night we could see the red hot hunks of steel on a track being cut off at a certain point.

When I got home in May, Dad and I talked it over—the expense, the distance, the home sickness. We decided I could switch to the State Normal School in Oneonta, New York. I lost some college credits but switched anyway.

I was happy in Oneonta. I could hold my own in any given situation. I joined many organizations, held offices, wrote for the school paper, joined a local sorority, and was elected to the National Honorary English Society.

In early November Mother was taken sick. She was in the hospital, then had a nurse at home. In two-and-a-half weeks she was dead. It was 1937. I had trouble coping, but Dad had much more trouble. He and

Mother had had ten years—the happiest time of his life he said. During the week he was alone. He had never cooked or made a meal for himself. I came home on weekends, cooked and cleaned. Eventually I brought other girl students home with me. There always seemed to be plenty of boyfriends.

In September of my senior year I met Vernon in his classroom. He doesn't remember. A month or so later we met again at a dance in Margaretville. He wanted to bring me home, but I already had a date. Some time later he stopped at my rooming house in Oneonta in the evening. The girls called up saying my date was there. I went down, but it was not my date. Next time he wrote me a card, "C U Fri 8 p.m." After that and for the next 50 years, he was my only date.

New Kingston

The high spots on my corrugated memory always go back to that Catskill Mountains hamlet. Not so much does it go to the hamlet as to the hollows and tree-embossed mountains that surround the valley hamlet.

The "hollers," as the residents called the hollows or valleys, each had its mud road that branched out like limbs from a gnarled oak, twisting and turning. The roads took the easiest route, usually following a creek until it disappeared. Only two of the roads went anywhere, that is except to the hillside farms.

One of these roads, narrow and steep, passable only in the fall and summer, went up and over to the valley beyond to Bovina. In the spring, there were deep mud holes and ruts that prevented any passage except by farm wagons. In the snow, only the farmers could get through with trucks or sleighs.

This Bovina mountain was like a hunk of heaven transported. Its beauty, even just to drive over on the dirt road, dappled with sunlight, was joy to me. Ferns lined the road edges, shinhopple with its arching branches and snow white flowers fell down over huge rocks. Smooth, grey-barked beeches rose like pillars and posts thru to the canopy of the woods. Jade green moss sparkled with moisture in the rock crevices and down the shaded north side.

This was where I rode my horse with nothing but the sound of his feet, the spring songs of the birds, and the chattering of a scampering chipmunk to keep me company.

We often drove over this mountain, road permitting, as a short cut to Delhi or Oneonta. It was even a joy to view from a car. We couldn't drive much faster than a horse could walk, and with the windows open, there was the sweet smell of the woodland.

There was a clearing just on top of the mountain. In the summer you could climb over the wooden fence rails, go out across the pasture, and on the big rocks build a fire and cook hot dogs and marshmallows. We had many roasts and picnics there.

In the spring you could walk over thru the unfurling brakes to the dense woods to pick pink and blue hepaticas.

In the fall two giant golden-leaved beeches offered beech nuts. We would spread out a sheet, and one person would climb the tree and shake the limbs. Three-cornered golden brown nuts would splatter on the sheets. Some would still be housed in their prickly burs.

In the spring before the leaves were full-green, I would stand at the mountaintop, look down at the miniature farms, with old wood-colored barns, white houses and red silos. (Seldom did the farmer have enough money to paint his barn. If he did, he painted it red.) Apple trees put bits of color here and there.

In summer, the tree foliage was deep green. I would stand in ferns knee-high to view the valley below. Some fields would be brown where newly mown hay stood in windrows waiting to be bunched. A field would be silver green, this was newly headed oats the farmer had grown for his horses.

The milk houses were nearly smothered in late blooming lilacs and single roses. The side-hill pastures were all mowed to a half-inch, neatly trimmed around every rock and wild rose bush, leaving only the brakes and buttercups untouched. The Jersey cows did the mowing and trimming.

In the autumn I often went up the mountain. We sometimes had a family picnic on Sunday. The view would have changed to a kaleidoscope of red, golds and yellows of the maple, ash and beech. I would pick up leaves, a red one here, a yellow, a green one with red veins. I still cannot resist an autumn-colored leaf. There is no place the autumn trees are as colorful as the Catskills.

I didn't mention that in spring the farm fields, our own farm especially, were filled with long stemmed large blue violets. In the summer there are white daisies, fields of them from stone wall to stone wall. Fall brings on the black-eyed susan, closed gentians, red woodbine on the wall, and the colored leaves of choke cherry, yellow to amber brakes (meadow ferns), and the purple leaves of the viburnum.

Nature always seemed to be at its best up these holler roads, even in the winter with snow sparkling on every rooftop and frosting the wooden gates and weighing down the hemlocks.

The other holler road that branched away to the right went over the mountain and down into the Roxbury Valley. From the last farm up, this had never been a car road, or even a good wagon road.

Dad, Vernon and I drove the Chevy over it once in mid-summer. Dad decided we would come back by way of a used road. It was a Sunday picnic worth remembering. At the foot of the mountain where the "trail" met another dirt road was one of those picturesque

Faulkner Was New Kingston Merchant

Myron J. Faulkner, 75, of New Kingston, longtime merchant there, died Monday, March 23, at his home after a long illness.

He was born Sept. 19, 1877, at Somerset, Orange county, Virginia, son of Lyman and Sarah Stokes Faulkner. His grandfather, Jury Faulkner, was not born in the South but at the head of Bull Run at Margaretville, moving to the South after the Civil war.

Myron Faulkner came back to the North in 1894, lived in upper Bull Run, where he worked on his uncle's farm. After staying there at a salary of $180 a year he went to Margaretville High school where he majored in teacher's training. He was graduated in 1898. He then taught in one-room schools in Bragg hollow, Hubbell hill, the Red schoolhouse near Dunraven and the White schoolhouse at Dunraven.

Started Store in 1904.

In 1904 he bought the general store at New Kingston, operating it for more than 40 years in connection with a filling station and feed business. For the same length of time he was a correspondent for weekly newspapers.

Mr. Faulkner was always a busy man. He was postmaster for 37 years and did some farming on the side. He was an elder of the New Kingston Presbyterian church and was active in cemetery work. He was a director and vice president of the People's National Bank of Margaretville and was active in the Democratic party.

Clipping from the Catskill Mountain newspaper, March 1953.

stone arch bridges, the perfect picnic place. Beneath the bridge, sparkling clear brook water spilled into sapphire pools. Forget-me-nots peeked into the cool pool to see themselves.

This Roxbury mountain road was just a short distance from Woodchuck Lodge, the home of the great naturalist, John Burroughs. My father was a great admirer of Burroughs. So we stopped at his house.

There were five of these stone arch bridges in the immediate area. They were perfect half-circles with a keystone in the middle of the arch. Uncle John had explained to me as a kid how these were built with a wood frame, and the keystone was put in just before the form was knocked out. I made drawings and paintings of these bridges when I was in high school.

My Childhood Home

Some stories have a way of crawling into a book all by themselves. I had hoped that this section would not be remembered. This came later, much later.

You can see that this little hamlet and these wooded mountains were so much a part of me. They were part of my growing up and formed my love of country and nature. It seems as though I could not be separated, even though I traveled and lived far from there, but I was. It was not miles or time

that snatched this treasure and turned it into trash, but people—the very people I had known all my life and believed in.

Dad said to me one day, "I am going to give you my house and its contents in my will. I know how you love New Kingston. Even if you have another home, you can use this for a vacation spot." This was a happy thought. Then after Mother died and Dad was married to his housekeeper some years later, he changed the will so that she could live in the house the rest of her life and then it would come to me. This was fine with me, but she became incompetent and was later put in a nursing home. This happened a few years after Dad died. The house was left empty. A tree had blown over and broken the porch railing, part of the porch, and put a hole in the roof. I wanted to get the house repaired. I wanted to get the house.

Curtis, my other stepbrother, was the executor of Dad's will. His attorney said that if I wanted to have the house, I would have to pay for the number of years that the lady would live, according to the actuary chart. I didn't have that much money. Time passed, I scraped, I worked, I borrowed. I finally got enough to pay for the house, even though I knew this was not Dad's intention. I was not up to or had enough money to hire a lawyer. This was only the beginning. The deed for my father's house had not been found. A neighbor had somehow gotten it and did not intend to give it up.

After I paid for my childhood home, Vern, our children and I went there, expecting it to be just as I had left it. The horror when we went in. The house had been completely stripped of every piece of furniture—the birdseye maple set in the guest bedroom, the brass beds and high old antique beds and dressers, the rocking chairs, the dining room furniture and mother's precious dishes that I loved.

Even the kitchen stove had been removed, as were all the little antiques that I had loved as a child. In the hall was a chest of wonderful old quilts that were gone, chest and all. The house was naked. All those rose-laced remembrances mashed into nothingness. Even the drawer that held my mother's handwritten recipe book was empty. Even my old worthless paintings and my little all-bisque dolls were gone.

In a small hamlet like New Kingston there are no vandals, just neighbors. Everyone knows everything. It was at this moment I decided I no longer loved New Kingston or the people there. New Kingston, in a single moment, had lost its charm, lost everything, that had meant so much earlier.

I had already arranged for a fine carpenter to come from Oneonta and replace and fix every spindle in the porch railing—to put the house back to its original shape. He fixed and painted everything, but my heart was no longer in it.

Another neighbor even tried to claim a strip of the lawn until I told him I knew exactly where the line was.

I was heartbroken, devastated, but one recovers. I advertised and sold the house. Just before the closing, something or someone put something down the drain to clog it. I sold the house anyway but had to pay to

have the drain dug up and replaced. I recovered more or less from my loss. Now I just keep that hamlet the way it used to be in the back of my mind. I don't go back to look and feel unhappy.

As I was writing this, Jeanne, my childhood friend, called and told me who she thought emptied the house and what he intended to do with the deed—thirty years too late!

PART 3

All Grown Up

State Teachers College, Oneonta, New York. This building, dear to the hearts of every alumni, no longer stands.

A ceramic plate that I made showing the six influences on my life.

College Professors

After leaving Muskingham College in Ohio and entering what was then called the Oneonta State Normal School. I found the relationship between the student and instructor to be entirely different and on a different plane.(When I earned my degree, the college had changed its name to State University College at Oneonta.)

The instructors became my friends, my lifelong friends. I often think of one of my art teachers, Rachel Taylor, a tall woman with steel grey hair drawn back in a knot and soft grey eyes that commanded both your attention and admiration.

The first half of the semester in her art course I did not make an impression on her with my art. She gave me a B. It was an unheard of thing to give me a B in art, I thought! Something had to give. It was like she didn't know I existed.

One morning in her art class, I sat daydreaming of possibilities to impress her. I noticed that about three days of the week she wore teal blue, either her skirt, blouse or dress was always that same beautiful shade of teal that went with her grey hair and eyes. I noticed other things about her and on her desk that were teal blue. The idea struck me. From now on, anything that I had to paint, construct, or choose a color for would be teal blue.

I saw my plan begin to work. Then one day when we were having a conference over the weeks' works she said, "I notice how much your work is improving." Then she added,

"All this aqua and teal blue you're using, I hope it isn't because I like this color." I hadn't put anything over on her, yet my plan had sort of worked.

I believe from that moment we became friends, good friends for the rest of her life. She was the teacher I worked for at the National Youth Administration (NYA), a Roosevelt program for students. I took all the art courses she offered, and never again was I offended by a B grade.

Rachel Taylor was a good friend. I consulted her when I was student teaching art. I was invited to her apartment to see the beginnings of new projects.

When Rachel Taylor and Mary Shepard, another teacher, started art classes at Craigsmoor, New York, a summer art school, I was a guest. The following summer I decided to spend six weeks at their mountain retreat and take courses for credit. The art in these two infected me. We lived, we talked art. We were painters, sculptors and weavers. It was all pure ecstasy living in the mountain cabins among the trees.

Both Rachel and Mary became Vernon's and my lifelong friends. They wrote letters and visited us through the years as our children grew. They watched our son Jay's art develop.

Dr. Mills was a small proper man who always wore a well-pressed grey suit. If he saw even a touch of talent in any student, he pounced upon it, always hoping to produce a great writer. I first knew Dr. Mills from his supervision of the *Pendragon* (the college newspaper) which I worked on, then as an advisor for the literary honor society. This group met in his home.

I then, on Dr. Mills's advice, took Writing III, which was nothing more than "a you report to me each Tuesday with a paper" class. I ate up all this individual attention and became a slave to that Tuesday two o'clock lesson. First he graded my papers with two marks, "F" for spelling and "A" for content. He wrote one day at the top of my paper. "You are the first student that I've had who could spell a common word three different ways on a single page."

Sometimes he wrote that I must learn to spell or learn to use a dictionary. Other than this, he dashed lavish praise on my writing abilities, that is until I tried fiction, a short story. This story and every other short story I ever wrote were nothing more than a waste of paper—disasters. We became friends.

As our advisor for the *Pendragon*, he arranged to take us to the *Oneonta Star* newsroom and have the city editor talk to us.

The *Oneonta Star* was a morning newspaper. When we got there at eight p.m., the room was wild with activity. There were clanky old typewriters and lights hung high from ceiling cords. The typewriter pounders wore green visors tight on their foreheads. There were ashtrays already overloaded, wadded papers overflowing in baskets, men talking to men. No one paid any attention to us. It was as though we weren't there. The place smelled of ink, stale smoke and oil.

The presses were already running with ads. The noise was unbearable. We were led along the side of the room to view the different processes. We saw the typesetter selecting type by hand and another man pouring hot lead to make a finished plate.

So this was the place where news, global catastrophes, six alarm fires, burglaries, murders, purse snatchers, and cats in trees changed from verbal news to the printed page—the news we read.

We were herded thru a hall into an office. The noise and the smell were left behind. We squatted on the floor, two to a chair, and on the window sill. We looked at the man at the desk, an Edward G. Robinson take-charge guy. He was in his shirt sleeves. When he spoke, the Robinson image faded, he had us in his spell.

He looked at us straggly students as though he knew all of us would turn into great reporters if we were given the right instruction. He had our complete attention by describing his first reporting job. It had been to cover a prison riot at Sing Sing. He told it in such descriptive terms and so clearly that we all felt that we were there experiencing the fear and anticipation he felt. We sat spellbound for an hour. No one so much as twitched.

Then he told us the basics of reporting—who, what, where, and when. He said the first part of the story told the basics, the next part explained further, the last part was the supporting detail. This style was for two reasons. If the story had to be cut, minor details were taken off the bottom without a re-write. The second reason was for the reader to be able to read just the first paragraph or two and get the basic story. He talked about newspaper language and vocabulary, and how different it was from everyday speech.

This experience carried with me, so much so, that I arranged for my children and their 4-H group to make a similar trip again to the *Oneonta Star*. This time I had to remember the basics of reporting to tell the children.

I was telling you about my college professors. I should tell you about the college president, Dr. Charles Hunt. I met him my first day on campus. They had arranged a picnic for the freshmen. We played softball and our pitcher was Dr. Hunt. From then on he was a friend. His office was open, we could talk to him. He lived on Maple Street and he usually walked to the main building. I sometimes walked with him.

If I could think of a reason, I was allowed to bring the car from home to Oneonta for a week or so at a time. I would drive the car to class in the morning and park it in the tiny circle that went around the flagpole. Early one morning, just making my 8 a.m. class, I drove the car into the tiny parking space. It was crooked. I backed up. Wham! I hit the flagpole. I got out to view the damage and see if anyone saw me. There stood Dr. Hunt. "Don't worry Pepper," he said. "See all those nicks on the other side of the pole, I hit it regularly." I was never sure whether he was telling the truth or just trying to make me feel better.

(I was dubbed Pepper by my high school principal one night at a basketball game when he said, "Screw down the roof, here comes Pepper." The name followed me for years. College friends still call me Pepper.)

Dr. Hunt was Vernon's and my lifelong friend, and we worked with him on many occasions in adult life.

Dr. Schumacher was at the retiring age when I started college, but he stayed one more year. He was an established part of the college. My sister Phoebe had had him. My father had had him in what was the Training Class. My husband had him. My whole family knew and loved him.

They referred to him as a fixture. He was a delightful, whisk-ered man with the heart and soul of a poet. He looked on us all as children. He called us children. He was a poet. His beloved volume of poems is still on my bookshelf.

We often walked up the hill at noon together. The side-walk was flagstone. In one place there was a hollow that looked like a footprint. He would stop (an excuse to rest) and step in the stone footprint. "Now you must do the same." I always obliged. As we parted at the top of the Old Main's steps, he would say, "Bring me a poem tomorrow. I haven't had one in a week now."

He corrected and criticized my many poems. He would always say, "Little girl, your poems intrigue me, write more, write more." "Shooe" as all the students called him was a loved figure.

One instructor, E. Louis B. Curtis, was something else. A tall skinny guy with imaginary itches. He itched, he twitched, he talked. He was convincing. He talked all the young men into being conscientious objec-tors (but not Vernon, who had him earlier). I never took a class from him. Just seeing him at meetings and in the hall with his continual itching made me squirm.

Dr. Johnson was a natura-list. I always felt like I was his favorite student. I loved his 5 a.m. morning bird hikes. I al-ready knew most of the birds, trees and wildflowers. I soon learned the weeds and grasses. When he couldn't think of the name of something, he would quickly turn and say, "Pepper, what is it?" We often had meetings at his new house on East Street.

I remember well the first morning I was in Anne Scotts's geography class. She looked at her list of students, picked out the longest name and said, "Miss Van Valkenburgh change your altitude." I started for the door. I was going upstairs—changing my altitude. She thought I was leaving. She yelled at me, and I was so embarrassed. I hated having my stupidity on display. "You could have stood on your chair," she said. I never thought of that. This experience left a nasty, bad taste in my mouth for Miss Scott and her geography.

New York City

I believe I was seven when I was taken to New York City for the first time. I did what children do, look up from the street at the towering skyscrapers, pat the policeman's horse, have a few extra rides on the hotel elevator, and put a postcard to Jeanne down the glass shoot that went the height of the building.

We went to see the Rockettes at the Roxy Theater. We rode the subways. The newest building was the Chrysler Building, the top not yet finished. We visited wholesale houses.

As high school seniors we spent one night and two days in New York City. We visited the Stock Exchange building. Dad was more interested in my report than I was. We took the tour and saw the beginning of television at Radio City Music Hall.

When I was in college, there was the annual Music Pilgrimage to New York City. Money was tight then, and I felt it an imposition to ask Dad for money for a fun trip. So I got a job under Roosevelt's National Youth Administration.

I had to state the reason for wanting work. I thought of a few lies that would surely get me a job, and then I decided they would know if I went on the pilgrimage. I decided to tell the truth. They gave me a job. The job was so perfect for me that I would have done it without pay. I was in my realm of glory. I arranged flowers, leaves, whatever I could find, for bouquets in the lounge and offices of the college. I took care of the plants, watering, turning, and breaking off dead leaves. I made arrangements of work from art classes in cases and on bulletin boards. I printed and arranged notices on the bulletin boards. I couldn't have had a more delightful job. It took me to New York City on the Music Pilgrimage.

New York City was different with a group of young people on a tight schedule. We went to two plays, *Arsenic and Old Lace*, and I don't remember the other one. We went to a musical and an opera. We took taxis and ate at well-known spots. It was an educational trip that sparkled forever for me, more than worth the work I had done to get there.

The next trip to New York City that impressed me was the

one to visit Vernon when I was teaching in Oxford, New York. We had no money, so we just enjoyed each other. We walked hand in hand thru the arboretum and sat holding hands in the planetarium, and on park benches. I made several of these trips while Vernon was in officers' training at Columbia University.

We made several trips to New York City as the children were growing up. The first one was at Thanksgiving to see Macy's and all the Christmas decorations. Vernon had a meeting so I took the children on a tour bus thru the Bowery, Harlem, and to the Statue of Liberty. We went to Radio City Music Hall so Colleen could see the organ. Jay wanted to see the aquarium, so we went there.

When the children were older, we went to visit the Museum of Natural History and to visit Alice Gray, the curator of entomology. By this time, New York City had changed. As we left, Alice Gray warned us to be careful.

We have not been to New York City since 1980. We hear tales and things that have happened to our friends. You couldn't coax me to go now.

Growing

Coming from a tiny hamlet and being pampered by a loving family slowed the natural process of growing up.

It was not until I was a college senior that I began to take my life and decisions into my own hands. I was still influenced by my father and his teachings. Vernon was humming *How*

My college graduation portrait.

Deep Is the Ocean and *The Girl That I Marry* and was trying to influence my decisions. Europe was in turmoil with Hitler and Mussolini. We lived under the shadow of war. There was still the deep Depression. Yet, this was a happy time, a growing up time, and much of this good feeling had to do with the constant attention of Vernon.

This was during the big band era. Vernon and I went to the college balls. I wore long, beautiful evening gowns as did all the girls. My date brought me corsages which I often wore on my wrist. We did the "Big Apple" and slow dances to Gershwin's *Rhapsody in Blue* or *Dancing Cheek to Cheek*.

It was after one of these delightful balls that Vernon seriously proposed for the first time on May 6, 1940.

Growing up for me must have been a slow process. Mother died my first year at Oneonta Normal. I had taken over the running of Dad's

house, the cooking, and the cleaning, as best I could. I took over Mother's flower garden. I had learned all these things from her through my growing years.

Planning my future was not easy. I felt responsible for Dad's well-being and realized how lonely his life had become.

I had signed a statement, as all Normal School students were required to do, that I would teach for two years. Vernon was considering going into the Service. He was teaching math and science in Margaretville Central School. I had no savings at this time. From school to work would be a big change, or should I get married. Say yes to Vernon now. That would be the easy way out.

But this senior year was a pleasant time. I was allowed to take Dad's car to college in Oneonta for two weeks at a time. Dad brought me a wonderful new wardrobe to wear for job interviews. As it was, I only went for one and got the job. But Vernon liked my new outfits.

This was the year *Gone With the Wind* came out. Vernon and I saw it together. We saw many movies together. He took me to restaurants, we walked in the parks, we spent weekends in New Kingston, we climbed mountains, we spent hours just talking. Periodically, he proposed in all kinds of roundabout ways. Sometimes I gave him a bad time, because I felt I had obligations.

Vernon decided to finish his degree in Albany State University. He was rejected by the

Air Force, but the Navy took him into officers' training—one of the ninety-day wonders. He finished his B.S. first, then went to New York for officers' training. This definitely cramped our style. Now he couldn't get married until he finished training.

This did give me a little more growing up time as I went off to my first teaching job.

Oxford

I graduated from Oneonta State Normal School in 1940. This was during the Depression and only a fourth of my class got jobs. I was surprised when I was the third one to get a job. My high school principal had changed jobs and was in Oxford, New York. He hired me to teach fourth grade when he came to the college to interview. He was filling Oxford New York Central School's vacancies.

Dad hired a housekeeper. This made things easier for me. I didn't have to work so hard on weekends. I also felt free to go to Craigsmoor for the summer. This was a summer art school. I studied sculpture, weaving and watercolor. I saw Vernon on weekends.

Fall came and I went off to my first teaching job. Teaching and living in Oxford was a whole new life for me. I lived in a single room. There were six of us, all teachers, in the same house, sharing one bathroom. Mrs. Stratton who owned the house made us breakfast. Her daughter who lived a few blocks away made us dinner four nights a week.

The grade teachers, a home economics teacher, and the music teacher had been teaching for many years and were well adjusted to this type of life. They were wonderful to me, making sure I did the right thing at the right time and included me in their activities.

Adjusting to being a teacher was easy. We all put in long days. We signed in at eight or before in the morning, had lunch or playground duty at noon, corrected papers and did reports. Sometimes I had Brownie Scouts until five in the afternoon. We went from the school to the home where we ate dinner. It was a long walk, a beautiful walk in the spring and fall, a cold one in the winter.

My first day at teaching could have been a disaster but it turned out to be good—all of my teaching experiences were mostly good.

"I could pick you up and throw you out the window," Alex remarked as he sized me up the first morning of school. He was two or three grades behind and a bully who had been dumped in my class.

I smiled at him and made him my helper, my errand boy. He knew the building and where everything was and how everything was done.

I made friends with each of the children. I found out all I could about their backgrounds, home life and learning abilities. I loved each and every child like they were my own and, in turn, I could see they liked me.

Teaching came easy.

Even so, it was good to escape

Here I am when I was teaching at Oxford Central School. Vernon took the picture.

to New Kingston and Vernon every few weekends. We were deeply in love.

On the playground one day when school had just started, a bitsy kindergartener came to me pulling another even bitsier one with her. "Her says her has to go bathroom. Her says, her does, right now." I could see it was too late.

The big war was going on in Europe. I had a little English girl in my class my second year of teaching. She had been sent to live with a relative to get out of the war. She loved to sing, her blonde curls dancing, "And the capons (caisons) came rolling along—." No one corrected her.

Vernon had come to Oxford to spend the weekend with me. It was Sunday evening and he

had just left to drive all the way back to Albany. When I came into my room, I turned on the radio—war had just been declared, President Roosevelt was speaking.

In February 1943, during my third year of teaching, Vernon and I decided to get married so that I could go with him— wherever. I went into see Mr. Franklin the principal, shuddering in my boots. I knew full well he would have trouble finding a substitute for my fourth grade.

I was surprised at his reaction when I gave him the news. "You and me too," he said. "I am going in the service in the middle of March."

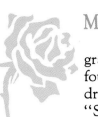

Meatballs

"Did you see that?" the first grade teacher wondered. The four of us had stopped at the drug store on the way to school. "See what?" Beth asked.

"I just happened to look over that man's shoulder at the paper. It said Blue Bird Diner Closed."

"Well what do we do now for our Friday nite spaghetti supper?" I asked?

This spaghetti supper had become a ritual for us poor $1,000 a year teachers. We had eaten the Blue Bird's Friday nite spaghetti and meat balls for two years now. It was good, cheap, and an end-of-the-week outing for tired teachers.

"When you go in the office, will you get the paper and see what's going on, Marion?"

I passed Beth as I took the children to the gym. "It was closed by the health inspector," Beth whispered.

"Johnny get in line. Barbara stop talking." I didn't see Beth, Etta or Marion until school was out that afternoon.

"The article was on two pages and I only got the first page." Etta said, planking the page down on arithmetic papers yet to get corrected. We poured over the article.

"Blue Bird Diner permanently closed by the health inspector. Routine inspection finds many violations, etc, etc."

Marion came running in. "You can't believe this." Marion was sticking the scrap of paper over my head onto the desk. I read aloud to the other teachers.

"Opened dog food cans found in trash, kitchen help found preparing meat balls of dog food for spaghetti special."

We looked at each other. Beth was suddenly sick. Etta blanched with the dog food thought. "I don't really feel like going to dinner!" I said.

The Hope Chest

In a way, the hope chest was a part of growing up. My sister, Phoebe, had given me a large cedar chest when I graduated from high school. These hope chests were family tradition. My mother and Aunt Lottie each had one as young girls, and my two elder sisters each had one. I was not very enthusiastic about hoarding things for a life that would come some day, but I think just to accommodate my mother, I put things in the chest. She put things into the chest. She said I would be glad later that I had saved a few things.

The first thing that went into the chest was a set of blue glass dishes. I believe these are now referred to as "Depression glass." These dishes came free with bread coupons. I got the ones from our bread, from people who bought the bread but didn't want the coupons, and the few extra we were allowed in the store. The blue sugar and creamer had a white print of Shirley Temple on them. (I saw her movies while I was in high school. She was the darling of the Depression.)

My mother gave me several pieces of silver that had been in her family. A year later, Mother added a small white linen tablecloth and a pair of nice pillow cases. Then, Mother took to adding things, little things like measuring cups, hot pan holders and dish towels when I wasn't around.

When I was a college senior, I wrapped my three bisque dolls and put them in the chest. I suppose this was a part of my growing up. I never put my all-bisque dolls in the chest. I thought of them as being of no value. When Vernon and I were ready to get married and expected to leave for Columbus, Ohio, right after the wedding, we unpacked the hope chest together. We were singing *The Bells are Ringing for Me and My Gal* while deciding what we would take with us. We put the dolls back into the chest along with other items that might not travel. I had not been to the bottom of the chest, really to the bottom, since Phoebe and Dad moved it into my bedroom.

Mother had been dead now for over two years. Here in the chest were her gifts and wishes for me for a long and happy marriage. Here she had packed many of the essentials for setting up the first housekeeping, two pairs of sheets, pillow cases, lovely towels, three of her favorite plates, more silver serving pieces, her little jewelry box and other little treasures that she might have given me had she been there.

When Vernon and I got our tiny, naked apartment in Columbus and unpacked the back of our car, we were ever so thankful for Mother's help. These were the "living things" that we carried for the next two years from base to base as Vernon's orders took us.

One of the first things we discovered missing from our kitchen was a spider. I went to a hardware store down the street to purchase one. It was a tiny hardware and the man explained they hadn't sold spiders in many, many years. As soon as we could, we went to a large hardware and found spiders in all sizes.

I told the lady we rented from. She laughed and said a spider was a fry pan with three legs on it used for outdoor cooking! Well, both Vernon and I had always called a fry pan a spider.

This same Ohio woman remarked one morning, "I was coming down earlier to see you, but I hated to drive the machine (the car) on the greasy (icy) streets."

There was something else missing, but I didn't know it. Vernon was two weeks away from a Navy paycheck, so we were living on my teacher's savings. After a few days, I needed groceries. I went to the small grocery store and picked out the things I needed most. I took out my checkbook to write a check and realized I had not changed the name on my checking account. The kind store owner looked at me, "Just show me something with your married name on it." I more or less emptied my purse—ration cards, teacher's card, my bank book—I had changed nothing

to my married name. I was so embarrassed and wondered what we would eat for the next two weeks. I left the store, walked a block and a half before I remembered the hundred dollar bill Dad had stuffed in the side pocket of my purse just as we were leaving.

Colleen has my cedar chest now. I never filled it for her. Instead when she set up her own house we bought her a washer and a dryer, vacuum cleaner, tools and whatever else she needed.

24 Plus 50 Years

Whenever Vernon had time off from officers' training he would go to New Kingston, and I would go from Oxford to meet him. Dad was always happy to have us around.

Vernon had a weekend off before graduation. This group of officers were known as "90 day wonders." Dad had picked me up in Walton. We arrived home at the same time as Vernon drove in. We were all frozen. Dad pulled his chair up and put his feet almost in the kitchen oven.

Vernon and I were getting warm over the living room register. This made a wonderful excuse to be close. I was wearing my new coral red dress. (I lived and taught in suits.) We hadn't seen each other for several weeks. We were so happy to be together. Vernon hugged me tight and said, "I think we should get married." We were hugging and kissing so much I couldn't answer.

In the morning we decided

we would get married right after his graduation, and that I would resign my teaching job and go with him. I was 24.

When I told Dad he said he would rather I wait until the war was over, or I knew where Vernon would be. Then he said, "I just hate to let you go." Dad gave Vernon my mother's engagement ring. We had the perfect little blue-white diamond reset in a plain gold setting.

Wedding Notes

Vernon and I discussed our wedding plans. We both agreed to keep it as simple as possible. We could go to New York City for a full Navy wedding at the Riverside Cathedral along with the other officers of his class. This didn't appeal to either of us. It would have been fun to walk under the swords, though. My thoughts drifted back some thousand years earlier when I had poured out my wishes. I was going to be married in the New Kingston Church in the month of June, wear Mother's old dress, and carry wild white daisies. (In New Kingston in June the fields are white with daisies.) I remember Dad's remark, "I'll make it happen." But now in the winter with this impetuous young couple he couldn't. The fields were white with snow, not daisies. The church had not been cleaned or heated in months. "Wait 'til June," he said. But this was war, Vernon's orders could not be bent.

I went back to Oxford and my teaching job. I decided that

we should be married in a simple ceremony at the Dutch Reformed Church I attended in Oxford. Vernon's orders had come through and we had just ten days. All school teachers are married on Saturday so that their friends can attend. I taught school until two days before the big day. I was scared that they wouldn't find a substitute for me.

The other teachers in the house were helping me with plans. They took me to Binghamton and made me try on wedding gowns. Being very practical, and this being a wartime wedding, I decided against a gown. Instead, I chose a very plain, dark blue dress with white trim to go with Vernon's dress blue uniform. I chose a dark blue suit for travel. The teachers were disappointed but still helped me pick out everything.

The other teachers went with me to the local florist shop to select flowers for the church and for me.

Thursday night a late snow storm got under way. At first it didn't amount to much, then it began in earnest. I never once worried if Vernon would get through the storm. I didn't even think about my college friends having travel difficulties. Then Friday afternoon the florist shop called to tell me that their truck couldn't get through. They had flowers they could use for the church but not my flowers—they picked pink azaleas from their bushes in the greenhouse! It didn't bother me; I liked azaleas.

Saturday, March 6, 1943, was

there. My college friends were in my room trying to help—or hinder—me from getting dressed. Thelma, my college roommate remarked, "Only Pepper has the figure to get married without a girdle." The girls were trying to fix the azaleas for my hair and some in the diamond broach a friend had loaned me for something old.

Vernon had gotten in on Friday with his brother, Glenn, just in time for a little party they gave him. Dad had waited until morning to drive out. He got caught in the worst of the storm and only got as far as Delhi.

Snow was coming down in large, wet, slippery flakes and building a foot of whiteness on everything. Nothing seemed to bother or worry me even if Murphy's Law prevailed—so not everything was perfect. I was too happy to notice.

I wore my boots to church and carried my shoes. (I stopped to kiss the three little girls from my class standing by the church door.) These heeled shoes were almost my downfall. As Vernon kissed me and we turned to come back down the aisle, my thin high heel went right down in the grille of the hot air register. I heard everyone gasp; they thought I was falling. At that instant, I decided I must pull my foot out of the shoe and go on down the aisle. But the heel quickly came loose and Vernon's arm guided me safely. My classroom children stood outside the church as we came out, two little girls cried.

The reception was fine, but dear Vernon could hardly wait

to take off. Oh yes, the cake had a Navy man in full dress, but with one too many stripes. Vernon at this point had just made Lieutenant J.G. We laughed as we cut the cake together.

I changed my clothes. The guests threw rice and confetti as we took off with all our worldly possessions and wet confetti in Vernon's gray Plymouth in a snowstorm. Vernon was on his way to Ohio State University where he was to study aircraft recognition after the honeymoon.

We were out of Oxford a mile or two when Vernon pulled the car over and stopped. He reached over and gave me a big hug and a good kiss. "We did it, we did it, I'm so happy." I was so happy too, I can hear him yet.

We stopped at about 7:00 for some dinner. It was just about time for the restaurant to close. Just as we went out the door, there in the slush of melting snow was a bill. I reached down and picked it up. It was a ten dollar bill. We went back in to see if someone had reported losing it. They hadn't. An elderly man, sadly humped over, was pushing a broom. Vernon said "Let's give it to him." We were rewarded with a full toothless smile.

As we climbed into the car Vernon said, "From now on in, I expect you will always be finding money."

We found a one-room apartment on the third floor. It had a murphy bed. Spring was beautiful in Ohio.

Oxford Teacher Is Bride of Ensign Vernon Seeley

In a quiet wedding in the Congregational church Saturday afternoon, March 6, at 2 o'clock, Miss Mildred Van Valkenburg of Oxford became the bride of Ensign Vernon D. Seeley, U. S. N. R., of Livingston Manor. The Reverend John Heidenreich performed the single ring ceremony. Attendants were Miss Lillian Eaton of New Berlin, and Glenn Seeley, brother of the groom, of Bay Shore, Long Island. Miss Laura Hamilton played the wedding march.

The bride wore a street length dress of blue crepe with white accessories. Miss Eaton also wore a blue crepe dress with white lace collar.

The bride and groom received the congratulations of their friends at the church following the ceremony, and at 2:30 drove to the home of Mrs. Robert Stratton where a reception was given them under the direction of Miss Miriam Bloomer, assisted by other members of the Academy faculty. Thirty-four guests were present.

Spring flowers decorated the living rooms; and bouquets of red, white and blue sweet peas added to the attractiveness of the dining room. The refreshment table held a beautiful three tiered bridal cake topped with a miniature bride and groom, and ornamented with flags. Mrs. G. Challiss Franklin poured.

After the reception, the bridal couple left immediately by car for Columbus, Ohio, where Ensign Seeley is stationed. For traveling Mrs. Seeley wore a blue suit with matching accessories.

The bride is the stepdaughter of Mr. Myron J. Faulkner of New Kingston. She is a graduate of Muskingum College, Ohio, and Oneonta Normal School. For the past three years she has been fourth grade teacher at Oxford Academy.

Ensign Seeley is the son of Mr. and Mrs. David Seeley of Livingston Manor. He is a graduate of Oneonta Normal School and Albany State Teachers College. Prior to his enlistment in the U. S. Naval Reserve last October, he was science teacher in the Margaretville High School.

Out of town guests at the wedding were Mrs. David Seeley of Livingston Manor and Miss Thelma Barlow of Schenectady.

We were married.

On our wedding day.

Mr. Myron J. Faulkner

announces the marriage of his daughter

Mildred D. VanValkenburgh

to

Vernon D. Seeley

Ensign, United States Naval Reserve

on Saturday, the sixth of March

Nineteen hundred and forty-three

Oxford, New York

In three months we had to go to Gary, Indiana, and then Great Lakes. Finding a place to live was nearly impossible. I would just get our dishes washed and put in the cupboard, when we would have to move again.

We found a room in Waukegan. Vernon got undressed to get into bed and found the bed had only a bottom sheet. I shut Vernon in the tiny closet because he didn't have a bathrobe and called the landlady. She spoke only Polish. I tried to explain I needed another sheet. I tried everything.

Finally her daughter came to see what was the matter. "Like hospital," she told her mother. I was afraid Vernon would suffocate in the tiny closet before I could get the sheet. I didn't want to live in Waukegan.

The officers' club told us to go to Lake Forest to find housing. We found the Strong Mansion. It was next to the Armour estate. Seven Navy couples lived in the house. We all cooked in the huge kitchen. The dining room was so big it had a fireplace on each end. The table was so long that couples set dinner here and there on ends and sides. Each couple had a bedroom and bathroom, and some had an extra little sitting room, we did. It was here that I introduced Vernon to the fun of modeling pieces in clay. He took to it like second nature

I started working in the therapy unit of Great Lakes Naval Hospital as a volunteer. I was teaching clay modeling. I found there was a Eugene Deutsch in Chicago who had kilns and would fire our pieces. The pieces we made in the hospital were taken there for firing.

He was German and had come directly from Germany with his glaze formulas. We asked him how to make a certain glaze. He said, "I drink a little beer, throw in some stuff, throw in a little beer and a little more stuff." This was his way of saying the formulas are mine, and I will not tell anyone.

This conversation made a lasting impression on Vernon and me. I decided then and there to share anything I learned. This was the beginning of the sharing philosophy that I carried thru to the doll business.

It was four years later that Deutsch died at 43. He drank too much and left four young daughters with no support.

We found a gardener's cottage nestled in the oak trees on the Donnely Estate. We took it with Frank and Doris Friden. Frank was a doctor on the base. It was close to the base and a good place to live.

Here we bought our first kiln. We worked at clay in the evenings and weekends. We both loved it. I taught some children's classes and worked at the Naval Hospital. I went to the Art Institute in Chicago two days a week for classes, sculpture, glaze formulation and painting. I rode the fast train in.

About the third day in painting class, my painting was so bad I decided to take it home and see if I could fix it up. At the end of the day I threw my smock over the 36" x 20" canvas, went up thru the museum, and out the front entrance. I was just pushing the outside door when a guard had a hold of my arm. He thought I was stealing a painting. I was not aware that if you wished to take anything out you had to have the professor put his stamp on it. He sent me back to get the painting stamped. He knew once he looked at it that it was mine.

I made the mistake of not paying the full amount and getting credit for my courses. I didn't realize that later I could use the credit to finish my B.S. and M.S.

There were good times at Great Lakes. We went to church on the base. We went to concerts. We heard all the great entertainers. We planted our first garden together. We met and were entertained by the wonderful people of Lake Forest.

I worked beside a famous garden sculptor, Sylvia Shaw Judson, and visited her studio and studied her works—all children. She made a lasting impression on me. Her children translated into dolls for me. I made small sculptures of children. I did these small sculptures for years before I started dolls.

From there we went back to Ohio then to California. We had moved in and out of all kinds of rooms and housing 19 times. Now Vernon was waiting for his ship, the USS *Brule*, an attack transport to be commissioned.

We said goodbye at a party the night before he left. I knew he was sailing at dawn the next

Above: Vernon taken in Neawah Park, Oneonta, NY. Right: Vernon and me after we were married. Below: Vernon, me and my dog Cammie.

Vernon took me fishing. He couldn't catch any—I kept him so busy taking the fish off my line and baiting my hook.

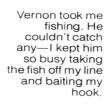

Me and Cammie.

Before I made dolls, I made many small sculptures of children.

morning. I got up and went to the base. I was the only one on the dock. I saw the ship move out. An officer came by and saw my tears. "You should see how those boys will eat on that ship. You can't believe the meat we loaded into her." This was all he could think of to say to me. I was familiar with the ship since I had been aboard numerous times.

I got home to New Kingston after having all kinds of trouble getting tickets and being stranded in Tucson.

I found a teaching job in Ithaca. I wrote Vernon every day. In the spring, Carolyn, my niece, then five, came and lived with me—in my one room. She was just delightful. I took her to nursery school in the same building where I was teaching, the Fall Creek School. We ate in restaurants and the home economics buildings on the campus. We visited the orchid greenhouse and the rose greenhouse. She and I loved the lush flower gardens. We walked the gorges with their waterfalls.

Santa Out of Season

Carolyn pulled loose from my hand and ran down to the end of the line. As she whisked away her excited childish voice said, "There he is. I told you I saw him before."

Four of us teachers and five-year-old Carolyn were standing in line for dinner at the cafeteria on the Cornell Campus. We ate there often.

I turned and tried to catch Carolyn as she ran toward the end of the line. "There's Santa Claus," she was shouting as

she headed for a white-haired, white-bearded professor on the end of the line. Everyone turned to watch.

"Sure I am. And what do you want for Christmas?" He grinned and gave her a pat. I tried to apologize and pulled Carolyn back up to our place in line.

I am sure Carolyn will always believe in Santa Claus no matter her age like Susan in *Miracle on 34th Street*.

When school was out, I went back to New Kingston before I left for California. In one way or another, Vernon had hinted in his letters he would be coming to San Francisco. I had trouble getting a ticket to San Francisco.

New Mother

"Can you hold my baby a minute while I go to the bathroom?" the very young mother asked, handing me what appeared to be more blanket than baby. I got out, "But," and found myself holding a complete stranger's baby in the airport at El Paso at four a.m.

Air travel was difficult during World War II. This was the second time I had been "bumped" coming from New York to meet Vernon in California.

I had been in the airport most of the night waiting, hoping that by morning they would find me a seat and I would get on my way. The young woman had also been there most of the night.

Now I sat with my small suitcase, my pocketbook, and a baby on my lap. I looked in at the small, red-faced infant who was fast asleep. Thirty minutes later, I was still holding the infant.

An hour passed. I was getting very nervous. What would I do if the woman didn't come back? Just then, there was a call for me, they had a seat to San Francisco.

Not ever having had a baby, I struggled with the baby and suitcase and got to the desk. The girl said, "Your plane leaves in 12 minutes. You are one of the lucky ones to get a seat."

I tried to explain to the girl about the baby—asking her if she would take it, just for a few minutes. "No. But I'll call on the speaker for the mother to return because you must leave."

"What is her name?" I didn't have the slightest idea. "Do you know where her luggage is?" I didn't.

"Is it a boy or girl?" "I have no idea," I said. Again, I pleaded, "Can't you take the baby back there until the woman comes back?"

She looked at me, "I don't want to be held for kidnapping." I could see that the girl did not believe my story. "I will call on the speaker for the no-name woman who left an infant to come and get it."

She did just that. The tone of her voice made it sound like she knew no one would come, or that there really wasn't any such person.

My time to catch the plane was evaporating. Minutes were sliding by like beads off a broken string. She called twice on the speaker, neither she nor I, believing for a minute the

I also taught the children arts and crafts.

baby's mother would show up.

She did. She rounded the corner with a sandwich in her hand. "I just had to have something to eat, but it took forever. Thanks for holding Johnny." She took the infant.

At that moment, I looked down at myself. The lower part of my blouse and skirt were soaking wet—the only suit I had with me.

I did get to San Francisco. I stayed with another Navy wife. We would go to the bridge twice a day to see if the USS *Brule* had come in.

Vernon came in and I met him. He left the next day for Seattle to get his ship repaired. Five of us wives drove to Seattle where Vernon and I had about three weeks together. The night before Vernon was to ship out again, the bomb was dropped on Hiroshima. He had to go,

and I returned to Ithaca for another term.

I loved the Ithaca fifth and sixth graders. Now I lived with five other teachers. Marion Dennison, one of the teachers, became my lifelong friend. Five of us teachers went to programs on the Cornell campus; we went to concerts; we ate on the campus; we rode horses in the park. Ithaca was a good place to live during the war.

The Gift

I had one very quiet girl, Bonnie, in my fifth grade. She was not only quiet, but quite alone. She was the only poor child in the well-off neighborhood.

In October I taught the children clay modeling for the art class. The children made small animals, and I took them to the local pottery to be fired and

63

Lake Bluff, Illinois, is where we lived in a gardener's cottage.

In Seattle, Washington, we met to wait for the repairs of his ship—the USS *Brule*.

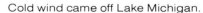

Vernon and me—we were already planning our rose garden.

Ration reminder of the time—1943-44. Below: Early unfinished sculpture.

Cold wind came off Lake Michigan.

Carolyn Fairbairn, my niece, lived with me for a time while Vernon was overseas.

glazed. The children were delighted with their projects. I discussed the results with them. Bonnie's little kitten with his straight-up tail and cat-like face showed more creative ability than the other animals. I admired it in class, and told the students why it was so good.

Christmas came. In this school, children were allowed to bring the teacher a present. (In other schools where I had taught, I had always told the children no presents.) The afternoon of the Christmas party, I did get presents, writing paper, handkerchiefs, all sorts of little things. Bonnie was the last one to go home. She went out to her coat and brought in something all wrapped up. I opened it. It was the wonderful little cat she had made in October.

I was so happy with the wonder ful cat. Bonnie could see I loved it and this made her happy. "It was all I had," she said. It was as if she had given me a piece of herself.

The First Married Years

We learned a lot those first four years together. It was really a great way to start a marriage. Living with the Navy in wartime, picking up and moving, irregular watches and hours, the uncertainty of daily life, of the whole thing—it all made us depend on each other. This was the first time I had really been away from my family and Vernon his.

I planned everything around Vernon's schedule, if he had one. I planned to be free if he didn't. We spent every moment possible together. Our love developed deeper, if that were possible. We traveled from one end of the country to the other and back again. When we were separated, we could hardly wait to be back together.

One horrible time that I remember was when we were in Long Beach, California. Vernon's ship, the USS *Brule*, was waiting to be commissioned. He would go to the ship at odd hours, sometimes stay one day, sometimes two. I never knew when he would come or go. I lived with nightmares when he didn't come.

In the dream, I was running, running. I couldn't breathe. Something was wrong and I didn't know what it was. But something was wrong. At that instant, the roaring and wailing sound shattered the night silence. Everything rocked. The hospital and the base sirens were deafening all around us.

I bolted from the bed to a standing position. I was paralyzed with fright. Awake I knew these alarms; they were the dread of every Naval wife. There was a catastrophe at the base, perhaps a Japanese invasion. Perhaps it was another Pearl Harbor.

I shook. Vernon's ship was at anchor in the bay and he was on watch. From the window I could see billows of smoke and flames. The sirens kept wailing. There was nothing I could do. Two other Navy wives were in the same house. We held onto each other. I don't know what time it started, but at daybreak we were still watching, weeping. All the next day, the three of us waited. We got the word about the big Naval fire and the number of men dead and injured, but no word from our husbands. At six o'clock that evening, our old Plymouth drove up. All three men got out. We hugged, kissed and cried. The USS *Brule* had just gotten in from a shakedown cruise and had missed the whole thing.

It was times like this that made us cherish every moment together. This was in the summer of 1944. Vernon and I were separated from November when the USS *Brule* left for Hawaii and the attack on Iwo Jima until his ship came in to San Francisco for repairs the next June.

We wrote each other every day. We not only wrote what we had done during the day, what we had thought, but also love notes. Vernon numbered his and put them in a notebook so that he could read them over. Sometimes they didn't come in order, sometimes we would get three or four one day and none others.

I don't believe either of us ever missed a day. The longest time I was without a letter was when Vernon was in a terrible typhoon. They were in harbor somewhere in the Pacific when the storm came up. They were ordered out to sea to ride the storm out. Only Vernon can describe the waves and how the ship would ride up, shake— another degree or two and it would have capsized. This was as scarry as the war itself. The *Brule* lost one man overboard. Many men and ships were lost,

Vernon and me.

mostly those that didn't get out of the harbor.

I just waited for mail and waited for mail.

These letters of our separated months were kept—that is until we found 13-year-old Colleen reading them. Then that night, after reading bits and pieces, we burned them in the fireplace. I wrote Vernon a poem once in a while and these he still keeps with his treasures.

Vernon's Return

Vernon was out of the service and returned at Christmastime. The girls I lived with loaned us their house to have a second or third honeymoon. When Vernon arrived, I was so excited that I couldn't get the door unlocked. Now for the first time we were making more permanent plans.

PART 4

The Children

From the time we had our children, until we felt the project of raising them was complete some 25 years later, everything evolved around them.

Both Vernon and I felt that they were the most important. Oftentimes our own lives and the business was put on hold to do something with, or for the children. From the time they were born, we saved for their education.

The children had first access to our time, especially mine. Whatever they needed, wherever they wanted to go, came first. We felt their at-home education was important. Vernon played ball with the children after buying a vacant lot next door and fixing a playing field. He taught them gardening and carpentry. I taught them entomology, cooking, sewing, trees, birds, horseback riding, and so forth. We bought music lessons and instruments for Colleen and art materials for Jay.

We wanted them prepared for a well-rounded happy life. We had a happy time doing with, and for our children. Child rearing was a good time in our lives. Following are a few episodes and memories from that time.

Like most children, ours grew up into responsible adults. Jay married wife Duby and they have a New England "barn" home. He became a professor at Wesleyan University, an author, artist, and collector of wood dolls. Colleen lives on her animal-populated farm and worked on the budget for Michigan State's Substance Abuse Programs for many years. Now she tends her animals, manages her apartments, makes doll plates, and has a small doll collection.

They are still our children, and we talk and consult with them each weekend, sometimes more.

"The woman paused fractionally, her mind's eye casting over the splendid life's bounty she'd enjoyed. Then, gently, she stepped forward. Placing a hand on each of her children's shoulders, she said firmly, 'These are my finest jewels!'" Author unknown.

So it is with me.

Jay arrived round, plump, blue-eyed, perfect in every way. I couldn't believe I had done it. I wanted a baby. He fulfilled my every hope. Vernon looked on as proud and happy as I was.

The day Jay was born on October 23, 1946, I came back—back to be a part of the world that had been running without me. Unless it has happened to you, you cannot know what months of isolation, nausea and cramps can do to both mind and body.

Let me backtrack. Vernon had been back from the Pacific about two months. We could not find a place to live in Oswego where he wanted to continue his schooling. I started to finish my B.S. at the same time.

We found a summer cabin down by the lake. It was January. The wind howled off the lake and blew ice until the visible world was crystal coated. The cabin had two rooms, an entrance shed, an outhouse and an oil-burning heater. We cooked on a two burner kerosene stove. The wind blew right thru the house. The roof lifted and heaved with Oswego's off-the-lake continual storms.

I walked up the hill to college. I could hardly stand up in the wind. I was taking art courses and the potter's wheel. Every day I would turn pots and line them up.

With the end of the week, the professor came with a wire and cut down thru all my pots. This was to show me the unevenness of the walls. This was the whole lesson. I was just beginning to get some consistency in my work, when I found my head to be going around with the wheel. I would get a drink. I would feel like fainting. I would go back to the wheel, and my whole being followed the grey mass of concentric circles. I was sick. I had the flu. I threw up and threw up. I was nauseated all the time. I couldn't keep anything down. I was pregnant; I did not have the flu.

The only thing that kept me from giving up was the wonderful thought of having a child. I had not made an acquaintance with others in Oswego. We had no phone and no contact with the world, other than the wind and snow. We really had no one. I had to stay in the cabin and in bed. I saw no one but Vernon. He had trouble trying to cook something for me after being in school all day. He had never cooked. Being just out of

Vernon and I with our Jay.

Jay in the antique carriage his granddad gave him.

Jay was just a delight.

We had no conveniences. Jay was bathed in a small enameled pan. Old iron wood-burning stove in the background.

Jay and his namesake Granddad (Dad—Myron J. Faulkner), along with my old dog Cammie.

I painted clowns on Jay's bedroom wall.

Jay and his dog Flash, given to him by the Palens. Right: Vernon and Jay on the steps of our Livingston Manor house.

Jay is two.

the service, he was not ready for this switch of events. The winter was hard; it seemed like it was forever.

The Babenzeins lived up the road. He was a student, and they had a one-year-old baby. She felt sorry for me being alone and would run down to see me once or twice a week. She was a lifesaver. My spirits were so low, and I was so lonely. Everyday I was sick. I saw a doctor only once, because we were too far out. The Babenzeins are still our dear friends.

Come spring Dad drove from New Kingston to see us. He brought me a white kitten. I wonder how we could cope with a kitten but we did. Vernon did. It was one of the best things that could have happened to me. I told the kitten how it felt to be nauseated all the time, and how glad I was he could sleep on my bed to keep me company.

Vernon finally found a car, an old car, a 1932 Nash. It smelled like rat manure—for good reason. The cushions were half eaten. (This was at the end of the war and housing and cars were not available.)

Vernon continued his studies thru the summer and completed his second B.S. so he could teach industrial arts. I continued with my vomiting. He took a job in Livingston Manor Central School. He drove the old car to Livingston Manor to find a place for us to live. I was horrified when he got back. He said he had bought a house in Livingston Manor, New York. We had money saved for a house, I had saved

every check he sent home while he was in the Pacific. I had also saved half of my teaching checks while I taught school in Ithaca when he was in the war.

He didn't know the people living in the house had a year's lease on the house, and we couldn't get them out. He found a summer house in De-Bruce that we could live in. This house, again, was not meant for full-time living. We had an icebox with no ice, we had electricity from a generator that would not take ordinary appliances. The old iron cook stove in the kitchen didn't want to burn green wood.

Again no radio, no telephone, no communication with the world. I was still isolated except when Vernon came home. At this point, I was hobbling around with a cane. I had pains in my leg and side. I was still vomiting nearly all my meals. I couldn't ride in the car for the pain.

A few days before the baby was due, Vernon took me to New Kingston. This was so I could get to the Margaretville Hospital. Dad would take me or Vernon when he came after school.

I weighed in at 100 pounds and now I had produced a beautiful 7½ pound baby boy. We named him Myron J. after his grandad.

Not ready to make the trip back to DeBruce, baby Jay and I came to Dad's house in New Kingston.

The second day I was home, the neighbors came in to see the new baby. My sister, her husband, and their children, and

the next door neighbors, the Scotts—the house was full.

I had baby Jay in a basket on a pillow. They had all seen the baby and he was asleep. I put the basket in the bedroom and went out to visit. Something made me suddenly return to the entrance of the bedroom.

As I did, I saw an arm and was aware of Dad's housekeeper, leaving by the other bedroom door. I checked the baby. The baby was all wound up with a blanket around his head and a pillow on top of him. I thought he was gone. I had gotten there just in time.

The baby was all right. I was in hysterics when Vernon came in. The next morning we took Jay to DeBruce. I never confronted her or told Dad. It was a thing that followed me, worried me. I always made sure I was where the baby was. This was the first time we had noticed that the woman had a problem.

I was back in isolation but now with our baby. Except for reading one small book, I knew little about babies. I heated water on the stove to wash his diapers and make formula. I didn't have enough milk to keep him happy.

The weather got colder. Panes in the window were covered with frost so you couldn't see out. Snow blew in under the cracks of the door. I was always cold. I hung diapers on an outside line to freeze. The kitchen was almost impossible to cook in. The oven didn't work. I got a single electric burner to help with the formula.

We took a small room in between the other two rooms and used it for Jay. We kept it warm with an electric burner. This ran day and night. One below zero night, I got up to give Jay his 12 o'clock feeding. He was ice cold; the room was more than ice cold. The burner had quit. We were scared. We took him into bed with us and got him warm. In an hour or less he could have been frozen.

All this time we owned a good house down in Livingston Manor. Spring came. I had survived what was probably the hardest part of my life. In April we got into our house in a very poor location. Old Route 17 ran by our front door.

Jay was pure joy. He was fun. He developed faster than most babies. He was always so happy, so alert. I told him about flowers, about birds. I taught him to count. He would wake up and sing in his crib. One morning he woke up and called to us, "The caw birds are back."

He had remembered the sound of the crows. His first fall we had planted bulbs at the back door. Early spring came and I hadn't noticed, but Jay began to shout, "crosits, crosits." He had remembered the name of the bulbs he had helped me plant. Crocus. He grew. He was never sick a day and never had a cold. He was a delight in every way.

Our best friends were the Presbyterian minister, Reverend Richard Neumann and his wife Ruth. (Ruth died of cancer in 1988.) We often went picnicking with them. We'd packed a picnic, met the Neu-

mann's, and a rainstorm came down. We returned to our house to eat. Jay was mad. Jay said, "Boy, if God had a telephone I'd tell him a thing or two about picnics."

The telephone was always important to Jay. He had his own toy telephone, one on which we used to carry on long conversations. One night we had company. He had been put to bed, and he wanted to get up. He tried asking for a drink—said he was cold—tried everything. He was coming down the stairs. "What's the matter Jay? You're supposed to be in bed." "My telephone is ringing," he said.

Jay learned colors, more than the primary colors. He called things by color before he could speak the word clearly. We had tree swallows in our birdhouse. I would tell Jay they were tree swallows. He said, "They are blue birds. I can see they are blue birds."

Jay played with blocks and wood pieces. He built everything either symmetrical or balanced. Having taught school, this amazed me. He could entertain himself in church or anywhere with an envelope of colored squares, oblongs and triangles. He made color patterns at two as good as my fourth grade pupils.

He liked paint and crayons. He used the wheelbarrow upside down and created "machines" with string, his tricycle and an old toy car. He loved kittens, chickens, anything that we used for teaching him about animals. He called the animals, the flowers and the many trees

by name. He made up other names.

He had an imaginary mouse that he kept in my old dinner pail. He carried it around. He talked to it. He chased it when it got out. This idea came about one day when the cat released a mouse in the kitchen, and I chased it with the broom. Jay wanted the mouse but I got it outside.

There was nothing on earth that could rival the joy of raising a little boy—such a happy little boy.

For him, everything had to be neat, clean and organized, including his play cupboard and toy box. If a drop of food was spilled on his high chair tray, it had to be cleaned before he could finish eating. He toilet trained himself.

We could take him anywhere —restaurants, school, the office—and expect this wonderful joyous behavior.

Jeanne, my New Kingston play pal had married Dr. Gilbert Palen. They gave Jay a German Shepherd dog named Flash. The dog, already trained, became part of the family. Jay was almost two.

In the spring before this, I had had a very bad miscarriage. We wanted another baby.

Along with cooking and cleaning for us and the two teachers boarding with us, I was teaching ceramics in our basement and at adult education at night. Saturday night we had games and dancing in the school gym for the teenagers. Vernon was doing the same. I was also doing ceramic projects

I painted cherubs on Colleen's bedroom wall.

The kiddie car that got her in trouble.

Colleen and Flash. Maybe this is where her love for animals started.

She developed very fast.

She taught herself to read.

All her dolls had to be fed and dressed. This carriage is the one I had when I was five. It is now in my living room.

Vernon and I taught ceramics at Oswego State University on Lake Ontario.

What can I get into? Right: Colleen a few weeks old, held by Carolyn Fairbairn, Granddaddy Faulkner, Jay, Jerry Palmer, Dick Fairbairn, and Bruce Palmer—grandchildren.

72

to use in his instruction book *Activities in Ceramics.*

Jeanne, who was a nurse, called that there was a baby without a mother in the hospital. We went to see about the baby born on August 15, 1949. We came home with our new little girl almost three days old. Dr. Holcom took care of the papers until we could get the adoption completed.

We named her Colleen. I painted her room with cherubs. We felt heaven blessed. We used old pieces of furniture that we had acquired for Jay. Jay got his big bed. Jay was so cute and loving with the new baby. He had no preparations for her arrival and needed none.

The house that we bought had four stories, counting the basement and attic. There was a flight of steps up the back to get to the garden, two flights down to get to the mailbox. We taught ceramics in the basement. The only bathroom was on the second floor. I carried babies up and down all day.

Colleen had some physical problems: both legs were crooked; she had an infection in one eye; her tongue was attached to the bottom of her mouth. When we took her to the local doctor, he said she also had a heart defect.

I worked and worried about all these things. I exercised and massaged her legs. Later we had to get corrective shoes. I had her tongue operated on twice. She grew fast and healthy. She walked and talked at nine months.

She was constantly in danger. She crawled and climbed over, under, and on top of everything. I could not take my eyes off her for a second. Once I answered the doorbell. She climbed up on a chair, across the counter, and stuck a finger in a hot pie.

I had her in her kiddie car playing on the front porch. She had never gotten out of the car before. I looked and she was gone. She had climbed over the porch railing and had fallen to the ground some five feet below. She was toddling around the end of the porch. She was only a few feet from the traffic of Route 17.

Vernon had refinished the hardwood floor in the hallway. He left his gallon of varnish in a jug with the cover screwed on tight by the entrance. Just in the few minutes while we were eating breakfast, Colleen in her kiddie car had unscrewed the top of the varnish, turned over the jar, and was playing—scuffing her feet in the varnish—all over the refinished part.

In the mornings, Vernon had to start making breakfast, so I could get up with Colleen. She always had to be cleaned before she was presentable in the morning.

When Colleen ate in her high chair she played with her hand in her food, always wanting to feed herself. If a drop of food was spilled on her tray, she quickly played in it. Parents soon learn children are not alike.

The nesting instinct in me must have been similar to the Rhode Island Red hen's I had used earlier to raise chickens. Raising two children, a 25-year

The front of the old store about 1948. That's Dad, Jay and me on the steps. Colleen is in the carriage.

Colleen's first Christmas.

project, was our happiest of happy times. Every day I saw them grow, learn, and come to us with creative ideas that only children, untrained, unstudied could.

No matter how much work I had, I always made sure the children had their time. They were read to and played with. I remember yet how Jay loved Dr. Seuss books and the heap of Golden Books. He loved his little record player. There was no television in our house.

Jay finished kindergarten and started first grade. He was the teacher's delight. Then the measles epidemic came. I was advised to take both children for a new shot that might prevent or ease the horrible disease. I took both children.

The very next day Jay was sick. The following day he broke out with a rash. He must have already been coming down with the measles or else he had a reaction to the shot. He got sicker and sicker. I couldn't get a doctor. He lay in bed like dead.

There seemed nothing to do but sit by and worry. His temperature got higher and higher. He ate nothing. I finally got a doctor, but he said there was nothing he could do. Never in my life had I been so scared. Then one day after two weeks, I saw my little boy coming back. It took time for him to gain weight and feel good again.

He went back to school. The teacher called me after a week or so, Jay could no longer count. He couldn't do the things he had been doing before the measles. He couldn't read.

Things were different for him. I worked with him, but his attention span was short. His delightful spirit returned, but the measles had taken their toll.

The measles did little to Colleen. She was growing and knowing more each day. She did whatever I did. She could set the table correctly at three. She could ride the tricycle, dress herself, make her bed and tend her dolls. Seven dolls had to be undressed each night and fed each day. She loved the kitten and the dog. Her growth, learning, and her one-jump ahead of me were both delightful and exhausting.

One of our ceramics customers asked about Colleen having an orphaned newborn lamb. It was a fun project. Off and on during their growing years, the children had lambs, Persian kittens, dogs, puppies, a skunk, a crow, a prairie dog, a flying squirrel, a rabbit, a chipmunk, a woodchuck, and anything else that came home with them. Jay even bought a duck in a pet shop in Philadelphia.

Jay's mouse project was one of his best. I believe he was in the fifth grade when it first started. He kept and bred mice in plastic boxes. Thru his science projects he developed scientific procedures and learned to keep records. He wrote and illustrated a little book which we had printed. It was called *A Mouse in the House.* He called his collection of plastic shoe boxes which housed his mice "Charlotte's Nursery."

We went to great lengths to get him special mice and special colors. Once we went all the

way to Bar Harbor, Maine, to get him mice. He made beautiful charts and entered the science fair. He was a winner. Everything he did was done with care and perfection.

I got so excited about the children that I forgot to say Vernon decided to stop teaching school and go into the ceramic business full time. We picked a place to bring up our children rather than a big city where business might prosper faster.

We carefully chose Oneonta, New York. On our tenth wedding anniversary we bought a lot on Woodside Avenue. We studied, checked, and made a list of things we wanted in a lot, a house, and a community. Vernon and I graduated from Oneonta State Normal School and this helped us decide on the city. It was a good choice! We had saved money to build a house, but it was only half of what we needed. I designed the house for growing children and it turned out perfect in every way.

Twenty-five years later when it was sold, we still loved the house. This was the first time I was blessed with conveniences. I had a washer, dryer, dishwasher, and later, our first television.

This was a new world for me, Vernon and the children. I had put a studio on the house that was large enough to teach ceramics in. (I only had night classes.) I had neighbors, made friends and enjoyed the neighborhood. Colleen started school in Bugbee (the practice school for Oneonta State Normal School) as had Jay. Vernon opened his first ceramics studio on Elm Street. Three years later, we bought a large building on 9 River Street, and also the house around the corner. Later, we bought a large building on River Street for making slip.

Colleen loved Dr. Hickmont in junior kindergarten, but when she got to kindergarten she was bored. She was ready for a much more advanced learning. One day in mid-winter I went to pick her up and the teacher said "Come in. Colleen is in serious trouble."

It seemed that Colleen had cut the buttons off another little girls coat and cut her scarf into shreds. My reaction was—how could this happen with dull round-pointed scissors, and two student teachers and the regular teacher in the room? It was not like Colleen. She had many friends and got along well with other children. Her teacher had already decided on her punishment. She must pay for the coat and scarf and apologize to both the girl and her parents. The child belonged to Dr. Sandley.

He hashed the thing out with his daughter and found she was putting black paint over Colleen's painting on the easel day in and day out. She had a coordination problem and could not do pictures like Colleen. This was her reaction.

Yes, the teachers knew this was going on. Dr. Sandley came to school and got Colleen off the hook. Being the mother, I just could never believe Colleen would do anything like that, but she did.

THE POTTER'S WHEEL —— Vernon Seeley demonstrates how clay may be shaped from bowl to vase to pitcher at will on a spinning potter's wheel, oldest machine known to man. (Star Staff Photo).

Oneonta's Newest Industry Operated By Man-Wife Team

By BOB WARNER
Star Staff Writer

Oneonta has a new industry—small at present but if past history of the firm is continued into the future, one that is bound to grow.

Two former teachers, both graduates of Oneonta State Teachers College a few years ago, left the teaching profession and started out on their own to establish a family ceramic service business. In the past three years, the business done by Mr. and Mrs. Vernon Seeley has tripled each year.

Both were acquainted with Oneonta from having attended STC. When they outgrew their quarters at Livingston Manor they looked throughout the state for a new location. Mr. Seeley said that they decided to come to Oneonta for two main reasons. Oneonta is a friendly town, and a good place to bring up children.

The Seeleys are building a new home in Eastland Heights, and have opened their business headquarters at 7 Elm St. Already the window display has attracted much curiosity, since many people had never before seen one of the oldest machines known to man—the potters wheel.

It is probable, Mr. Seeley said, that he and his wife will undertake to do some teaching in ceramics. Mrs. Seeley is a former art teacher, and Mr. Seeley was an instructor in industrial arts. However, the mainstay of the business is supplying schools and individuals with materials and equipment for making ceramic articles.

They now serve some 150 schools in New York State, and have between 50 and 100 individual customers from coast-to-coast. Their 24-page catalog lists dozens of individual items, ranging from clay to glazes, and from molds to potters wheels and tools. Even electric kilns are included.

More than the bare materials, however, is the specialized service which they are able to render to schools and individuals in the teaching of ceramic art.

For example, Mr. Seeley has just completed preparation of a pamphlet on materials, project ideas, etc., to aid schools in getting started on a ceramic project. The pamphlet is to be published by the University of the State of New York for the benefit of schools throughout the state.

Their catalog, in itself, is almost a complete instruction manual, telling in detail how to prepare and fire kiln ceramics.

The service is designed to serve both those interested in the fine arts and in industrial arts. In the fine arts field, there is modeling and casting in molds, and in the industrial arts field, the use of the potters wheel, which makes a stronger ware.

A couple of our many pots. Vernon threw them, I decorated them.

Left: A clipping from the Oneonta Star, 1953.

Mother I Lore you very much. You are so nice to me, ant you do so many things for me. I am sorry about that Last note. I wove you I wore you said the little blue man. I Love you and I hope you Love me,

Love Colleen

I found this treasured note written by Colleen when she was in the third grade.

The first grade teacher said Colleen was crazy about the piano in her room; all she wanted to do in free time was play the piano. I must back track. At Christmas when Colleen was three we gave her a little red toy piano. She loved this little thing and played and played and sang songs. The second week of junior kindergarten she decided to take her little red piano to school. Nothing I could say or do would change her mind. The rough little boys smashed it to bits. She was heartbroken.

I hunted around and found an old upright piano for her. When the men brought it they could not get it into the basement. They gave up. (Vernon was not home.) I said take the casters off and unscrew the front legs and it will go down. It did.

I got Mr. McLaughlin to teach her piano. He came once a week. Colleen played, played, played. I never had to tell her to practice. Sometimes I told her not to. She would get up at 5:30 in the morning and play. This was her thing. At eight she asked for an accordion. (She still plays it.) At ten, she wanted to play the church organ. Churches weren't very excited about having a ten year old taking lessons on a church organ.

The Presbyterian church let her for a time, then said no. The Methodist church with their huge pipe organ let her have lessons. I had to sit with her for both lessons and practice. I did this thru high school —whenever she was going to play.

When Dad died he left both children a little money that was earmarked for college. I decided to use some of the money to get Colleen an organ.

Kitten Cherubs

When Colleen was five, her best friend was Muffie Dietz. They spent a lot of time together, in school and out.

Muffie's parents Sarah and Bud Dietz were medical doctors and had wonderful ways with children.

Muffie's kitten died and she came home with Colleen to help forget about it. The girls were playing with clay in the studio when I heard Muffie explaining to Colleen that she didn't feel bad about the kitten anymore.

"You see, Mother explained to me how cute the kitten would be flying around cat heaven in pink wings. Every time I close my eyes and think of the kitten, I see my kitten flying around with pink wings. Don't you think a white kitten with pink wings would be cute?"

I reminded Colleen of this last spring when she was feeling bad about losing her mother cat.

Colleen loved the organ and the piano, practicing like no child ever practiced. She played for everything from grade school, junior high to accompanying the high school chorus and the musicals—she played for everything. She was substituting in churches almost every

Colleen at her organ.

She hooks a rug, sews her clothes.

Colleen grows up with butterflies...

Persian kittens and her awards.

Colleen

She paints dolls for the Farmers Museum, Williamsburg and Sturbridge Village, by the thousands.

Jay bought this duck in Philadelphia, and named him Monday.

Left: Colleen wins a ''Freddy'' (the highest award in hobby ceramics) and is on the cover of Popular Ceramics.

Colleen throwing pots on the potter's wheel.

Jay watching Vernon at the potter's wheel.

One of Colleen's many ceramic sculptures, this one is called "Monday."

Sunday. On the side she played the guitar, and off and on had a hootenanny group of her own. It seemed music was her life, but no, the child had so much ambition and talents, music was only part of her. She had top grades and was an honor student. Anything she did, she did the best. If she played games, she played to win. She kept me busy. I knew the minute she was without an interest or a job she would be in trouble.

In her first year of high school she and another girl skipped class and got on top of the suspended lighting island over the stage. Don't ask me why. There was only one way off when they were caught. Colleen jumped to catch the curtain, missed it, and fell to the stage. Another two feet and she would have gone down another five feet. The nurse brought her home. Nothing was broken, but she was in bad repair all over. Her legs and knees hurt her for months after.

She got her license and drove to school. One night I let her take the car to the movies. She took a bunch of her friends on a wild ride. She ended up against a tree in the woods above Oneonta. No one was hurt.

Jay was something different. I knew from the time he said to Daddy on Christmas morning, "You and Santa Claus didn't do a very good job painting the tricycle," that he saw things in a different light. I watched him draw, paint, make charts, arrange and create. That was total joy to me.

I decided at a very early stage not to, in anyway, try to influence Jay's creativity and art work. I had had teachers make fun of my art work in school, saying I couldn't even trace a picture. I was humiliated in grade school for my attempts.

I knew what criticism and even ill-timed instruction could do to a would-be artist. I supplied Jay with art materials. I gave him space to grow. I felt I had to remain hands-off for him to develop in whatever way his art took him. This was as hard, in a way, as it was with my constantly being with and guiding Colleen. Children are different and must be guided differently. I couldn't know if I was doing it right.

Vernon had been a Boy Scout and a scout leader. We put Jay in the scouts. He hated it. He didn't like the uniforms, the marching, or anything he had to do just like everyone else. His creative inner self balked at meetings. I could see scouts were not for Jay. I had a Brownie troop. Colleen was happy and loved the activities with the other children.

Then I remember how I had loved 4-H club as a child. I inquired into the 4-H. No, there were none. There never had been a city 4-H club. Never hesitating to be the first at anything, I started one. Colleen was eight, Jay ten, just the right age. Their friends filled the club.

I had a good feeling about 4-H clubs. I like the Cornell materials and teachings. I felt this started where school left

Colleen, Muffie Dietz and other friends on her sixth birthday. She wanted a house cake, other years she requested pink ponies and other wild things I loved producing.

And then she ran and picked armfuls of flowers.

Ponies are her wishes.

Colleen does a 4-H demonstration on Binghamton TV on Pink Paper Dolls.

Jay and Colleen at Christmas.

She plays the accordion yet today.

Harvey came for Easter. Colleen bought him in the dime store. Far right: Colleen was chosen queen of the National Asbury Park Ceramic Show in New Jersey.

COOPERATIVE EXTENSION   NEW YORK STATE 4-H

THE NEW YORK STATE COLLEGES OF AGRICULTURE   AND LIFE SCIENCES AND HUMAN ECOLOGY
CORNELL UNIVERSITY

Awarded to _____ Mrs. Vernon Seeley _____

THE

Certificate of Community Service

in recognition of _15_ years of

4-H LEADERSHIP

in _____ Otsego _____ County

Co. Ceramics Instructor
4-H Club
Entomology
Cooking
November 10, 1973
Date

Bill S. Wilson
Cooperative Extension Agent, 4-H
Betty S. New
Chairman 4-H Program
George J. Broadwell
Chairman Youth Development 4-H
Edward A. Smith
Director of Extension

THE 4H AWARD OF THE

PEARL   CLOVER

Is hereby presented to

MRS. VERNON SEELEY

in recognition of fifteen years of 4-H Club leadership
by the Cooperative Extension Service, U. S. Department
of Agriculture and   **New York State Cooperative Extension Service**

Edward A. Smith
STATE EXTENSION DIRECTOR
George J. Broadwell
STATE CLUB LEADER

Edwin L. Kirby
ADMINISTRATOR, FEDERAL EXTENSION SERVICE

Date   NOVEMBER 10   , 19 73

Both Vernon and I worked for 4-H for 15 plus years. Entomology, landscaping, cooking, sewing and demonstrating were the areas we worked most in.

off. It gave the children a wonderful background for living. We studied flower and vegetable gardening, we learned the weeds, the wildflowers, the forest trees. We sewed, sawed and cooked. We learned to tell others by demonstrating what we learned. We made exhibits at fairs, we went on television, on radio and made books of our collections. I probably had more fun than the children—these Woodside Chickadees. They were the top club for years in the county.

At nine, Colleen announced she was going to be an entomologist. I am not sure where she got the idea. Later I know she read Jean Stratton Porter's *Girl of the Limberlost*. Anyway, I said, "Not in my house. You can't have insects." She won, of course, and I worked steadily with insects, mostly lepidoptera for ten years.

In the back of my mind was always that childhood desire I had to preserve the beauty of a butterfly. Probably my own disastrous results hovered over me. I couldn't let that happen to my children.

I got everything I could get from Cornell. None of it was workable for an 8-11 year olds' insect study. I started experimenting. Carbon tetrachloride certainly was not safe for children's insect killing jars. Not only that, but it stiffened the butterfly's wings backward so that they were impossible to spread.

I tried nail polish remover. I talked to the druggist. We found ethyl acetate would work, and the resulting butter-

The house on the hill in Livingston Manor, New York.

Left: Vernon starts Seeley's Ceramic Studio in Livingston Manor—note the snow-covered sign.

Below: Building the house on Woodside Avenue, Oneonta, NY.

The finished house where we lived for 25 years. The magnolia was a Mother's Day gift the first year in the house. I designed the house for raising children—it worked. We love the house.

The family grows up.

Citheronia Regalis—one of the rarest of rare moths we raised.

Left: The two sections of Seeley's Ceramic Service, River Street, Oneonta, New York. Vernon also owned the house around the corner on Main Street, the one across Harvey Street, and a mixing plant on Broad Street (below left).

fly would be limp. Later I found that if we were hunting in our own yard or it was something we had raised, we could kill it and store it in the freezer.

Both Jay and Colleen worked at lepidopetra, studying, setting specimens and working out life cycles. For the last 100 years, butterflies and moths have been set on a pair of slanting boards with a string drawn over to hold the wings in place. This, of course, was far too difficult for children.

I developed a method by which they could pin the butterflies perfectly. I used a smooth foam packing material, dug out a hollow large enough for the body to fit in, then spread the wings, held them down with wax paper and common pins. Jay perfected the method, and Colleen, having unusual motor coordination, found it easy at her early age.

Jay was preparing his first case of butterflies for the county fair. Something fell and knocked off the antennae of two butterflies. With Jay there must be symmetry and perfection. He took the antennae off all the other specimens. I waited to see what would happen.

The 4-H agent stopped by and commented on the fact that the antennae were missing. Jay set out to make a whole new collection in the three weeks before the fair. I helped, Vernon helped him, Colleen came with her surplus specimens. His effort paid off with rosettes and blue ribbons. Over the next few years, both children earned gobs of blue ribbons. They were blue ribbon kids. Jay

became 4-H landscape winner and went to the National 4-H Congress in Chicago.

Each butterfly and moth must be pinned so that the bottom edge of the top wings are in a straight line. The bottom wings are pulled up so that all the markings show. The antennae are pinned at a V above the head. The entomology pin goes straight down thru the butterfly's thorax. About a fourth of the pin is above the thorax of the butterfly to act as a handle. I taught the children to use wide tweezers to pull up the wings, because their moist little fingers take off too much of the wing scales.

Quite by accident, or heaven sent, men came to my door one day and asked if they could set up a trap for gypsy moths. These conservation men had a black light arrangement in a funnel-like metal container. I explained we would be delighted, that my 4-H club would be especially interested.

The children and I watched the trap, no gypsy moths, but in the morning around the trap were other moths, both dead and alive. We expanded our collections. When the men came back for the trap, we begged them to leave it. I had an idea.

We pulled the black light from its casing and Vernon installed a sheet behind it. This was the beginning of "black lighting" for moths for collections. It is a regular practice now all over the country.

We collected perfect specimens of the large silk moths, plyphemus, cecropia, prom-

ethia and hundreds of smaller but still exciting specimens. We studied their time schedules. We knew when to expect each. In the beginning, I started working on this to help the children, but I became so interested and fascinated, that I spent any extra time I had working at methods of growing and collecting lepidoptera.

We found if a female moth came to our light we could put her in a brown paper sack and she would put eggs all over the sack. Then, if we could find the correct plant food, we could feed the larva when they had hatched and grow our own cocoons.

We had wire "emerging cages" and plastic cases for growing larva. We found if a female moth emerged, we could get her a mate by simply making a little string harness and tying her on the rough bark of a tree outside the door. It was so exciting, like nothing I had ever played with.

We moved our black light to a friend's hickory grove. We caught the beautiful green luna moths. There is nothing that can awaken the excitement of an amateur naturalist like the sight of a pale green luna with her tapering swallow-like tails fresh from the cocoon.

This was a different kind of project for each of the children. Jay saw the beauty, the colors, the miracle of change from larva to moth or butterfly. Colleen studied the eggs, the chrysalis, the cocoons—it was her science project. The children filled cases and riker mounts. Colleen wrote a little book

Moths of the Woodside. Jay illustrated it for her. She sold cocoons and started The Teen International Entomology Group (TIEG). It was a correspondence and specimen exchange group.

She started a TIEG newsletter and corresponded with a little girl in Australia, a couple in England, and before you knew it, the newsletter was too big for us to mimeograph for her. Cornell saw the educational value in the TIEG and took it over. It is still going now under the direction of Michigan State.

Colleen's exhibits and demonstrations were tops in the county and state. She was the National Entomology Champion and was awarded a travel-study grant to go to England to study under Hugh Newman, a noted entomologist. She was not yet 16.

We hesitated to let her go but we did. She came back with a head full of new enthusiasm. She was awarded a Cornell scholarship, and at the same time, she got one for music at Ithaca College. She had been runner-up in the Miss Teenage State contest, and then again in the Junior Miss Pageant.

There was never a dull moment in Colleen's world, nor did she let there be one in mine. I had to hang on with both hands to stand the spinning. I loved every minute of raising her. She was indeed a challenge.

She chose Cornell. My neighbors wondered what I could possibly do when Colleen went off to college.

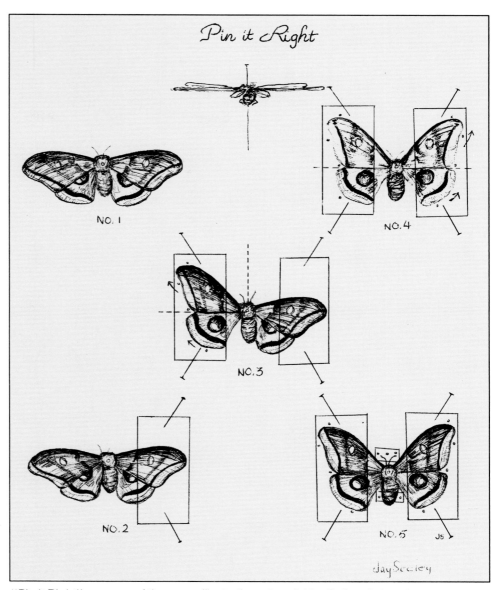

Pin it Right

"Pin it Right" was one of the many illustrations Jay did for Colleen's brochure Moths of the Woodside. This was a method we developed to make it easy for children to set butterflies and moths perfectly.

The Butterfly Farm of "Uncle" Hugh Newman. Colleen was given a study-travel grant to go to England. Right: Bags on the trees are growing larva.

Area 4-H

COLLEEN SEELEY
Oneonta

Three area 4-Hers, two from Oneonta, have been awarded $500 scholarships at the National 4-H Club Congress in Chicago, Ill., for the excellence of their work in various fields.

A 15-year-old Oneonta girl, publisher of a pamphlet on the life cycles of moths, organizer of a 4-H entomology club, and active in an international teenage group of entomology students who exchange specimens, has been named a national winner in the 4-H entomology program.

* * *

COLLEEN SEELEY, daughter of Mr. and Mrs. Vernon D. Seeley, 47 Woodside Ave., was one of six young scientists who received a $500 college scholarship from Hercules Powder Company, during the 43rd National 4-H Club Congress in Chicago this week.

A six year 4-H member, Colleen has been invited to study next summer with Dr. L. H. Newman, English entomologist. Next October, an International Teen Entomology Group member from Australia plans to study entomology at Oneonta with Colleen.

The youthful national winner rates the making of a 4-H educational movie of her moths and demonstrations, the most important thing that ever happened to her. This experience rates well with supplying moth eggs to the Cornell Experiment Station at Geneva, and showing Dr. Mansingh of India how to grow an insect species. Miss Seeley also supplies moth eggs to entomoloists in England, Australia, North Dakota, Wyoming, New York and the American Museum of Natural History. Last summer she assisted with the teaching of a field biology class at Hartwick College.

With the proceeds from the sale of her moth pamphlet and sale of dolls, the winner hopes to pay her way through Cornell University as an entomology major.

Colleen is National 4-H Entomology winner. She received a scholarship from Cornell and at the same time one from Ithaca College for music.

The Junior Miss Pageant for which she makes her own gown and plays the organ for her talent.

In the meantime, Jay had quietly selected Buffalo State to study art. He had spent some time in the last three summers teaching at 4-H camps.

Jay worked at gardening and his exhibits. He wanted to be a radio announcer. He worked on all the technical stuff and went off to New York City to take his test. He passed his test and did some Sunday announcing. He had a shop set up in the basement where he cut hundreds of wood blocks for printing. They were beautiful and exact. I was his greatest fan. I was still practicing my "hands off" policy with Jay's art. He experimented with colored inks, colored papers, with block on block. His work was so good, I could not believe he was ours. He was so modest, nothing was ever quite perfect enough.

Jay graduated from Buffalo, but never went to his graduation. He didn't go to his high school graduation either. He didn't like this kind of thing. He knew what he wanted to do; he wanted to teach in college. He got a scholarship to the Rhode Island School of Design to get his masters degree. He had now changed interests from printing to photography.

With Jay there was always that secure feeling that few parents have. We always felt we could depend on him to do the right thing at the right time. He was absolutely reliable. He always did what he said he would do.

Cornell was no place for Colleen at this time. There were riots, buildings were being burned; she was scared for her

Colleen spent the summer working on Vernon's Railroad Project—The DO line.

Colleen at Christmas during her teen years.

The beginning of Jay's block printing.

Jay taught numerous summers at 4-H camps, both block printing and entomology.

Jay runs the Woodside fair each year.
He has his own hot dog booth.

Jay wanted a goat.

Jay gets first award for his 4-H new
reporter's job.

The woodchuck that ended up on
the Captain Kangaroo show.

The skunk, de-scented of course.

Jay's crow, Filmore. Filmore was the ugliest
thing, but he grew up to be quite a clown and
handsome.

Jay and his prize-winning science fair project.

One of Jay's pro-
jects that won him
the horticulture
award and a trip to
the 4-H Club Con-
gress in Chicago.
This was a model
of our house and
his landscaping.
Right: The family.

life. There were drugs. Her first year was terrible, one problem after another. We didn't know everything that was going on.

Finally she got a hold of herself and from then on was an honor student. She had her own money that she had saved from 4-H, her scholarship, and dolls. She moved off campus, she bought a car. We never knew from one minute to the next what she would get involved in—good or bad. She always left us in suspended state, hanging. She was beautiful and brilliant. She was capable and talented. She could do anything she set her mind to.

Back to the ten years I spent with entomology and the 4-H'ers. This may have been a project started for the children, but soon I was so involved, it was my project as well. This was a new and exciting dimension for my nature-loving mind.

I was working out life cycles of butterflies and moths. It sharpened my eyes to hunt for butterflies depositing eggs on certain plants—you had to know that particular plant for that butterfly or moth in order to rear them. I studied and worked at it continually. We happened on the 1870-1890s Holland Butterfly and Moth Books. These I used as texts. We went butterfly hunting, with or without, the children. I had plastic containers, screened cages, nylon sacks on trees full of growing larva. I timed larva growing. I timed the chrysalis. I knew when eggs would hatch. I discovered how to delay them in the refrigerator. I taught the

children to put together life cycles which consist of the four stages—egg, larva, chrysalis or cocoon, and adult moth or butterfly—for preservation and study usually in a riker mount. We did 37 different life cycles. Once we discovered a new moth on our black light. A beautiful tiger moth. We didn't know or realize we could have named it and gotten credit for it. Cornell registered it.

We went to see Alice Gray at the Museum of Natural History in New York City. From that time on, she and Colleen had an ongoing correspondence. Max Richter of East Durham, New York, then an 80-year-old German entomologist, helped us get rare specimens from other countries.

Nothing in nature could intrigue me more than this study, partly because there was nothing much to work from, everything I must find out for myself. The biggest help was my built-in knowledge of the trees, seeds and flowers. When we traveled we carried killing jars, butterfly nets and plastic containers for live specimens to study.

We hunted butterflies in Florida several times. We caught Zebra Swallowtails and Heliconieas in Edison's Garden. We caught Giant Swallowtails in the orange groves and exciting Peacocks in the Everglades. I should have been a lepidopterist.

I can hardly imagine a project that would engross an adult like me to the extent it did. I could have spent my life studying either butterflies or moths. Now and then in my old age of 75, I still grow a few, set a few,

Jay in front of a Model T.

work out a life cycle—just to see if I can still do it.

Jay created, planned and managed the Woodside Fair. He used our extra lot and let any child (no parents) set up booths of games, rides and sales. He set up a hot dog stand. Colleen had pony rides. Other children sold candy, popcorn, ice cream, homemade projects. Others had game booths. It turned into a big annual project until Jay went off to college.

Colleen needed a little project she could sell. I came up with a little clothespin doll, then we found a little turned piece of wood that was better. At nine, her coordination was super. She painted these.

Someone from the Cooperstown Museum said the museum would like a gross of them for the museum. Colleen came to me. "What is a gross?" This was the beginning of a business, Colleen's Dolls. Colleen made these little wooden dolls for Cooperstown, Sturbridge Village and Williamsburg, Virginia.

She had a little stamp that said, "Colleen's Dolls, Oneonta, N.Y." She turned them out by the thousands for college money. I helped her make them while she was getting her masters at Michigan State University. Vernon even helped. When she finished her masters, she said, "I quit." The little doll business had provided the extra money she needed.

I was reminded of my own fudge deal with Dad. We had the little figures turned, supplied the paint, and did the shipping. Colleen got the money. Colleen's cousin, Jeannie, was given the supplies and patterns, and she has made the little dolls for the past nine years or so.

The Spook

I wonder if Jay will remember. I'm sure Colleen won't, but the "Spook" was a thing in our household for a few years while the children were very small.

We had a white cat we called Spook. The children, especially Jay, used the cat to take care of all problems—little things like spillings, lost things, sometimes little teasing things.

The cat took the blame for almost anything the children did that they shouldn't have done. "Spook did it." Spook never complained. It was a neat way of taking care of small problems. Long after Spook was gone, we blamed her. It was a way of saying, "I did it, I'm sorry."

The Accident

We loved taking our children on trips. Vernon had a convention in Kansas. We planned that after the convention we would vacation with the children along the way home to New York.

At this time, I was teaching Jay, nine, and Colleen, seven, to collect and enjoy bits of rocks and minerals gathered along the roadside. I had done the same with them gathering shells on the coast of Florida.

We were coming thru Tennessee when we spied glittering rocks down by a creek. Colleen was putting on her shoes with the car door open. I was some ways from the car waiting for her. She yelled, "Mother the car is moving."

I thought I must get into the car and get the brake on. There was a huge cliff behind the car. Colleen was still in the car. The car was moving faster than I anticipated. As I tried to climb in the car, the door caught me and dragged me.

I fell directly under the front right wheel. The car, a big heavy Buick, rolled over me from my left ankle, to my middle, to my chest, and grazed the left side of my head, loosening my teeth. The car turned and went in the ditch on the opposite side of the road. Colleen was safe.

I was in the road smashed, broken and unconscious. Jay went down to the car and brought his father our first aid kit. Some car stopped, saw what had happened, and sent for the ambulance.

We were in a mining area of Ducktown, Tennessee. There was a small mining hospital nearby.

In the hospital, my first worry was the children. My first recollection was that I could not see; everything was black. The next was that I had no arms. They were there, but I could not move them. It was some time before I realized my left leg would not move. Days went by. Vernon was trying to take care of two lively children and see me in the hospital. I could do nothing; he had to feed me.

The hospital was small and short of help. Everyone in the hospital had a cough. This was a copper mining town with a smelter. Acid in the air was so strong there wasn't a living tree or plant in sight—just bare red earth. It was a strange place.

I had not seen the children. Vernon assured me they were fine. Jay told Colleen that I was probably dead. He said later he really thought I was.

Vernon took the children around to the hospital window so they could see in my room that I was still alive. He put them in school. The people in that town were most gracious.

My sight had come back the day after the accident, and one day I discovered two fingers on my right hand would move. I was in terrible pain, probably from all my broken ribs. I was having trouble breathing. I had oxygen from the beginning. My sister came to help us. She would drive the car back, and we would fly, once I could be moved.

I was determined to get better. Everything was working but I was in such pain.

Teaching a class in ceramics. I also taught copper enameling.

Dad, Sister Dot, Sister Phoebe, me and Colleen taken on a family picnic.

Ducktown, Tennessee, where I had the accident. Copper mine and smelter in the background. The hills were bare and red, no trees, no grass.

Our family growing up.

SEELEY'S EMPIRE CITY

Camphene and Alcohol Distillery.

AARON SEELEY,

Camphene, Alcohol, Coal Oil, Burning Fluid. Tar, Pitch, Rosin, Spirits Turpentine.

Seeleys' have been around a long time. Note sailing vessel.

Left: Taken in Edison's Gardens, Florida. We were allowed to catch butterflies here. Jay gets his first Zebra Heliconia by trading Reverend Good a Tailed Skipper.

I can feel for Vernon, yet trying to get me home. Our plane came down in Washington at ten p.m., and we had no place to stay all night. I was in a wheel chair but could hardly stand the pain. Two unhappy, tired children and one complaining woman was almost too much for Vernon. He did get us home.

Oh yes, people are wonderful everywhere. While I was in such bad shape in the Ducktown hospital, Jay's tenth birthday arrived. I had planned him a party since we expected to be home. The nurses in the hospital gave him a party. The doctor loaned us a car and driver to get to the airport. Afterwards, Colleen corresponded with the classroom she had been in. Everyone had been wonderful

My injuries eased, but my chest and lungs were permanently damaged. It was slow, but I was determined to get back to normal.

These are the kind of things from which one never fully recovers. I still have breathing problems.

The Black Witch

During the ten years of 4-H work, the underlying music was always the same—lepidoptera. Colleen would thumb thru the Holland Moth or Butterfly book and say, "I want that one," like wishing on a star. There was one full page of a moth called the Black Witch. It was not that it was beautiful— just mottled grey, black and white—but its tremendous size, and the fact that no one had

ever seen or knew about it, must have intrigued her.

Anyway, it became a family joke. When anything flew over the house, was out of reach, or got away, we said, "It was probably a Black Witch." This went on for years.

Colleen was in high school. She and a friend had gone to the movies. My phone rang. "Mother, you won't believe this, but I have a Black Witch." Of course she had never seen one. A boy from her class had a moth in a paper sack. He was looking for her. She didn't believe her own identification, but I did. The moth was over six inches across. She was so excited, she could hardly wait to get home.

Now she must make a decision as to whether she would keep the moth alive to give her some eggs to raise, or would she kill it and add it to her collection. It was so rare, so exciting, she spent most the the night trying to find information on what the moth larva ate. Nothing, not even the Holland Moth book told her what the larva ate. Then too, the question remained—was this moth a male or female?

She usually could tell the sex by the feathered antennae of the male. She couldn't tell on this one. She finally gave up and decided the safest thing was to kill the moth and add it to her collection. She didn't come down to earth for several days. The boy who brought the moth wanted his name on the identification slip below the moth.

Now, Black Witches do not come to Oneonta, New York,

nor do they grow there. They are a tropical moth appearing in Hawaii and Central America. Their plant food is unknown, as is their life cycle. For a young, aspiring entomologist to get one of these, even second hand, was a high point in her collecting.

The boy had found the Witch in the lumber yard on a new shipment of lumber. Could the cocoon have come in on the lumber? There had been a big windstorm left over from a tropical hurricane the day before. Could it have been brought in on the storm? We will never know how a Black Witch got to Oneonta and filled the wildest dreams of a young collector.

The saying in our house, even some 20 years later, "It was probably a Black Witch," still goes on.

The Monarch

For Jay's first-year college biology project, he came up with an interesting experiment using his entomology background. He wondered if he could reduce the size of the butter fly by feeding the larvae poor quality and insufficient food. Monarch larvae eat nothing but milkweed so he thought that would be a good butterfly to work with.

He took eggs from four females and divided the eggs, half from each female in the control group. He fed the one group of larvae frozen milkweed and only enough to keep them growing. The control group had all the fresh milkweed they could eat.

The resulting butterflies were spread and placed in a riker mount (glass-covered box). The ones fed on the frozen milkweed were only about half the size of the others. He lost one third of the growing larvae. The control group came thru one hundred percent, and the butterflies were the usual size. The results of the experiment hang on our bedroom wall with other life cycles.

For the New York State Fair the year before, our 4-H club had made an exhibit with Monarchs. We found we could grow, and then delay the emergence of the butterfly from the chrysalis by placing the chrysalis in the refrigerator. We found that the butterfly would emerge from the chrysalis seven days after removal from the cold.

We made a butterfly tree. We took a well-shaped three-foot piece of thorn apple tree. We dried it so there were no leaves. We grew hundreds of Monarch larvae and put them on trays in the Seeley refrigerator. We started taking them out of the refrigerator, ten in the morning, ten in the evening, seven days before the fair started.

The tree was set up and the branches and thorns hung with shimmering, pale green and gold speckled Monarch chrysoli. We timed our project so carefully that, from the first hours of the fair until the end, Monarch butterflies were emerging, stretching their wings, and before the day was over, flying away.

We carried a new supply of chrysalis every other day to put on the tree. It was the most exciting exhibit the entomology department had ever had. I'm sure neither Jay, Colleen, or the other 4-H members will ever forget the Monarch Tree.

One winter when we were in Florida, Vernon was giving a lecture. All the seats were full, so I was wandering around near the flood-lighted entrance. I had a killing jar, scooping up a moth. A teaching Sister from the nearby Catholic school stood and watched me. She struck up a conversation and was just fascinated with lepidoptera. She asked me if I would come to her fourth grade class tomorrow and talk about butterflies. Well, having been a fourth grade teacher, I said yes. I went.

We were on the third floor of the building. After the last child had left, she said, "I want to show you something that I don't believe anyone knows about." She took me to the window, there, in some type of pine tree were thousands of Monarchs hanging in the branches. She said they had been there since some time in November—or that is when she first saw them. I have never seen a record of the Monarchs ever wintering in the Florida Keys.

In 1985 Vernon and I went to the Westward Look Hotel in Tucson for lunch. We parked our car under a pine tree. I looked up as I got out of the car—there were several branches hanging with Monarchs. The next year, we went back about the same time to look for more—the tree was gone.

We once went to Monterey, California, just to see the wintering Monarchs. Just last fall I grew some Queens, similar to the Monarch, once I found the plant food. You see, I have never lost interest in the butterflies!

The On-Going Thing With Dolls

As Colleen was growing up, I just delighted in making her soft dolls. When she needed gifts for birthday parties I came up with a doll for her to take. I spent some time doing needle sculptured dolls. Colleen still has Rip Van Winkle, a soft doll I made for her. She played with Ginny dolls. I made clothes for these and bought other dresses for them.

One day she took her Ginnys to school. They used the dolls to make Romans dressed in sheets. All her Ginny doll clothes never came back. Just this last year I gave her her box of naked Ginnys, wondering if she would remember.

Like most little girls, Colleen wanted a bride doll when she was five or six. I got the doll early and was working to get it dressed before Christmas, taking care that Colleen never saw it. One night she woke up, came out of her room, and found the doll on the table where I had been working. She went back to bed and never told me she had seen the bride doll until years later. She didn't want to spoil "my" fun on Christmas morning.

I gave Colleen my play doll, an Armand Marseille walking and head-turning doll, when she was six. I was six when I got it. She took great care of the doll which she still has.

Candle in the Window

I was meandering amongst my memories that evening. I guess I was anticipating Christmas and a time for the children to return, when I thought of a Christmas when Jay was nine, maybe eight.

I was teaching a copper enameling class in the studio—eight to ten o'clock. It was the last class before Christmas, and my students were getting pieces finished up for gifts. The children were in bed and asleep—so I thought. I had decorated the living room, dining room and hall with greens and many, many candles. Jay had helped me.

With copper enameling and our tiny kilns, there is always the smell of heat and sometimes bits of design paper burning. The room was alive with ladies' chatter.

I emerged from the studio at about ten, and there was the smell of wood burning. The whole living room and dining room was aglow with candlelight. Jay had lit every candle. Two candles on the bottom of the hutch were too tall. They were burning the shelf above. It was charring, not yet flaming.

I was upset. I looked in Jay's room. He was sound asleep. The next morning I talked to him. The night had gotten me calmed down. Jay said, "I wanted to make everybody happy for Christmas. It was so pretty, I wanted to surprise you, too." I showed him the burned spot, felt sure he understood the danger, and let it go.

The Collector

After Colleen came back from studying with "Uncle Hugh Neumann" in England, she had an urgent request from him. He needed live mourning cloak butterflies. They were filming part of the movie *The Collector* at his butterfly farm.

We had shipped lots of moth cocoons and moth eggs, but we had never shipped live chrysalis of butterflies before. From the time the chrysalis is finished, and when the Mourning Cloak butterfly emerges, is just seven days. There would be no time to lose. I was not sure that delicate chrysali could be shipped, or that they would emerge after the ordeal. Colleen was insistent. She was going to do it anyway—so I helped her.

It isn't just any time that you might have a Mourning Cloak butterfly growing. It just so happened that Colleen had caught a female. The butterfly liked her wire cage and the branches of fresh elm that Colleen supplied each day. The butterfly had deposited eggs up and down the branch, and now several plastic boxes were filled with growing larvae.

They were in their last instars. Most butterfly and moth larva molt four times. The plastic boxes had to be cleaned and the frass (excrement) cleaned out each day. We could tell by the color of the larva, as well as the shed skins, which instar the larva were in.

The beautiful dark larva with tufts of black dispersed between the bright red-orange triangles and blue along each side, told us the larvae were ready to make their chrysali. We prepared the box. We decided to send eight, hoping that at least one or two would make it.

Monday morning, chrysalis morning came. There wasn't one but perhaps 20 of the dark spiny chrysalis hanging from the branches provided. Vernon helped Colleen cut the branches into little pieces to leave the silken thread that attached the chrysalis. We wrapped and padded each chrysalis. We prayed a little as we packed. Then Vernon took the box to catch the first mail out.

Colleen got a card from Uncle Hugh that they arrived and some were surely okay. She never heard if the butterflies really emerged into perfect butterflies.

The movie *The Collector* came to Oneonta. Colleen went off to see it with her friends. We went, not because it was supposed to be a good movie, but because we wanted to see the part done at Hugh Neumann's butterfly farm.

The movie opened—there was the dark-winged beauty with her cream-colored border and azure blue dots—the Mourning Cloak filled the screen.

"There's my butterfly," Colleen shouted from the fifth row, standing up in her excitement, the whole theater filled with people were told.

Teachers Teaching

Vernon and I often say when we are working together at something "Let I do it."

When Jay was just beginning to talk he would say, "Me will do it." I would correct him and say, "use I instead of me." His next sentence was, "let I do it." This pair of school teachers, teaching!

With two very lively children in the back seat of the car for either long or short trips, our aim was to keep them happy. We also wanted to teach them to watch and learn from what they saw. We had seen other people's children scrap and wrestle in the car. We encouraged ours to play little watching games. They had one they concocted themselves—"I see it first." When we went to Liverty, New York, they watched for two things and in a singsong voice announced, "I see the steam crusher." This was a stone crusher, and because steam came rushing out of the top, Jay knew it was a steam crusher. Next was "I see the castle." This was the stone home of Otto Hillig, a well-known photographer, built in the form of a castle overlooking the valley. They had another one that they used when going anywhere, "I see the blue house." Later, they saw smiling or frowning faces on the front designs of automobiles.

In our older years, Vernon and I play such games in air-

Birthday party when I was seventy.

ports or other spots to shorten the waiting times. "I see a Marque or a Jumeau." We watch the children's faces and find features that look similar to our dolls.

In our file drawers, even today, we have "vanilla folders." When Jay was in kindergarten the teacher sent him to the office to bring back a manila folder. He went to the office and asked for a "vanilla folder." The office got such a kick out of that they told everyone about Jay and his "vanilla" folders. Now, Jay, with his interest centered on vanilla ice cream, it seems the right name for something that color.

Vernon and I have nothing but "vanilla" folders in our files.

Birthday Party

Did I tell you about the birthday party Colleen made for me when she was ten?

Colleen always got up before the rest of us to practice her music, so we were used to her getting up early. It was Sunday morning and she begged off going to church. Vernon and I went.

When we got home, the dining room table was set and crepe paper streamers came from the chandelier. The fine Wedgwood dishes and Fostoria crystal were on the table, all perfectly set. Crepe paper hats were by each place. In the center of the table was a layered, decorated birthday cake. I couldn't believe it. The whole thing was a complete surprise. She had gotten up at four o'clock in the morning and baked the cake, frosted it, and decorated it. She made dinner and decorated while we were in church. Everything perfectly timed. She had planned for a week how she was going to surprise me with a birthday cake and party.

Most children at ten are thinking of themselves, their

friends, their own fun and games—but not Colleen. Even at an early age, she was thinking of others.

I didn't have another birthday party until I was 70. I was having a doll seminar. I think Vernon told the girls, and they made me a party—complete with darling little gifts, cake and love.

Sewing Clothes

I made Colleen's clothes. This was not only an economy measure but I loved to design her dresses. Hardly a holiday passed that I didn't design her a new dress. It was fun for me and she just loved it, often telling me what color or what she wanted. I often took her to choose the fabric.

Once she wanted a Valentine's Day dress, designed with a big red heart on the front. Her Bugbee School teacher took her on an errand to each classroom to show off her Valentine. I made her clothes until she was about three years into 4-H when she took over her own dressmaking. She made everything, even her evening gowns. She made the gown she wore when she participated in the Junior Miss Pageant.

One day when Colleen was five she was real angry with me for not letting her go some place. She said to me, "I'm going to run away." I said don't wear or take anything I've made for you. In a few minutes Colleen came out of her room with her little doll suitcase with nothing on but underpants. The front door was right across from her room, but to be sure I saw her, she paraded thru the kitchen to the back door. She went out and sat on the back steps. In a little while I went out and talked to her about why I wouldn't let her go. She came in, got dressed, and helped me make a batch of cookies.

Colleen Makes Christmas

The first Christmas that we had Colleen, she didn't do much to make Christmas except to be there. She made us so happy. Now we had a family.

Now we look forward to Christmas. Colleen always comes home for Christmas. She comes with fruit cakes, cookies, her own honey, jams, piles of packages, and the wonder that makes Christmas. She's the one that is first out of bed on Christmas morning, turns on all the lights, and makes a super holiday breakfast. Everything done to perfection.

When Colleen was three, I was putting her to bed on Christmas night, she asked, "Will it be Christmas tomorrow too? When will Christmas come again?"

From the time she could walk she helped make cookies, Christmas breads, and helped with the decorations. Her drive to get things done, to make Christmas, were apparent from early on.

She had the ability to keep a secret which was so unusual in a small child. She would make something, bring home something she had made in school, and hide it away for a Christmas surprise for mother.

Once, I remember we were on a trip to Arizona in the fall. I couldn't believe it when I opened my Christmas present— Colleen had bought me a little pair of glass candleholders to match my other pieces. She had bought them in Old Tucson without me seeing her. She had gotten them home and kept them until Christmas. I could hardly believe it.

Colleen always made Christmas parties for her friends, her class, her 4-H club. Her music, organ, piano, accordion—always helped with the Christmas spirit. Then too, there were always school and church occasions that she played for. In high school there was the annual Christmas Concert. A couple of Christmases she had her organ taken to school for the concert. Then they moved the concert to the big Methodist Church, and she played the big organ both for the choir and a solo.

The house was always alive with music. Wherever and whenever Colleen is or was, she made Christmas and still does.

Colleen was always thinking of others—what would this person like? How will that person look when they open the package? Even as a small child she didn't say, "I want this and this for Christmas." Instead, she was planning what she could make or do for someone.

This generous, unselfish attitude has gone on all thru her life and all her activities and business dealings. Other people always come first with her.

Sometimes parents take these wonderful traits, like Colleen's unselfishness, for granted. This wonderful inborn unselfishness of Colleen's cannot be ignored, even in this peephole memory of mine.

Some of these fine traits our children exhibit could have been taught in their upbringing. We, as parents, like to think so.

With Colleen, her gentleness, compassion and fairness were there without teaching. It showed in little things from the time she was tiny, such as each kitten getting the same size snack and the same loving. Or when dividing anything with Jay, she would always take the smaller piece. I saw this trait again recently when they were deciding which dolls from my collection they wanted saved for them. I suggested they draw straws to see who got the first choice. Colleen said, "I know Jay wants the boy Marque, so let him have first choice."

When Colleen's old dog Kava was dying, she never gave up. She provided the dog with hospital care, then care at home, even when the dog could not get up. It is the same with all her animals—tender loving care.

When Colleen was working for 4-H in Michigan, one of the 4-H'ers lost her horse that she intended to ride in a show. Colleen loaned her her mare. The girl did so well with the mare that Colleen could never take the horse back.

Recently, Colleen, out of job, was raising Samoyed (registered, pedigreed pups) to help with her income. One pup ran

away. People who found it washed it and put a collar on it. When Colleen went to claim it, she couldn't. She let them have it. Would you believe another one got lost. She finally tracked it down, brought it home, got to thinking about the children crying, then took it back. She also took them the pedigree papers and her book on Samoyeds.

The Put-Togethers

This year Vernon needed a new wheelbarrow for Christmas. It wasn't quite like giving a woman a mop, as gardening is his love. The wheelbarrow came in a carton—all in pieces. He had to put it together.

He always been quite an expert at this putting things together, that is until we got the new Sony television and he tried to hook up the VCR. The instructions were translated to English by a Japanese! They were next to impossible.

Whenever something comes flat in a carton with instructions I think of Jay's farm. We bought the farm for his fifth Christmas. We waited until the children had gone to bed before we lifted the beautiful lid showing a lovely red barn and all the animals. I guess we expected them to pop into place when the lid was removed!

Vernon dumped the box on the floor. There appeared to be 2,000 pieces, some as small as half-an-inch. The fire in the fireplace was already burning low. Vernon says, "Let's just give up and put the pieces back in the box. Jay's got enough

presents." I suggested that we just put the barn together. I did little more than encourage the master builder. I did push out and stand all the animals. It was long past time for Santa to arrive, and we were still putting on doors and standing up trees. Vernon did it—he did the whole thing.

I wonder now was this a great success as a play thing? I don't seem to remember anything except the wild struggle to get it together.

The first Christmas we were in our new home in Oneonta, I found a sink and cabinet unit in the Sears Catalog. It was just perfect for our recreation room downstairs. I ordered it. When it came in several flat boxes, I hardly dared to tell Vernon what I had done. There were 278 pieces. Nothing, absolutely nothing, was assembled. I forgot how many screws there were, all numbered with instructions. Again, Vernon decided it should be done before Christmas. It was.

It does seem that Vernon and I have either been hunting for something we need, or putting together something, all of our lives. Looking back, it was fun and a part of the way things were and are today. I have always been surprised that we didn't buy Shandele' in boxes and put it together ourselves!

Pony on the Doorstep

As a kid of seven, I often escaped the real world by dreaming of ponies, my very own pony. It was always the same pony, shining black with white socks, a long flowing mane and tail, and a bit wild in nature. If I had seen the movie *Black Stallion* at that time, I would have said "That's him. That's my pony."

The first star at night, the birthday candles, the load of hay—all these were for pony wishes. The good fairy's wish box was jammed full of my pony wishes. My wish did come true, well partly. When my Dad got me my own horse, it was a dappled white horse with some age speckles—spirited, it wasn't. But when I looked at the horse it matched my dream perfectly.

When Colleen was six or seven she sometimes escaped reality by dreaming of her pony. I'm sure in her dreams, it matched my black stallion. She just expected her pony to show up on her doorstep any day, like magic. At this time, we lived on the edge of the Oneonta city limits on an acre lot with neighbors all around.

It was one cold autumn morning just after the last leaf had fallen from the maple tree, half-rain half-snow was pelting the windows and sliding down. Vernon and I were up and getting dressed, when Colleen called in her high-pitched excited voice. "There's a pony on our doorstep. My pony has come, he's on our doorstep." This was on Woodside Avenue in the city of Oneonta, how could this be? There was, we soon discovered, a wet shaggy black pony with his head under the eves at our front door. Clods of wet snow were sliding

from his back. His head was hanging.

This was an odd way to have a little girl's dream materialize. She was jumping with joy, getting on her jacket to go out and ride him. We tried to calm her down and told her the pony was not hers. The second she touched the doorknob, the pony flew off in a gallop beyond the trees.

After breakfast, Colleen and I put on our warm clothes and boots and followed the pony's tracks. He hadn't gone far. We had an apple but no halter. He eyed the apple and let us come almost within reach, then shied away. Finally, hunger got the best of him.

I put my hand under his chin and started him toward the house. He came readily into the garage. He was wet and shaking with cold. We found a little leftover hay and grain. We got him a pail of water. I kept warning Colleen to be careful as this pony could be wild and could kick and bite. The pony appeared to have a cold.

With tears running down Colleen's face I called the police station to see who had lost a pony. Nothing. I called the newspaper. Nothing. I called a pony farm on the other side of the city. Nothing.

I could see all kinds of problems developing. I dared not leave Colleen with the pony for fear she would try to get on him. I tried everything I could think of to locate the owner of the pony. No luck.

The next day I said to the mailman that we had a pony in our garage. "Have you heard of

anyone who is looking for one?" "Yes," he said. "There is a college student down on Center Street going house to house looking for one. When I go back down, I'll tell him if I can find him."

The student, a college freshman, showed up at our door. He said he guessed it was his pony. He had a couple of pieces of rope.

Colleen was crying again. I questioned him why, how, and where did he have the pony. It seems that he and some of his friends went on a Friday night binge, then found themselves at a livestock auction. "I don't know just how it happened, but I bid on this pony. We shut her in the garage, but she got out."

"And what are you going to do with the pony?" I asked. "I called my father and he is coming to get it for my little brother."

"I named him Midnight," Colleen said. "Can I ride him before he goes?" The young man improvised a halter from the rope. The pony seemed very nervous. "I better try him first," the young man said. He took the pony out of the garage and after a couple of tries was able to get on, only to be thrown with gusto to a lump on the lawn. He got up. "Now I remember, they told us the colt was four years old and had not been trained."

Colleen's excitement was turned off. It was like a dream, and the thud of the young man landing on the lawn awakened her. The student left with the pony, not even offering to clean out our garage.

The next spring we rented "Queenie," a friendly black mare, for Colleen. Queenie spent that summer, and many summers to come, with us.

Once out of college and on her first job, I bought Colleen her own "Tez," an Arabian gelding. Now she has three and her own farm.

Christmas Remembrances

Christmas 1991 I went to Wal-mart to buy the old film *Miracle On 34th Street*. Vernon liked to see this each Christmas, and it was not listed anywhere in the television guide. I believe we have been viewing this film for some 30 years, and we still love it.

The young clerk said, "We have one," and went to get it for me. "It's gone, we must have sold it." Then with a twinkle, and revealing that he was very familiar with the film, he said, "Try K-Mart." Again, we ended up renting the film.

When Jay was little and we took him to see Santa in one of the stores, he always told Santa the same thing. I want to be a Santa Claus helper. I want a red suit and to give out gifts. Next Christmas, I think Jay was five, I made him red pajamas and Colleen a red nightie for Christmas. Christmas afternoon Jay put on the red pajamas, made paper whiskers, and put a pillowcase over his shoulder. He pretended he was Santa. This went on for several years. Eventually, I made a Santa suit for him.

One year he took Colleen's sawhorses and put branches on them for horns to make reindeer. There always seemed to be a party where he could play Santa.

What a beautiful quilt all these red and green Christmas memories would make if they could be stitched together! There would be a few blank white patches for the Christmas after Mother died, the Christmas Vernon had Valley Fever, or last year, when I had a broken leg. Some of these are better left blank or forgotten.

PART 5

The Doll Business

Mixing Molds and Tragedies

Ideas are born when they get good and ready. The mind producing them seldom has a choice of time or place. Sometimes, ideas come in litters like kittens, each one crowding to get full attention.

All morning while I was washing the clothes, folding and ironing, even when I was making Vernon's favorite apple pie, my mind was some place else. For weeks, I had been trying to figure out how we could expand our ceramic business to include dolls. Now, mixed with apple pie and laundry, I had a whole litter of ideas. I said to myself, "I will try them out on Vernon when he comes home for lunch."

Lunch finished, I hurriedly slipped the dishes from the kitchen table into the dishwasher, removed the tiny bouquet of roses, and pulled out pads of paper along with a couple of cups of coffee. "I've got it, I've got it, try this on for size," I said as I pulled my chair in and proceeded to tell him of the wild plan to put *molds* (not dolls) of precious antique dolls in his ceramic mail-order catalog. The plan was really far-out. We would make molds and I would write the procedure to mail with each mold sold. "It will make such a wonderful hobby for women everywhere," I told him.

Vernon considered the ideas and kept adding to them, always being enthusiastic, but more practical than I was. Vernon usually hurried back to the store after lunch, but today he was still adding more detail to the plan. It must have been 1:30 or later when he finally stacked the paper, the doll mold plan, and took off for 9 River St., Seeley's Ceramic Service.

As Vernon was pulling out of the driveway, the phone rang. It was Betty New, wife of Dr. John New, from the street above. She was calling to see if I was judging the 4-H demonstrations on Saturday. "You can ride with me and—wait, something's happened—just a minute. She left the phone and turned up her T.V. I could hear only excited voices in the background. "They think President Kennedy has been shot in Dallas."

My first reaction was that it was a mistake. I turned on the T.V. Walter Cronkite, looking ghost-like, was saying, "The President has been seriously wounded." I left the T.V. and called Vernon as he was just entering the store.

There were immediate flashbacks of the shooting, all cameras had been on the presidential car. They had taken President Kennedy to the Memorial Hospital in Dallas. The reporters were waiting. "All we know is that the President's condition is critical, but there are no new bulletins in the past minutes." Still the news had not become a fact. I stood spellbound, glued to the T.V., not realizing tears were running down my face.

It was just about two o'clock when Walter Cronkite told the waiting Americans the President was dead. I shivered with chill-like waves. A strange sensation went thru me. It was like the day my brother Lyman was killed in the tractor accident. It was like the day Dad died. It was like the world came crushing in with nothing but sadness. My feelings were for Jackie, the despair, the loss—they came back to me as though it were yesterday.

Over and over we saw the cars and the shooting. Now the President's body was on Air Force One headed for Washington. The killer supposedly had been apprehended—Lee Harvey Oswald. Lyndon Johnson was taking the oath of office. Jacqueline Kennedy stood in the same pink, blood-stained suit. I thought of two small fatherless children. I thought again of my brother. It was like my father had died all over again.

Daughter Colleen came home. They quickly closed her school for fear of riots and sent everyone home. She sat glued to the T.V. for the next three days. We all did. The city was closed, everyone watched the coffin drawn by the black horses to the Capitol. We saw Jackie filled with grief, kneeling beside the casket.

Colleen was knitting a white sweater with an intricate pattern of blue and green on the front. She never stopped, the click of her needles sped up and slowed down as she couldn't see the instructions thru her tears. The drum beat, the riderless horse of Monday's funeral procession made me ache with pain

I had known before. Colleen's tears were a sadness, a new sadness, she had not experienced. Tuesday she stuffed the finished tear-stained sweater into a plastic bag. She returned to her studies.

Vernon said that we must go on where we left off—pick up the pieces. It was he who got me back on track after my brother's accident and Dad's death.

It could have been four months later as I moved a pile of papers saved from the Kennedy tragedy that I found the original pages with the doll mold plan. The shock, the excitement, the closing down of everything had closed down our minds too. We had not thought of the plans or remembered even making them until months later.

I gradually returned to writing, with how-tos being my best and most loved types of writing. The dolls were my best subjects. I started to buy dolls. I had saved my play dolls, but hadn't purchased any until Colleen was finishing Cornell. The family money had to see her thru college first. Her scholarships worked.

Now my greatest desire was to make dolls, perfectly wonderful dolls like my own bisque ones. I spent a year experimenting with low-fire clays. I sculpted a doll I called "Colleen" with solid parts, pressed clay and yarn hair. I sold a bunch of these, but I was not happy with them. Fifteen or 20 years after they were made, one came up at auction. It went for $700. I was horrified. I had sold them for $6 when they were new.

Making dolls was not a new desire in me. When I was tiny, my mother helped me tie up a sock after Dot gave away my Susy, my first doll. I made dolls from one thing or another for as long as I can remember. I made heads for dolls of mother's jelly wax. I used corn husks. I used salt and starch mixtures.

When I finally got into clay during college, I made little figurines. I guess I really always had a desire to be a sculptor of garden statuary. Dolls were the next best thing. When I was teaching grade school, I made dolls for my classes. Later, I was always making dolls for Colleen.

I did a large display of low-fire doll figurines from one mold to show the possibilities in originality and variation. This was a teaching aid for my ceramics classes. Dolls were like an infection, a delightful infection, that emerged and receded from my childhood forever.

With both children out of college and at jobs, I had time to experiment. I put away the entomology projects. I stopped teaching copper enameling and ceramics. Vernon saw what I was trying to do with dolls.

There were no molds for good antique dolls on the market anywhere. We had searched. If we wanted molds, we would have to make them ourselves. This was a new idea surrounded by unknowns. No one in this country or Europe was making any kind of a porcelain reproduction doll.

Our ceramic store, Seeley's Ceramic Service, sold ceramic supplies to schools, colleges and hospitals. Our mail-order business reached customers scattered across the U.S. We had a few customers in Australia and Europe. Vernon and I had been making ceramic pieces and writing articles for magazines since our marriage. The nucleus for our business really started in 1943, the year we were married.

The ceramic business needed a pick-me-up, especially in the summer months.

I bought a J.D.K. Googlie for my collection. Vernon and I started working together to make a mold from it. We taught ourselves. We wanted porcelain to make reproduction dolls of the J.D.K. Googlie. We developed a porcelain recipe over a period of years with help from Mr. Issacs of the Kentucky-Tennessee Clay Company from whom we bought our ceramic clays. I figured out how to tint the porcelain slip to get a smooth allover color.

This same formula, "French Bisque," is being sold worldwide today. It is still the best porcelain on the market for reproduction of the old dolls.

Once we had the porcelain and a mold, we had to have an instruction booklet. I wrote and mimeographed the first. Eventually I could afford to have the booklet printed with pictures. It wasn't much, but the sales prompted and encouraged me.

We made more doll molds from my antiques and put a

Vernon makes a mold of the rare and expensive Marque doll. We had decided to produce a limited edition reproduction of the Marque dolls, the very first limited edition doll in 1977-78.

couple of doll molds and porcelain slip into our ceramics catalog. I put a price of $90 on the first Bru mold. Gordon, who worked for us, said "Mil's idea is crazy. I'm not interested in working with any dolls." He later became one of our best help—our foreman—and an expert in the doll molds.

Our accountant said, "I suppose we will have to put up with Mil's playthings." Later, he wanted to buy into the business. He changed his tune concerning dolls as time and success came into sight.

I had one idea in mind. I thought dolls would be a great hobby for women like me. I thought they could make dolls for their children, for their grandchildren, for fun, and to build a collection of antique reproductions if they could not afford to buy the original antiques. I thought dolls would be a good retirement hobby for many women. I thought dolls could make people happy.

Whenever I could, I bought another antique doll. We attended auctions as time went on. I bought out a tiny doll museum in Florida. There wasn't much I could use out of the collection to make molds from. I bought another small collection. I traced down every doll I heard of. I skimped on everything else to buy dolls.

I am still wearing inexpensive canvas shoes to save for doll shoes. Jumeau shoes run about $300 now.

I studied dolls, their painting, construction and markings. My mind was completely void of the idea this could become big, real big business. It never occurred to me that other companies would jump on our doll bandwagon, or that they would take our molds to reproduce and copy them. They did. We got more antique dolls and made more molds. We learned to make, not only molds for production, but the cases to produce the molds. This took time, study and errors.

Every time we got one thing worked out for the dolls, there was another that had to be developed. You couldn't make good dolls, good French and German dolls, without bodies. For a year we tested formulas from Goodyear Rubber Company and other companies. We made body molds. They were difficult.

Most antique bodies are a paper mache composition which will disintegrate when wet plaster is poured over them. We could not afford to lose bodies from expensive dolls to make molds. I finally solved the problem of the body molds.

We still searched for a formula to reproduce the bodies. We finally found one that was being used for mannequins. Now this is the formula that is used worldwide for doll bodies by many doll companies. We originally called it Milvex.

I set up a body production room in the top floor of our store. I poured, I cleaned, I worked out methods of putting bodies together. I figured out how to color the base material to change it from grey to a natural body color.

Much later, we found it was better to paint the finished bodies. We had to locate elastic and develop methods of attaching parts. The making of the bodies was not my cup of tea, but it was necessary. Vernon was busy with the ceramic business.

Then I found the material wouldn't dry hard enough. It was fine in July, but the rest of the time it stayed spongy. We located and purchased ovens for drying (curing) the bodies. This worked after we figured out how long and how hot the ovens had to be. We got the body production underway. Before this, people were putting heads on shoulderplates, cloth bodies and on all-bisque bodies.

I wanted everything to be like the original old doll. I searched and experimented with china paints. I worked with different oils. I worked out methods for cleaning the greenware and the bisque. There seemed to be just one stumbling block after another. I was never satisfied with the results. Through it all our molds were selling. These were the first good French and German doll molds ever put on the market. Everything we were doing was a first.

To be first at anything is always the most difficult. There is no reference material, no one to go to. For solutions, I had to rely on me. Along with each new development, I wrote how-to books. I started the *Dollmaker Magazine* so I could tell my ever-expanding groups of dollmakers what was developing. The whole doll thing was experiencing an explosion.

I needed pictures. Jay, now teaching photography at Wesleyan University, took some pictures, all black and white. Vernon took a few. Duby, Jay's wife, made some illustrations for me. She helped with the *Dollmaker Magazine.*

Nothing came easily. Now we had a doll with a painted head and a composition body. I had to find wigs, or figure out how to make them. We were painting the eyes because there were no glass eyes of any sort available. Then I happened on Gus Schoepfer in New York City who had bought eyes from Germany and stored them from 1921 when the Fulper Doll Company collapsed. They were old German round blown glass eyes. He traded these eyes with me by the hundreds for ads in the *Dollmaker Magazine.*

Now we had to learn how to cut out eye holes and bevel the inside of the doll head. Vernon made a tool for me after he saw what I was trying to do. We produced these tools and sold them.

Now they have been copied in all kinds of variations by many companies. They are in every dollmaker's set of tools. I had to develop a method of setting the eyes so everyone could do it.

Well German eyes are fine for German dolls, but the French dolls did not look like much with these flat German eyes. There were no paperweight eyes available anywhere. I tried everything because I wanted French dolls that looked like the French dolls with paperweight eyes.

One day Vernon coated an old desk top with epoxy. He forgot to wipe the bottom edge. The next morning when I went to pick up the desk, there were rows of tiny pools of clear epoxy on the bottom edge—I thought eyes. I worked out a method applying epoxy to the crystal lenses on the old German eyes. I wrote the method up for everyone to use. We had French dolls with paperweight eyes—the first since 1900. They were not perfect, but we all used them, the best we could get. (Now gorgeous glass paperweight eyes are being made. Glass and plastic paperweight eyes are just another business developed from my little idea.)

I made a broad plan for developing each type of doll in turn, which included writing the dollmaking books and teaching the methods for each type—the German, French, babies, all-bisque, and the lady dolls. Everything had to be studied from the doll itself. There were no doll books except mine.

Dollmaking and my books were a success from the start as far as popularity was concerned. I, in order to get more dolls, was putting in more money than I could possibly get out with the cost of printing books and continually buying dolls for more molds.

The doll business was doing just what I hoped it might, giving us business in the summertime when ceramic classes weren't offered. I worked hard and long hours. Vernon and I did doll business at night after a full day.

It was probably 12 years from the time I said, "I want to make dolls," until I felt the business and its little components were working. There was always more to do to get better. At the same time my asthma was getting worse. We decided to spend a short time in Arizona during the winter. We had been going to Florida for a week's vacation. We tried out Sun City, Arizona. We stayed on a Tucson ranch. One day Vernon bought a lot in Green Valley. My asthma was much better in Arizona. We rented a place for a couple of weeks the following year.

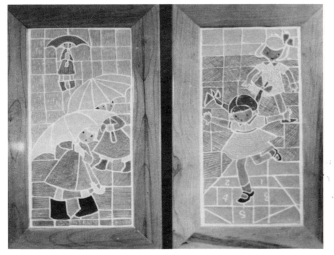

One of the projects I did for publication—they were handmade tiles.

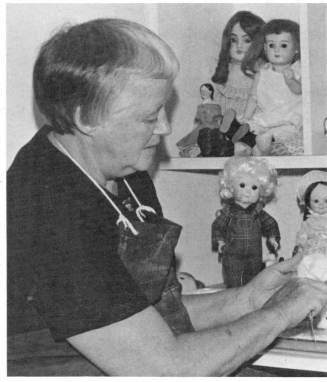

Demonstrating dollmaking.

The many ways to adapt a mold to create different looks was a teaching project that I did.

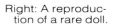

Right: A reproduction of a rare doll.

Left: One end of the Nature Museum that I set up in our extra room at 9 River St., Oneonta, New York. School children and adults enjoyed it. It contained labeled rocks, minerals, moths, butterflies and dolls.

We bought a ten-year-old house. We both adjusted to the weather, the open-air living. We liked it. We loved Arizona and the people. We considered moving our business. We looked for a suitable place but none could be found. (That was in 1974.)

While in Arizona, I did the doll advertising and conducted doll business over the phone. I selected and we made molds and cases for the next group of dolls and bodies to be produced. Vernon made a nice shop, and I took over the master bedroom for my studio. We built shelves and doll cases and put in an outside door. We stayed a month, then two months....

From my very first molds I have had wonderful communication from the dollmakers. They call, write and visit. Now there is a worldwide following with stacks of mail telling me what dolls and dollmaking have done. Each individual, in his own way, tells me what he or she is doing with dolls. I go to shows or conventions, and people I've never seen before hug me, have their picture taken with me, and bring me things to add to my dolls. I cannot ever quite conceive the truth—that we did it—we have helped in our small way to make a happier world.

At the same time as we started dolls, Vernon and I kept looking for other areas and other craft items that we could use in the store for making money. I taught copper enamel-

Vernon and I are given the Meritorious Alumni Award by the State University College at Oneonta, NY, for the revival of the old time art of porcelain dollmaking.

ing, and we sold the little kilns and material that went with the hobby. Then there was the craft of making jewelry from fried marbles, and we sold the materials for that. We devised many projects with handmade tile. We designed clay jewelry and worked it into a project. We wrote a little newsletter, *Ceram-O-Gram*, with projects for schools and clubs. We wrote articles for the ceramic magazines, and the rock and mineral magazines.

We kept an open mind, hoping to find some craft area to expand our ceramic business.

Diamond Hunting

Vernon and I turned into rock hounds. We joined the Rock Club and went to gem and mineral shows. It was not only a fun outlet for us, but

Vernon thought it could be an addition to the ceramic business—the sale of lapidary tools and equipment. The business never matured, but our interest did.

Whenever Vernon went to shows or conventions, I outlined the rocks, fossils or minerals that could be collected in the area. We once made a trip to Thunder Bay, Canada, to bring back a carload of amethyst. We hunted trilobites on the lake outside of Ithaca. We found, quite by accident, beautiful fern fossils outside of St. Clair, Pennsylvania. We stopped to drink our thermos of coffee, and here under our feet were the finest fern fossils I have ever seen!

We read *Keokuck Geodes*. Vernon was headed off for

Sculpture made of me as an old lady.

Nugget and us at our home on Vista Del Rio, Green Valley, AZ.

Plates were our thing and one of our best projects. The Snow Angel was a best seller.

Nugget and Joyce Wolf's *Baby Millie*—this one is Colleen's.

My play dolls: A walking Armand Marseille given to me by the Lunns, Mother's doll, and my birthday doll given to me by Mildred Whitney on the day I was born. I was named for her and this was her doll.

Kansas City. We took a "detour" by way of Iowa. It turned out the young man who wrote the book had just taken his grandfather's writings and submitted them for his masters! The landmarks, the railroad station and other buildings had been gone for 40 years! Anyway, we were good hunters. We brought home from Iowa tiny geodes filled with crystals, water, and even one with oil.

After the conference we were on a side road near Morgan, West Virginia. I was out in the ditch looking for a geode. Along came a young girl in a truck. She stopped to help us. I told her what we were looking for. She said "Oh, nigger heads. I have always tried to get someone interested in them."

She took us to a tree-lined large creek. There, every rock was a geode, each specimen better than the next. We could not stop looking. We picked up a couple of bushel baskets full. We also came home with a huge geode for a special specimen. It was about 18" across and contained seven different crystals inside.

Another time we were directed to an old mine dump— I believe it was a coal mine— at the edge of Illinois to find concretions with ferns in them. They were not at all like the Pennsylvania fern fossils.

Another time in Cave-in-Rock, Illinois, we visited a man who was an expert on fluorite. We traded him specimens of other minerals. In Oklahoma we hunted desert roses with Jim and Grace Snelling. (I had taught with Gracie in Oxford,

New York. Friends are forever in our small world. They have visited us in Arizona numerous times.)

We found apache tears in Rock Hound Park, New Mexico. We found pink quartz, garnet, diopside in the Adirondacks of New York.

Our little nature museum was in the front room in the ceramic store. It just emerged as an extra. The walls were covered with butterflies and moth specimens, the room was filled with glass cases of rocks and mineral specimens. I labeled them all and arranged them. I was so proud of the colorful and educational museum. Area school children visited the museum.

I saved the best until last— the diamond hunt. In the area of Middleville and Herkimer, New York, deep in the dolomite of the hillside, are pockets where doubly terminated quartz crystals exist. This is the only known place in the world where this occurs.

There is a place to hunt just outside of Middleville. Most people hunt by walking over the ground and picking up small bits. Not us, we took crowbars, ten pound sledges, pry bars, wedges, heavy hand hammers and stone drills. We wore boots, heavy clothes and gloves. We carried hot stew, coffee, sandwiches and our old black Lhasa apso, Sheba. I carried tools and graph paper.

We studied the dolomite cliff. We hammered, we listened. If we thought we heard a different sound, we would proceed to hammer, chisel, pry and

Herkimer diamond

wedge to get a hole into a pocket. Often Vernon moved a ton of solid unrelenting rock. His hands were bruised and his body aching.

A pocket was a hole anywhere from four inches to two feet wide and perhaps six inches high. It was a place that no one, not anyone, ever had peered into. It was like a buried treasure that had been buried when time began.

Once the outer surface was cracked you could hear the air rush in or, if under water, see the bubbles. Some of the pockets that were near the surface were sometimes cracked by frost, and the mud flowed in. But if you opened up a solid one, the dry crystal would be clean and pure—many of them perfect.

Some pockets had one fine cluster centered on the roof of the pocket. This usually fell to the floor of the tiny cavern while you were getting the pocket open. On the floor you could scoop them up by the handful. Here were all the exquisite crystals, some were little clusters, some had inclusions, some even had water bubbles.

A bit of the diamond collection.

Herkimer diamonds in the matrix.

Cutting, prying, moving tons of rock to get to the pockets.

Aching back, joints, battered hands.

The general area where the doubly-terminated quartz crystals are found.

Once you get thru the rock you might find a pocket of treasure.

108

The crystals were from the size of specks to four inches. One time we found a large one only partly formed, a skeleton.

Once you opened the pocket large enough to get your hand in to pull out the crystals, the hunter becomes infected with a mania for more—like a miser for gold. You can't stop. We couldn't stop.

We worked until we hurt all over. Vernon worked so hard and long one time, he couldn't let go of the hammer. My neck hurt from the shock of the hammer hitting. Sometimes we worked into the night. If a pocket was opened late in the day, you had to finish emptying it or someone else would have it in the morning.

I studied and cleaned crystals. I tried to figure out how these loose crystals could be there with points on both ends, no place for growth. Then we found a pocket, half filled with large calcite crystals. Imbedded in the calcite were the quartz crystals. One side where the water had seeped in, the calcite had melted and freed doubly terminated quartz crystals. Some had fallen out. Mystery solved.

To find the pockets I kept a sheet of graph paper with the layers of dolomite rock and the rock above marked. I put on the graph where we got pockets and reasoned where there might be another. Our graph served us well—we opened some 52 pockets.

This became wild. We hurt, but we still wanted to hunt. We had boxes of crystals—we still do. One day I said I am not going to do this anymore. I quit. Vernon went once without me, but he knew too that we should quit. Now he likes to tell people about our diamond hunt.

Selling Seeley's Ceramic Service

We had worked long and hard at the ceramic business and the dollmaking business was well established. Both were very prosperous, but we needed to be there the entire year. Vernon was at retirement age, so we thought we should sell the business.

We had three chances to sell. The first was a concern in New York City who wanted us to make dolls for them. This was a nightmare and I backed out.

The second was to the American Art Clay Company (AMACO), one of the largest suppliers for the ceramic business. On our way back to New York from Arizona, we were to stop at AMACO in Indianapolis to meet with their president and attorneys to sell the business.

In our meeting Vernon was asked how much a year he needed to live on based on the number of years he was expected to live—this was to be the price for the business. Then they outlined my work—how I would continue to write a book a year, give lectures, and set up exhibits and sales booths eight times a year. I think Vernon was horrified when I said, "I wanted no part of this deal." I knew it wasn't right for me.

We arrived home in Oneonta and Bruno, our accountant, who couldn't see the value in the doll business, said he could sell the ceramic business, but we must go light on the doll part. He advised me to sell the *Dollmaker Magazine*. I did. The business was sold in 1977 to Rolf Ericson.

The new owners knew nothing of either ceramics or dolls. We agreed to teach them. The ceramic part was all set up and was relatively easy. Dolls were something else. In the contract I was to teach them the doll business from scratch and work for the next three years, which turned into ten.

I was to buy dolls, produce new molds and write books. In fact I was to do much the same as I had been doing. I did. I wrote the books and came up with matching molds and instructions. It looks today like I wrote 20 books in 20 years, produced about 200 molds with matching bodies. I also wrote articles on dolls for the new doll magazines—five different ones —that were popping up. I liked this work. I liked the fast pace I set for myself. At this same time, I was completing my masters degree. Every time I turned around, I came up with a new idea. Dolls were a joy, people I met in the doll world were fun. The doll thing spread, expanded.

At the end of the first year after the business sold, I was working very closely with the new owners, Rolf and Ragnild Ericson. I came up with the idea of having doll pictures on

After Sheba died, we bought Nugget. She was a little gold ball of fluff.

plates. We developed this business as a partnership. I did the designing and advertising, and they did the shipping. We did very well, but we could have done better.

Oh yes, just as we sold the business, I came up with the idea of the Doll Artisan Guild. I planned it so that there would not be the hassle and scrapping of other organizations. Our new organization would belong to Seeley's Ceramic Service and be controlled by them. It still is. I knew now that selling the *Dollmaker Magazine* was a mistake. So I came up with a new magazine, *The Doll Artisan*. It is still going under the Ericson ownership.

The dollmaking business grew and grew. The Ericsons were and are doing a multimillion dollar doll business worldwide.

Vernon Gets Sick

Vernon got Valley Fever in 1979. This disease is from a desert fungus. He was in and out of the hospital. He didn't get better. It got into his spinal column and he collapsed. He had meningitis.

My world evaporated overnight. The doctors told me there was no way he could survive this. The doctors told the children when they came. I had a feeling I could make a difference. I could make him want to live. I went everyday to the hospital. I sat and worried.

Then I decided I must do more. I tried to make his mind work. I discussed business. I asked about bills. I made him add. I talked to him about our puppy Nugget. I tried everything, every angle, to get his mind to think of home and getting better.

Coping with everything in the house, my work, the new puppy, the car—everything was a hassle. I was used to Vernon doing more than his half. In our beautiful garden the watering system would not go on. I fell thru the slats. I couldn't eat.

One morning I woke up knowing I was also dying. I crawled out on the floor. They sent me to the hospital in an ambulance. I had diverticulitis. I got better and came home. Two days later it returned, and I was back in the hospital. This time in the same room with Vernon. I was sure I was dying. I would pass out, come to, pass out again. In a few days I did get better. I had to. There was the house, the dog. I had to get Vernon better.

His treatment was the most painful thing anyone anywhere could go thru. I felt the pain myself. They gave him amphterican B in his spinal cord. At first it was every day, then every other day, then finally down to twice a week on an out-patient basis.

About noon he would get his terrible injection. He could hardly stand it. I could not stand it. The doctor would ask me to leave the room, but I couldn't leave him. I disliked the sloppy doctor. Vernon thought he was doing all he could. He would not agree to change doctors.

One day at five o'clock I had just brought Vernon home from the hospital and gotten him in his chair when a storm hit. A wild Arizona thunderstorm broke loose. With the first startling crack of thunder and at the same time lightening flashing, I was somehow aware the house had been struck. I could smell it.

I had some experience with lightning back in New Kingston when lightning struck our big maple tree and house in one storm. It crashed the water tank behind the toilet and thru a large piece all the way across the room and into the bathtub. My mother had coaxed Dad to wait until the storm was over to take his bath. Wire all over the house burned out. It killed the maple tree. It would have killed Dad had he been in the tub.

I tried the phone. It was dead. I guided Vernon out of the house and got him into the car. I put the dog in the car. I drove to the fire station in the pouring rain. They came. The fireman found the lightning had come down our high palm tree and blown a large hole in the bedroom roof. It was leaking. There was some smoke, but no fire. I began carrying dolls to the car. (It didn't take much smoke to make you see your lifetime's investment go up in a cloud.)

The firemen saw my situation; they put a large canvas over the roof hole. They reassured me. I was more than a little shook up. Vernon was too sick and hurting too much to realize what was happening.

The pain from the treatment just got worse and worse. The doctor decided he could help Vernon's pain by adding cortisone to the ampheterisen shot. Vernon's medical doctor had not suggested this, but the doctor did it when the other doctor was off duty.

By eleven o'clock that night Vernon was paralyzed from his waist down. His leg had fallen off the bed and he couldn't get it back. I called 911. They couldn't get the stretcher into the bedroom. They more or less hauled him out by his arms, I knew they were hurting him. We got him back to the hospital.

In the morning the doctor finally got to look at him. He had had a stroke. His left eye was closed. From his waist down he was paralyzed. The doctor said it could be permanent. If I fell thru the slats before, I fell thru the cracks and melted down into goo-like syrup now. My world dissolved into nothingness. I have always, with all the things I did or wanted to do, needed the support and encouragement of Vernon. We were always a team. I really did nothing alone.

I got him out of the hospital. He was getting some strength back in his legs. He said no more shots even if he died. We read Norman Cousin's book Anatomy of An Illness. I gave him huge doses of vitamin C.

We made phone calls everywhere to see what we could find out about Valley Fever. We found there was a Dr. Bauchsbaum in Tucson who was considered the best in the area. I got Vernon to see him. This was the beginning, the high spot with new treatment and a new doctor with know-how. He began to recover.

I worked on his mind each day, having him figuring numbers and doing little jobs. He could not remember or concentrate. He would walk away from the house and I would have to find him. I took all the cords and plugs so his tools could not be started.

I watched him like a fearful mother of a three year old. He weighed 135 pounds. I made special foods for him to eat. He was improving. He liked the new doctor. The new treatments were not painful. By noon after a treatment, he was able to come home from the hospital. He still got nauseated just by going past St. Mary's road. (The road to the old hospital where he was first treated.) I did, too.

Along with this, I was still under contract to produce a book and ten molds along with ideas and advertising for the doll business we had sold. The company was constantly pushing me.

Now that Vernon was getting better I took my work with me to the hospital. I wrote one whole book perched on a hard stool in the emergency room where I waited for him. (That book still sells.) Vernon was Dr. Bauchsbaum's prize patient. He wrote about Vernon's case in a medical journal.

Vernon wanted to drive the car, but his eye was still not working as it should. His legs were walking. He insisted on driving. I never let him take the car alone. He would forget he was driving.

It was a very dangerous situation for us both, but he improved rapidly. It helped him. We made a trip by plane to St. Louis to a doll convention. It was so good for him and good for me. He talked to a friend who had gotten along for years with only one eye. It took eight months for Vernon's eye to come back completely.

Time smoothed out the wrinkles. I got him back working and gardening. He even got back on the golf course. He told me how good it was to be out, even though his golf was pretty bad. Things became all pink again after the gloom of grey for several years. We were happy again and living—doing dolls. The roses came back into bloom. The dolls smiled.

Again we started to look for a new house, one already built. We looked and looked. It was discouraging. Our dolls and our life style were jammed to the limit at "Desert Dollkins"—the

I used the garden room that we built on our Vista Del Rio home in Green Valley to paint dolls. We also ate there. It was so cheerful and flower filled.

Vista del Rio house. We found a wonderful lot and bought it. Vernon got scared we could never build a house. He wanted to change our minds. I had planned and supervised the building of our home in Oneonta. I was old, but I could do it again. I took over the complete planning.

I fired the first builder. I wanted certain things in the new house. I wanted it to be special for us. I wanted a bay window. I wanted built-in cases for our wonderful doll collection that we had acquired over the years. We moved into the new house on February 9, 1986.

I didn't tell you that at one time just after we sold the business and we were still spending the summers in Oneonta, New York, I had a chance to buy a Marque doll—two Marque dolls. I found these in a closed museum in North Carolina. I had tried to buy them earlier, but the owner would not sell them. I had no idea how much they were worth. It must have been three years later when I called her and she wanted to sell. This would take my life savings. Would it be a safe thing to do? I knew it was a risk. She wouldn't send the doll. I would have to come and get it.

Vernon and I drove down from Oneonta to North Carolina to get the doll. All the way down and back we planned on what we could do with the doll to get some of my money back. We came up with producing a limited edition. A limited edition of one of

Our wonderful pair of Marque dolls. They were made in 1913 by the French sculptor, Albert Marque. Their clothes are original.

Vernon making a doll mold. His molds are used by dollmakers all over the world.

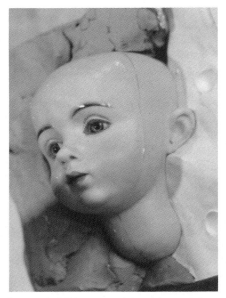

A usual doll head mold can be made in two parts. The Marque has five.

The reproduction was smaller, about 16''.

Left: Pam Lembo paints the heads to match the antique dolls.

Left: Vernon and I with the *Snow Angel*. I'm painting a larger A.T. Above: Firing the kiln is like a magic process.

the world's most-sought after doll! This was a success. It was the first—the birth of the limited edition dolls. It was 1978.

The next spring we drove down and bought the girl Marque to go with our boy. I have never felt as rich as I did when I put that girl in the case with the boy. These two dolls have graced the covers of many doll catalogs and doll magazines. They are probably the best known of all the French bisque dolls.

The next spring I did the research on Marque. I found his name, his obituary, and all about his work. Others wrote this up and claimed the research was theirs, but I did it thru the library in Tucson. It was I who had the idea we could find him under sculptors, not dollmakers. Until then, Marque dolls were an unknown as to date and maker.

Again things were coming up dolls and roses in Arizona. The house building was a great experience, a great risk at our age, but we did it. We wanted the children to come and spend the first Christmas in it. It didn't happen. The house was not quite finished, but the children came. We had a happy, jammed-in holiday, and the fun of showing off the new house. The next Christmas we did it up round, the giant tree and all.

Our rose garden was a joy from the start. We now had 100 bushes to keep our house filled with happiness!

Six years and two books in the new house. I couldn't believe I could do it. I stopped teaching seminars on judging dolls after the *Judging Dolls* book (published by Scott Publications) came out. Groups and clubs are still coming to study and I have two or three seminars a year on antique dolls.

Dolls—The Collecting

At first, I thought a good doll collection would be one with a specimen of each type, kind and age. I started out to collect this way. My sister Dot, a longtime antique dealer, explained to me that collections of anything were more valuable than singles.

People like to study and see variations of the same type. If you want to sell what you have collected, it is better that they be similar. I saw what she was doing, making a collection of cut-glass, or Stuben glass, and sterling silver pieces. She spent years putting together a collection, then sold the whole collection for a high price.

I am no antique dealer or seller of anything, nor did I aspire to be, but I saw what she was doing. I decided she was right and my doll collection should have a theme—a single thread running thru—as the collection expanded.

I made mistakes, expensive mistakes. I cleaned my doll closets, took out all the dolls that did not conform—dolls that had been purchased in groups. I sent them all to the Withington's auction.

These dolls came up on the third day of a three-day auc-

tion. People either had gone home or had spent their money. I barely got enough to buy one French doll. I did as I had planned though. I bought the one French doll. Lillian Sprowl was closing her doll museum near Albany, New York. She had sold most of her dolls before I heard about it. Yes, she had a Bru doll left.

We went up to see her and the Bru. It was a little Brevette. I bought it. I was proud of myself for having carried thru the plan. Now instead of clutter, I had a doll, a valuable French doll.

I now was convinced that this was the way to go. I had a direction. Our doll mold business required good bisque dolls, both French and German. I bought dolls where I could find them. I repaired them, cleaned them, and made them clothing. My collection always had to take second place to what we needed for the doll business.

When I was preparing to do a group of baby doll molds, I bought baby dolls. These I used for the books on baby dolls at the same time. I put together a wonderful collection with Kestners, Heubachs, Simon Halbigs—a collection anyone would be proud of.

Sometime later, when I needed money to buy another group of dolls to do another set of molds and another book, I sold them. I sold all 52 of my baby dolls, including my wonderful Hilda and Heubach Billy. I thought I was getting a check for the lot. The dolls were picked up. He gave me a small check and then paid for them in dribbles. By the time they were paid for, the value of Hilda alone had gone up enough to be more than he had paid for the lot. I lost again. I am a slow learner.

When I finished *The Dollhouse Doll* book, I sold the dollhouse dolls. I thought, I'll never need them again. We had made a complete set of molds. I must have done a good job on the book—it's still selling.

As soon as we sold the business, I was to put together a large group of all-bisque molds and a book of instruction to match. I had the project well underway when we left Oneonta for Arizona. I would finish the molds and the book in Arizona.

I packed the little all-bisque dolls in one box. We took them into the motel each night. I guarded them as my book depended on them—my income depended on them.

We unloaded in Arizona and decided to leave the boxes unopened until we painted the inside of the house. In two weeks, painting accomplished, I hunted for the box of dolls. No dolls. We searched. We called the painter thinking perhaps he had carried out the box thinking it was paper. We called the last motel we stayed in.

We covered everything, every track, every box in the house. The dolls were gone! They were not insured—neither was the book or my income. I did have some all-bisques that we had brought out the year before, but not enough. I had no solution to the problem.

I remembered visiting a collection in Tucson the year before. She had some all-bisque dolls. I called her, and she let us go in and photograph many from her collection. This saved my doll life! I bought a few more to make molds. I did the book. In 1991 I rewrote and rephotographed a completely new version, *The Complete Book of All-Bisque Dolls*. It was published by Scott Publications in hard cover. It came out in January 1993.

The box of all-bisque dolls was never found. I now have acquired a fine collection of the finest all-bisque dolls. We win some, we lose some.

The Flood

It wasn't really a flood. The water meter broke in our Oneonta home's basement and flooded the basement within a foot of the top with nice, clean chlorinated water.

We were not in Oneonta but in Arizona. We had been there about three weeks. The Ericsons, the new owners of our business, called us when we were just getting home from an auction, it was ten p.m. Rolf said he had been up to check on our house. The water was crystal clear, and the whole basement looked like there was nothing there.

The next morning, Monday, the rug company was coming to lay carpet in our Arizona house. There was no way I could get to them. Vernon said that he would go alone and take care of the situation. He got a flight at 1:20 a.m.

By the time Vernon arrived, the fire department had come and gone. They put down two massive suction hoses and siphoned the water out. It was like a tornado hit. The swirling water drew every piece of furniture, including Colleen's piano, all the articles over the years that we had written, Colleen's music, books, albums, movies of the children, and the movie projector.

Everything was beat and mixed with water and clay like the doings of a massive food processor. We lost cases of rocks and mineral books, butterfly and moth books. We also lost all the doll molds stored in Vernon's shop, along with most of his tools and machinery. Only a few tools were salvaged.

To understand the extent of the damage you would have to know the house. I had designed the lower story (basement) as part of our living area. Vernon had a well-equipped shop in the far end. He had mold cases of all kinds, lathe, kilns, and hundreds of plaster molds.

The large room had a fireplace, television, books, files, leather-covered furniture, and antique pieces, including a Shaker rocker, a chair made by Vernon's great-grandfather, and on and on. There was a furnace room, a small room with shelves and shelves where we kept partially completed cases of butterflies and extra butterflies.

On a shelf in this room I had the material for my "best seller" book, the story of my cousin (that I called aunt), Emily Carpenter. She had polio when she was a senior at Oneonta State Normal School and hadn't walked since. Her whole life story would have been an inspiration to anyone who was physically handicapped.

She had given me her diaries that went all the way back to childhood, along with many many old photographs and clippings. I had named the book *Ann Temily and Her Giants*. (When I was eight, I wrote a letter and addressed it to Ann Temily, believing that was her name. It seems I had been calling Aunt Emily, Ann Temily all my life, and my family hadn't told me.)

The material for the book, photographs and the first and last chapters went down—never to be seen again. This is the best excuse I can come up with for never having produced a best seller.

Vernon traveled all night, arriving the next morning with a terrible headache. Jay came in from Connecticut to help. Colleen said she would come from Michigan if we needed her. It was terrible, our treasures in this unbelievable mess!

They got a dump truck, truly a dumpster, and started carrying and shoveling the mess out. Vultures came and salvaged stuff from the truck and pushed into the inside of the house when possible.

The furniture and piano pieces were carried out, the big tools covered with rust were set outside. Jay was seeking out some of the hundreds of photos and reels of film to dry them

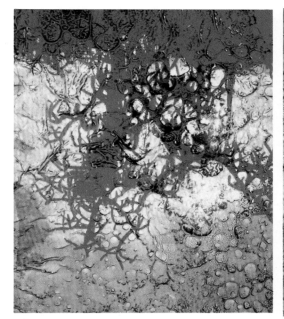
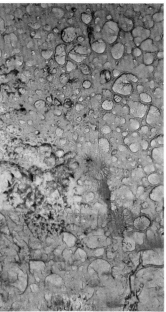

This is what the water of "the flood" did to our butterfly slides. Could they be some special kind of art?

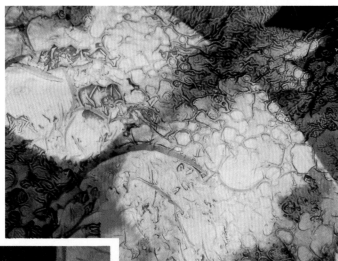

Left: Emily Carpenter and her boyfriend, who died of influenza while attending Cornell. Emily had polio, then called "infantile paralysis," when she was 19. She used a metal brace on her paralyzed leg. Her courage, her stamina, and working-intelligence was to be the subject of my book *Ann Temily and Her Giants*.

Baby Millie was sculpted by Joyce Wolf of Florida. She did it from my baby picture.

out in hopes of salvage. These things had been soaking, perhaps two weeks or more, who knows.

Neither Vernon or Jay were aware of the things, like the Shaker rocker, other antiques, and childhood photos, I treasured most.

Back in Arizona, I saw the carpet job finished. I realize what a giant hole had been taken out of my life when we returned to Oneonta in April. Insurance on this kind of thing—forget it.

I had given Jay a little iron stove, a salesman sample, just before we left for Arizona. I had given Colleen my cedar chest that housed my old play dolls.

Both of these things had been in the basement. They were saved from the flood.

Wolf's Baby Millie

I was judging at a doll convention in Oneonta, New York. We expected more baby dolls than dolls in any other group, so I was going to work with the baby dolls. At the last minute they divided the baby group, and I was changed to work with the French Be'be's.

Following the judging, Joyce Wolf and a group came and handed me a good-sized original baby doll. I got a funny feeling when I looked at the doll. I said, "It's odd but this doll looks so much like my sister Dot did when she was a baby." Then they told me. Joyce had taken my baby picture, enlarged it, and had made the portrait of "Baby Millie." I was really speechless. It was such an honor. The card on the doll read "Sculpted by Joyce Wolf as a tribute to Mildred Seeley for her contribution to dollmaking."

I loved the doll from the moment I saw her. She sits by my table in her high chair. I believe she is Joyce's masterpiece. She wears an 1890 family christening gown given to me by my neighbor Deloris Crebs.

Joyce and the other girls had intended to put the doll thru where I was to judge baby dolls. Their plan fell thru when I moved to French dolls. I am sure I would have broken up had the doll come thru to be judged. Joyce, you'll never know how much this doll means to me. I love it.

The By-Pass

For perhaps a year or so, I had, just off and on, a dull ache in my left arm. I noticed it more if the air was cool or I was walking or carrying a purse. It seemed to be occurring more often, but it was nothing I couldn't stand or a little rest wouldn't take care of.

One day we were at Harlow's Nursery in Tucson and after walking around the nursery, my arm was aching. Vernon said, "We are right next to Dr. Parker's office, lets go over and see if we can find out anything."

The doctor's office was full. He couldn't see me. I told the nurse my trouble and she took me in for a cardiogram. They called a heart man from across the way. He took a quick look at the cardiogram and said "You have had a heart attack. Any first year medical student could tell you have had a heart attack. Go immediately to the emergency ward of the hospital."

Dr. Parker sent his assistant-in-training with me with the cardiogram. The nurse in charge looked at the cardiogram, remarked that it looked normal, but they still proceeded with the routine for a heart attack.

I was scared, scared skinny.

They gave me nitroglycerine under my tongue. They set up an intravenous thing to give me medication used for dissolving clots. I passed out and knew no more until I was in the intensive care unit.

I did not and would not believe I had a heart attack.

I woke up and my mouth was bleeding. The heart doctor came in and said I should have an angioplasty, but first I should have an angiogram to see what was blocked. Dr. Parker's assistant came in later and said the chemistry did not show that I had a heart attack. They were poking medicine down me at a great rate. I wanted to go home. A few days later I came home.

The clot dissolving medicine had not made a difference. The medicine the heart doctor gave me had not made a difference—I should say it made the arm ache worse. It did get worse. Vernon took me back to the hospital.

They ran a tube in from my leg to see my artery blockage. Vernon and Dr. Bob Hughes saw the video. It did look as though one entrance was partly blocked, but I thought too, this could just be the angle, the way it curved under. They left the thing in all night and I was to get an angioplasty the next morning.

They kept me full of tranquilizers so that I didn't care. I watched the video as the doctor worked to get the angioplasty in. He tried and tried again. I don't know if he had ever done one before or not. I heard him say, "I'll try once more—I am going to tickle your heart a little." That is the last thing I remembered.

I woke up in intensive care. Vernon was there. He told me I had a heart attack on the table, and they had done a heart by-pass. My whole body had been ripped apart. I hurt all over. I was alive or partly alive.

This was something that shouldn't happen to anyone. Every part of me complained. The children came. I wondered if when they doped me off to sleep at night if I would wake up in the morning. I did.

I could feel Vernon worry. I was so happy the children were here. If I didn't make it, they would help him. I came home, much before I was ready. My surgeries in both my leg and chest were still oozing and dripping. I felt like I could not move my horribly sore body.

The second morning I was home, my blood pressure ran way up. I told Vernon I was going to pass out. I thought I was dying. The ambulance came and they wanted to take me back to the hospital. I could just see my chest and leg opening up in the bumpy old ambulance. I had ridden in that thing before. I decided quickly that I'd rather die here at home.

I hate having holes poked in my world. I hated worse having a hole as big as a year torn from me, it didn't seem quite fair. I had work to do. I was sure my doll world needed me.

Vernon coddled me, pampered me, waited on me, fed me, got me up and down. If it had not been for him, I would not have bothered. It was too hard.

I did recover but I never felt like I had felt before. It could never all come back. I will have to do with what I have.

All the time Vernon and I wondered, was that treatment, that by-pass necessary? Now, of course, we have read many times that it was not. The doctor needed another patient's money to make his planned trip to Europe. I took care of his trip and his next one too. I hope I never run into that doctor again, under any circumstances.

PART 6

Life in Arizona

In the rose garden at Shandelé.

World Doll Day logo. I established the World Doll Day to be the second Saturday of every June to mark a special day devoted to dolls.

Happiness

Happiness is a big new house —Shandelé—with everything I ever wished for in it.

Happiness is a rose garden of 90 bushes producing a multi-colored foreground for snow-capped mountains. Happiness is roses lending their fragrance and soft colors to every room.

Happiness is a pile of published doll books and articles that I can leave to the world of dollmakers, doll collectors and my children.

Happiness is the hobby of collecting. Joy comes with every doll I collect, clean, study and place in my cabinets.

Happiness is helping other doll collectors and makers.

Big happiness is a fabulous collection of antique French and German dolls that fills our house to overflowing.

Happiness is World Doll Day, the second Saturday of every June, that I dreamed up to spread happiness. World Doll Day appears on doll calendars and is celebrated by doll collectors and dollmakers around the world.

Happiness is being alive, hearing a bird sing, smelling a rose, watching a butterfly, touching a doll, cooking a dinner.

But most of all, happiness is daily living with Vernon.

Our Shandelé

We "haunted" the real estate agents. We went in and out of the many houses that were for sale, but found nothing that we liked.

One day, our agent Mary said, "Buy a lot and build your

own. I know where the best lot in all of Green Valley is located. A California man owns it and was saving it for his own retirement house, but I think I can get the lot for you."

The lot, sprinkled with its original mesquite and pa-loverde trees, overlooked the emerald green of a golf course. Two small lakes reflected Arizona's ever-blue sky, and the 7,000-foot snow dusted peaks of Mount Wrightson and Mount Hopkins.

We paced the lot. "Perfect," Vernon said. I agreed. In three days' time the deed was done. We had bought a lot and now we must build our home.

Vernon suddenly had second thoughts. We were both about 70 and considering building a new home! We must be getting senile! Our old house, now about 20 years old, really was good enough.

We had added a wall to keep out the rabbits and keep our dog in. We had built a fireplace, a workshop for Vernon, a studio for me, and completely rejuvenated the kitchen.

But the dolls were squeezing in from all sides. At night they jumped around, rattled the furniture, and played their music boxes in hope we would provide them with better quarters.

I decided we could build a house. I wanted to build it without an architect. We would use a builder—a cost saving plan.

We went to the lot. I studied the view, the directions, the slope, the existing trees. In our imaginations we picked up our house and turned it this way

Breaking ground on our Shandelé.

Shandelé under construction.

and that way. We knew what we wanted.

I drew the house from the inside out, placing the rooms just as I wanted them—a guest room and a bath at one end of the house, and my studio (that could double as an extra guest room).

I wanted a massive living room with a cathedral ceiling, fireplace, and windows that faced Mount Wrightson. Most of all, I wanted big wall cabinets for the dolls and another wall with recessed pockets for our mechanicals. I designed a special spot for the Brittany Wedding Couple, a pair of very old French Fashion dolls that had been dressed in Brittany with the date attached to their clothing: 1869.

The kitchen had to be very special. It had to be large enough so we could both work in it at the same time and also have it filled with doll guests. It got everything: microwave, grill and instant hot water. The kitchen eating spot was designed with arched bay windows with a view of the rose garden and mountains.

Our bedroom was to open off the kitchen. It was designed to

Plasterer wears stilts.

Inside Shandelé under construction.

The fireplace for the study.

All cabinets were lowered 4'' for me.

be a quiet room with a special Mil-designed bathroom, which included his and her washing areas, mirrors and closets, a whirlpool tub big enough for two, and showering area.

The laundry room became a multi-purpose area with a lower counter for sewing, and a counter for washing dolls. I designed storage area everywhere.

Our study, with its brick fireplace, built-in television, doll cabinets, and lounge chairs became a loved and comfortable spot. We put Vernon's shop and gardening tool storage on the outside edge of the garage.

I worked every spare minute on the house plans. I spent many nights in bed thrashing around for fear I would make a mistake. But I loved working on it.

When all the designs and measurements were done (and Vernon and I were both happy with them), Vernon redrew the plans. The plans then went to a computer service in Tucson, Arizona, that provided blueprints based on our designs. Very little was changed from Vernon's plans.

We hired and fired a builder who would not do our bay window, fireplaces, or many other details the way we wanted them. We eventually found a young builder who wanted to do things just the way we wanted.

The house, our Shandelé, came to be a reality. We named it after one of our Brus—a big, lovely Bru named Shandelé. We had named the doll after

Vernon and me inside the finished Shandelé.

The first Christmas in our new home.

Kitchen area.

Studio cabinets.

My studio.

200-year-old rocking horse in the brick inset made for him.

Setting for the Jumeau sculpture.

Summertime brings rain and rainbows.

The view of our home from the rear.

A Long Face Jumeau is carved into our front door.

Wisteria blooms over the arches.

Lake Shandelé, a quiet, beautiful little spot in the heart of the Catskill Mountains of New York State. Bru Shandelé was to have a prominent spot in our new home. So we decided to call our home Shandelé, meaning "loved place."

It was an expensive project, but the dolls didn't care. All they wanted was space and a husky security system—and they would finance it. I found house planning a challenging and fun project.

Happiness is a big new house, our Shandelé.

The Rose House

We were in Hawaii one Christmastime, and we stayed in the rose-colored Royal Hawaiian Hotel. Not only was the outside painted rose, but the walls, carpets, sheets and towels—everything—was a soft rose color. On top of this, the elaborate Christmas decorations in the lobbies were dominated with huge rose-colored balls and rose ribbons.

I never realized how color could affect me. It was like pure relaxation with a smile embedded with happiness. I decided then, that when I decorated my home again, I would use the soft rose color. Vernon liked it too. That is how we came to want a rose-colored house.

When our house was underway, we hunted the paint stores for just the right color of pink. But nothing matched what we had in mind.

One day while traveling north of Tucson, we saw the new buildings of La Paloma, a hotel complex, being built. It

Simplicity roses and the garden walls.

The Chanticleer sits on the wall overlooking the golf course.

Shandelé from the golf course. Vernon's half-acre of daisies.

Our tree roses accent the path in our rose garden.

was rose—just our color. There was a newly painted wall at the entrance of the complex. I asked Vernon to stop.

I went up to the wall. On the ground were numerous stones where a sloppy painter had drizzled the fabulous color. I picked up one of these stones and took it to a paint store, which happened to be the one that had mixed the color for the complex. It was called La Paloma Pink.

I was at the new house every day. My neighbor, who often reminded me of how much time I spent "supervising" the building of our home, asked what color we planned to paint the exterior. "Hot pink," I said, never believing for a moment that he would take me seriously.

He wasted no time in getting to the housing committee. The committee showed up. I had to convince them I was kidding and showed them the sample color.

One of the men on the committee had built his home up the street and he had gotten into the same kind of pickle. He had built a six by four foot recess in his foundation for a wine cellar.

When people asked about it, he told them he was having a new experimental "atomic heater" put in. He was having so much fun with it that he had a sign made that read "First experimental atomic heating plant installed in a home."

Well, you can believe he got visitors—a whole uproar was created. So I got lots of sympathy for my "hot pink house" lie.

The Statue

I designed the rose garden at Shandelé three steps down from the house to give us a better view of the roses and the beautiful green of the golf course.

We wanted something for the center of our rose garden. We studied pieces of statuary. Nothing was nice enough; nothing suited us. One day while we were in Phoenix, we stopped at Des Santana Handcrafted Fountains.

We asked about having a custom design carved for us. They said there was a sculptor in Mexico named Pablo who might be able to do something. We went home and thought about it for a week or so.

I decided a doll was the appropriate thing for our garden. I carefully measured just the right size and height we wanted. We decided on the Long Face Jumeau. I took photos from every angle of the antique doll. We had a mold of the doll, and we cast a head to provide the sculptor with an idea of the doll's features.

Part way through the job, the company sent us photos of the big piece of lava rock they had quarried, and of the sculpture in its earliest stages. We were getting excited.

Two months later we got a telephone call. The statue was finished and it would be delivered on Sunday.

On Sunday, two skinny young men and two girls arrived in a truck with a crane and a huge crate. I didn't believe these skinny kids would be able to handle the crate.

The crude beginning of the statue.

The Long Face Jumeau sculpture under construction.

The boss checks the workmanship against our photos.

Thank goodness Vernon was there. He replaced the thin little pieces of plywood they had brought to move the statue with planks and heavier plywood. If he hadn't, the statue would surely have ended up forming part of the gravel in our driveway.

They managed to get the crate off the truck and moved it inch by inch into the rose garden, breaking the bricks in the walk as they went.

I was running around the crate, trying to see what we had. It was packed in sawdust and paper. I couldn't see a thing. I told them it had to face in a certain direction. They said once the crate was off the statue, they couldn't move it again. I still couldn't figure out why the crate was so big and

129

Pablo's masterpiece.

heavy. It weighed over a ton.

Finally, they got it on the right spot and opened up the top so we could see the head of the sculpture. It was huge. They removed the crate and pulled away the papers and sawdust. The statue was six feet tall. It was the biggest Long Face Jumeau anyone had ever seen! Pablo had carved every detail so carefully—her face, dress, the eyelets on her petticoat—even her locket. Every curl was in place.

But I was still horrified at her size. The four chatted in Spanish as they cleaned up the statue and chiseled out the props that had been left attached for shipping. Then I realized that I had given the statue's measurements in inches, not meters. We liked it. And anyway, the only way this Long Face Jumeau will ever be moved from the garden is in pieces. So here stands Pablo's masterpiece surrounded by roses.

Dinner Time at Shandelé

And guess who came to dinner? These guests live here, some just board with us in the summer, others are full-timers. They *do* take advantage of our generosity. They call us. They talk to us. They sit on the back of our chairs. They tap on our windows and hammer out codes on the metal fireplace chimney cover. They are our birds, demanding attention and food.

A *Says Phoebe* bird picked our house while it was under construction. She watched every day from a nearby tree. Then, as soon as she could, she built a nest under our home's eaves. She used pink gravel from our yard as a base, then built upon it. Up before daylight, she is the first bird to call to us each morning with her "chee, chee, chee."

When we sit at the table in our bay window eating, we watch Fritzie, a male vermilion flycatcher. He is the brightest red of any bird. He usually sits on the uppermost branch of the mesquite tree, and flies up into the air to catch his meal and back down to the same perch. When the sun is setting, his fiery coat is a wondrous show of nature.

Vernon's favorite boarders are the roadrunners. He buys hamburger to feed them. Our first pair were charmers, Mr. and Mrs. Woody. They built their nest in a mesquite tree beside our home to be nearer to the food supply. We put up a ladder to their nest and left it there so we could inspect the family every day or so.

They laid seven large white eggs, but only four hatched. The pair had one slow learner. We called her Blunder Boo after the Kewpie. She flew into everything. If you held food for her, she would miss the food and hit your hand.

Then our wonderful Mr. Woody was hit by a car, injuring his leg and wing. For three days he sat under a chair, anticipating death. Finally, he hopped on one leg up to the nest and resumed his paternal duties of feeding his kids.

Roadrunners are part of Arizona life.

Mr. and Mrs. Woody's nest.

Blunder Boo sits on the back of Vernon's chair.

Hamburger, please.

Rosie, the tame Paraloxia.

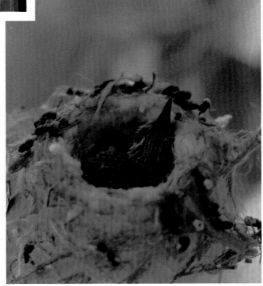

Our hummingbird's nest.

He went back to taking his turn sitting on the nest at night. Soon, Droopy Drawers (named for his several feathers that hung down in the back) was dumped from the nest into our garden to be fed. Before we knew it, Vernon and I were regularly feeding all six road-runners.

Mr. and Mrs. Woody started a new nest in another mesquite tree. We watched the nest, but then one morning, we found Mrs. Woody dead in the driveway (probably shot). Mr. Woody was so lonely; we hoped he would find a new girl—but no.

He found a place to sleep under the back roof. He always went to bed early and slept late. On Christmas morning we found his feathers. We believe an owl got him in the night.

It wasn't long before Blunder Boo and Droopy Drawers grew up. Droopy Drawers grew into a large handsome fellow, and Vernon changed his name to Mr. Brown. Mr. Brown knew the secret of quick food, all he had to do was say, "please, please, please."

Sometimes he would knock on the door, and we would feed him a piece of hamburger. He would grab the piece, almost as large as a golf ball, and swallow it. If Vernon was gardening, Mr. Brown would follow him around and pester him until Vernon would go into the house and get him a piece of hamburger. When Mr. Brown was full, he would often sit very close to Vernon and just watch him.

Now you know that roadrunners are clowns and they belong to the cuckoo family. Mr. Brown's "love antics" include jumping straight up into the air and chasing a potential bride with a stick or a wad of hamburger in his beak. Or, he would put his head on the ground with wings outspread. He always seemed to come up with some new performance to coax his girl into submission.

My favorite boarder is the pyrrhuloxia. I have a female whom I call Rosie. She has been with us for four years, appearing at the window, fluttering her wings and tapping the window.

I take out hamburger, she sits on my finger, says thank you, and flies away. She comes three or four times a day. One cactus wren and towhee will also light on my finger for hamburger.

Vernon buys big bags of grain for house finches and quail. Doves, flickers and curved bill thrashers make up the rest of our boarders.

One of the very best birds to watch was the hummingbird who built her nest in our potted ficus tree. While watching her gather spider webs, I decided to offer her some white mohair. She used it, probably creating the first nest ever built of mohair purchased for doll wigs. We became such friends that she even got used to me photographing her nest. When her little bird fell out of the nest twice, I picked it up and replaced it.

We enjoy our birds and their lives happening just outside our windows.

Doll Books

Doll books (all 22 of them), including the instruction books that I write and have been writing for 22 years, are a part of me. Each has taken the larger part of a year to prepare. The books are my way of sharing my dolls, my experimental work, and my know-how with the world. I love to write and to photograph—but most of all—it's the feeling I get from sharing and spreading the fun of doll collecting and dollmaking.

Each book is a piece of me, a picture collection of a group of my dolls, and a little of what I have learned in the last 50 years. I planned and made sure that something new was in each and every book.

At first, I mimeographed the dollmaking instructions and gave them away with molds. Next, I had a small printer in Cooperstown, New York, print my first two books of dollmaking instruction which Vernon sold thru our business, Seeley's Ceramic Service.

The books were essential to the success of the doll molds. When the business was sold in 1977 to the Ericsons, we moved to Arizona and the instruction books continued. The Ericsons paid for the printing, and I did the writing, photography and layout. The Ericsons did not see the books until they were shipped to Oneonta, New York.

I met the Fishers who owned HP Books, and they wanted to do a doll collecting book. I did the writing and photography, and the Fishers published it.

Our first magazine.

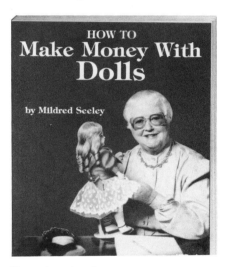
Two of my books.

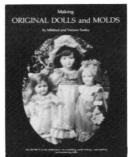
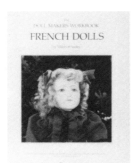

A German translation of one of our books.

Some of our
books produced
over the years.

The Fishers sold HP and the new owners published two more collecting books. Again, the company was sold—this time to Price, Stern & Sloan in California. They decided not to continue publishing doll books.

At this point, I either found Scott Publications in Livonia, Michigan, or they found me. They revised and reprinted *German Children Dolls* and *Doll Costuming* and published *Judging Dolls*. They published *Fabulous French Bébés for Collectors and Crafters* and *The Complete Book of All-Bisque Dolls* as hard cover books. The company is great to work for. I can talk to the owner, and they pay me on time. I thoroughly enjoy working for them.

Along with the books, I have written hundreds of articles on dolls. I write each month for Scott's *Doll Crafter*. I write for other magazines such as *Dolls, Dollmaking, Doll Artisan, Doll Reader, Doll News, Puppen* (the German doll magazine) and *Doll Life*.

Ages ago I started and edited the *Dollmaker Magazine*. My daughter-in-law Duby Seeley helped me with the illustrations. I write as the magazines ask me, or I come up with ideas. My dolls are often on the magazine covers.

I get paid for the articles and photographs, but it is the sharing of the dolls and my materials that I like. I am sure much more time, effort and expense goes into the articles than I get out. Writing satisfies my constant urge to share—before it is too late.

I do my own photography in my kitchen bay window. In Arizona the sun always shines, so I use it. My doll photography came to be perfected one day when we were at Colleen's. She showed me close-up photos she had taken. She said, "Here, try my camera."

I bought a Pentax just like Colleen's for $32. Today, my photographs are everywhere—in books, magazines and on covers. I don't know one f-stop from another or anything about exposures. I just know what works for dolls, and I do it.

Twenty years later, I'm still using the same old Pentax to photograph dolls for my books and articles. I shudder at the thought of it wearing out!

Millie Winner

We were guests of honor at the Doll Artisan Guild International Convention in Oneonta, New York. It was the last evening of the convention. The banquet food was consumed, and we moved from the speakers' table to give room for the awards. The speeches were over, and the awards were given out. The last thing on the program was a gift to all conventioneers.

My new book, *Project Milettes*, which was finished just in time for the convention, was the gift. It had not occurred to anyone that the minute the convention was over, the conventioneers would descend upon us to have their books autographed. The late hour made no difference. They came at us, Vernon and me, from all sides.

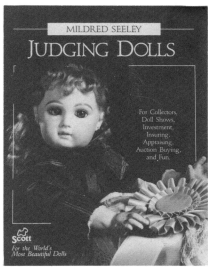

Three of my recent hardcover books published by Scott Publications.

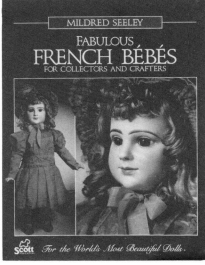

That's Vernon and me in the center of the crowd signing books.

This is Mary Stevens' doll —it even has sleep eyes.

They put books over our heads and shoved books on top of books. Some wanted special messages written. It was a madhouse, totally unorganized and unplanned for. These were the people I knew from letters and phone calls.

Weary me looked up at the sea of faces. In it was Mary Stevens with a little box. She put her little box on top of the three books in my lap waiting for autographs. "Open it now," she said.

I opened the little box and here was her dollhouse doll that she had entered in the convention competition with its blue ribbon and all. "It's for you, you were my teacher. I couldn't have done it without you. I want you to have her."

I was so honored that she would give me her prize-winning doll! All I could do was hug her. (At that time, Mary Stevens was the only three-time Millie winner—an award named for me that is given for the very best reproduction dolls.) This doll is one of the few reproduction dolls in my collection.

I returned to autographing books. Lights flicked, they were closing the auditorium. It was still half full of people. I signed a few books on the way out, and a few more at the hotel. The next morning there were people at my door and in the dining room with books to sign.

I came out of the dining room, breakfast finished, and here was Mary. Would you believe I hadn't even thought to autograph her book?

The Collection

A broad smile came over her face. She was looking at the rare laughing character Jumeau doll. Another lady was already on the floor with a sketch pad in front of the Marque dolls. An older lady stood with fingertips just touching, studying or worshipping the little A.T. made by Andre Jean Thuillier.

"There she is, there is the Snow Angel I've heard so much about." Another excited pair of doll collectors were looking in the big glass dome.

"Can you believe I've counted 20 Brus?" one young lady remarked to another.

"Kubelkas, your wood pair, I understand there are only three of these in this country?," a white-haired collector commented.

"Where are your H-dolls?, the Halopeau dolls?," asked the young, excited collector who was afraid she would miss something.

This was a seminar group of doll collectors from six states. They had been in the house only a few minutes.

I mentally record peoples' reactions to the collection, to each doll. I have very carefully selected these dolls over a lifetime, collecting them as I would fine art, studying their makers, faces and costumes.

Each doll was collected for its beauty, rarity, marking, or perfection. They are all choice dolls in excellent condition. These dolls represent the many different doll companies—the many different faces. All are works of art.

A seminar group in my home in the late afternoon.

Vernon showing the mold process.

The seminar groups usually stay at the Quality Inn in Green Valley.

137

Jumeau character dolls.

Three of our four "H" dolls.

When I started to collect, I thought one of everything would make a great collection. Later, I realized a collection of one type makes a more interesting and valuable collection. So I collect antique bisque dolls, almost entirely French.

A doll collection like mine is not something you can go out and buy, no matter how much money you are willing to spend. It takes years and effort to locate these beautiful specimens, to select the best, and to know where and how much to spend.

We laughingly say dolls built our new house. They did, of course. These dolls that look smilingly at me from their cases have loaned their heads for molds which we sold to large doll companies. These dolls loaned their images for articles, plates and books. They loaned their clothes for patterns, and their faces to paint from. These dolls hand me checks regularly, yet they still stand in my collection.

I have clubs that come in for the day, sometimes two days. I take them thru my collection. Quite often I prepare a special exhibit on one dollmaker, such as Jumeau or Bru. Other times, it is on costuming, wigs, shoes or all-bisque dolls, etc. Besides seeing lots of rare dolls, I like visitors to go home feeling they have learned something. This is all very time consuming, but I love sharing my dolls.

A doll collection this size takes time to care for. Cases must be cleaned, glass polished, dresses have to be washed, and

Some of my collection.

Five Jumeaus in original clothing.

I am always hugging A.T.s.

Doll arrangements from the living room.

sometimes dolls redressed. Records of the dolls must be kept. I have each of my dolls catalogued and a picture in my safe deposit box.

My house is decorated with gorgeous French and German bisque dolls. The dolls are a wealth that give me happiness each day that I live. There are certain ones that, even after 40 years of living with me, still give me a jolt of happiness every time I pass them.

There is always something refreshing about my big 32" 15 Long Face Jumeau in her white child's dress. The 36" Bru just says, "I'm still here to keep you happy." Mein Liebling stands by the door, looking just like my daughter did when she was eight. The row of big-eyed Steiners reaches out to me. The Bye-Lo lies quietly in her carriage.

I like their costumes. I always prefer to collect dolls in original costumes. I believe in preserving them as a bit of history, an artifact. Dolls have worked their way under my skin and into my heart and head.

Now dolls are a part of me. Day in and day out, I am never without letters, phone calls, guests. Doll-related activities fill my day to the brim, sometimes overflowing. I feel rich, I feel wealthy, I feel I have made it. I am on top of the world of dolls.

Happiness is a large collection of French dolls.

Doll Study

Groups of people, antique collectors, service clubs and church groups are always calling me to see my dolls or to

Conducting seminars
in our home.

More seminars.

have me speak about dolls. I don't do this anymore unless it is a doll club that requests it.

One of the last groups who came to see the doll collection for entertainment convinced me that sticking with doll clubs is best.

I had spent two-and-a-half hours taking the large group thru the dolls. I had explained and directed their attention to extremely rare French dolls, to dolls such as the Marque (only 22 exist), to the fabulous dolls made by Bru and Jumeau over 100 years ago, to the gorgeous large-eyed Thuilliers, to the vintage costumes the dolls wear.

I gave them bits of history, doll stories, and had removed the dolls from the cases for their close inspection. I answered their questions with care. I felt sure I had done a good and thorough job.

The group was well out to the sidewalk, but thru the open door I heard one woman exclaim, "She doesn't even have a Shirley Temple!"

Doll Plates

"Yes, we have a few doll plates left. Yes, they are in the original boxes, Yes, perfect. Just four different heads left—three French and one German doll." I was on the phone with a woman in California.

We had discontinued our doll plate business about six years ago. All the sets were gone. The only ones left were the Girl Marque, Bru Jne, Long Face Jumeau and the German K&R 109.

Selecting dolls and photos for our plates.

Vernon and me during a seminar.

The Doll Collection
The Most Loved and Appealing Baby Dolls

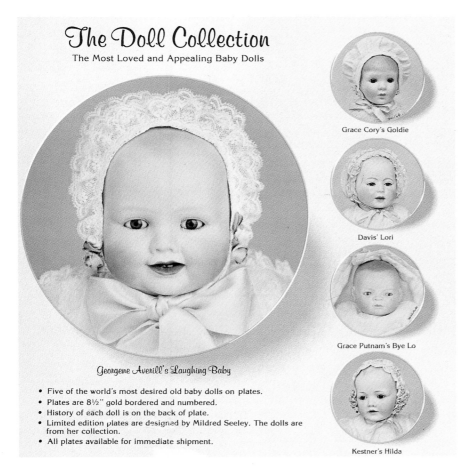

Grace Cory's Goldie

Davis' Lori

Grace Putnam's Bye Lo

Georgene Averill's Laughing Baby

Kestner's Hilda

- Five of the world's most desired old baby dolls on plates.
- Plates are 8½" gold bordered and numbered.
- History of each doll is on the back of plate.
- Limited edition plates are designed by Mildred Seeley. The dolls are from her collection.
- All plates available for immediate shipment.

Early plate series.

Choosing baby doll photos for plates.

MILDRED SEELEY DOLL PLATES
GREEN VALLEY, AZ.

The Seeley logo.

143

The Doll Collection
The Fabulous French Fashion Dolls by Mildred Seeley

Floridel
1st limited edition

Goldonna
2nd limited edition

Shamaré
3rd limited edition

Jewelette
4th limited edition

The French Fashion Doll Plate Series.

I designed five sets of plates and some single plates. The plates were all done from my doll collection. Plates were a fun, but a difficult and risky project, because so much start-up money had to be invested.

Our first plate almost became our last. The Bru Comfort plate, which now sells for around $300, had almost unsurmountable problems. First we had problems with the decal colors, then the firing went bad, and then the percentage of good plates to bad plates left us in the hole.

We had advertised before the plates were finished, and we couldn't fill our orders on time. We had to return money.

The project was set up for a series of six plates. We didn't know whether to go ahead or take a loss and quit.

Suddenly, everything came up roses. We got the Bru plate out and the next five French plates followed. They sold like hot cakes. We were finding out how to do it.

I didn't really start at the beginning. I found an advertisement for a substance that could be applied to a picture to create a type of decal that could be applied to a plate. I wanted to put doll pictures on plates.

I carried this advertisement with me for a long time. I finally bought the material, but never tried it.

There were collector plates on the market but nothing with dolls on them. Vernon and I started writing, telephoning and questioning everyone at conferences about how the plates were made.

We finally came up with people and addresses for lithographic transfers (decals). We went to Ohio and found a factory that made dishes and would apply the decals and fire the plates. Then, I had to design and locate packaging. It was quite a process and took us months. Finally, there were the problems of photographing dolls close-up and maintaining perfect coloring with the decals.

In the meantime, we had already sold our business to the Ericsons and we asked them to join us in this venture. They would do the advertising and shipping, and we would design the plates from our rare dolls, take the photos, and get the decals made. We did three sets with the Ericsons—The French Dolls, The Baby Dolls and The German Children Dolls.

Later we took over the plate business and began shipping the plates from Green Valley, Arizona. We designed a new set of French Bébés. Then we designed plates for Commemorative Imports.

On the whole, the plate project was the very best project we have ever done, probably the most lucrative. I loved the doll plates because people could have very expensive dolls in

The Doll Collection

The World's Most Magnificent French Dolls
on the Finest Porcelain Plates

"H's" Bébé Halo

Bru's Faith

Steiner's Easter

Marque's Alyce

Jumeau's Gaynell

Popular plate series from the past.

146

their homes at a very low price. The project gave me money to buy more dolls.

Idea Factory

Somewhere stored within me is an idea factory. This is the kind of thing that must be held in tight reigns. It could get away and run wild all over like bindweed.

The minute all is quiet, I sit down with a cup of coffee, put my feet up, and the idea factory opens and fires up its furnace.

Thoughts make big circles. For instance, I look up into my lady doll cabinet. There, along with a Bru lady, is an antique poodle. A doll friend, Georgia, brought me the dog. So I thought of Georgia and her collection of cloth dolls. I thought of the Arnold print of Little Red Riding Hood (patented in 1892) that I had rolled up in the back of my closet. It had been there 20 years or more.

I got right up and called Florence Theriault of Theriaults' auction house and asked her if she would like to copy it to sell. She said yes, and I packed it up and shipped it out the next day. When the original comes back, I will give it to Georgia who will appreciate it.

Little projects like this come out of the idea factory as well as big ideas and working ideas. All have to be sorted out into what might work and what may not.

Examples of ideas that have been extra-special include the creation of doll molds; books of

Vernon working in the garden room.

dollmaking instruction (*Project Milettes* and the Milette molds were especially good); the two doll magazines—the one that I published, *The Dollmaker*, and the one that I conceived, *The Doll Artisan*, which is in its 15th year of publication.

The idea factory came up with doll photos on collector plates and these were super successful. Now Colleen and Scott Publications are producing a new set of French plates based on my dolls. Also, the limited edition Marque dolls

and the Doll Artisan Guild were triumphs.

The idea of doll seminars at our house was good, but too much for this old lady. In the next two weeks I will do two more. A group of 20 ladies will fly in from San Francisco for a two-day seminar. The other is a one-day seminar for a doll club.

The ideas for Shandelé came out of the idea factory—the set-in nooks, the extra closets, the room arrangements. This is how the idea factory works. It started when I was little and my mother and stepfather encouraged it. I could always think of a way to get around an obstacle, to earn some money, to get where I wanted to go. Now that I am old, I still take a problem or dream up an idea, turn it around, and work on it from all sides. I immediately try the ideas out on Vernon. He fills in the blanks and always helps me to find how this idea can be carried out.

The idea factory produces simple, everyday ideas concerning doll books, doll articles for magazines, reproduction dolls, and doll displays, as well as lifelong projects.

I believe other doll people, perhaps my children, also have their built-in "idea factories" which must be used continually in order to function well.

This idea factory is one that must be fired up, but then the products that come out must be scrutinized carefully, thought thru, turned over, looked at from all sides before being put into a project. Sometimes, a person with an idea factory like mine needs someone to hold up the red flag before they jump in where they can't get out.

Later

The late afternoon of life turns all too quickly into evening. Here I am old already. I'm not finished with the things I would like to accomplish or enjoy. I look into the mirror and see my aunt Charlotte, not me. I just can't picture myself as old and white haired with aching bones. It's not me. There is still much to do, much to learn, much to share.

I used to be a good doll-maker, as I used to be a child —a little girl. But these things are gone forever. I seldom look back. Now I get a warm and wonderful feeling from looking at the fine dolls of today's dollmakers.

You can assume I love both the dolls and flowers, but I also have two other ongoing love affairs. I love life. I wake up in the morning and think "I made it. I've got another day." This was especially true just after I had open heart surgery.

Loving dolls, roses and life are fine, but my best ongoing love affair is with Vernon. For nearly 50 years, our relationship has been infused with understanding and affection. (Vernon's 1992 resolution was to hug me everyday, not that this was anything new.)

We hear what each other is saying. We do not smother each other's talents. We share our problems and our blessings. Today was no exception. It was cloudy, cold and raining, so we built a fire in the fireplace, made homemade soup, and worked out a small problem.

PART 7

True Doll Stories

This is my 22'' H-doll incised 3 H just under the rim, center back of the head.

Doll Marked H

Suddenly, as if stroked by a magic wand, people are talking about the doll marked "H." There was no magic, just doll-appeal, that let the gavel fall at a recent auction at $100,000 for that lovely doll.

One always wonders what makes an over-a-hundred-year-old plaything that valuable? We look to see what this doll has that the run of the mill dolly-faced dolls don't have. The first and foremost thing with any H-doll is the unrivaled appeal. You have but to combine the H-doll's beauty with her rarity and there is the answer.

But, there's more. Consider the workmanship: the bisque is perfect and the painting is perfection plus. Her body and the original wig are exquisite. Add to this an antique costume fit for a princess, and the picture changes from a plaything to a work of art.

H-dolls have been little known and little collected, simply because there are so few of them. I have been collecting dolls for 40 years, and know of only eleven. Until recently, four of those have resided in my cabinet. The recent auctioning of the H-doll was a first—thousands upon thousands of dolls go through the auction houses each year, yet until now no H-doll had ever been catalogued.

This had been my 22'' H-doll and was incised 3 H just under the rim, center back of the head. She has dramatic blue paperweight eyes with mauve blushing above. The doll was dressed in antique pale green silk lace over sateen, with a matching bonnet. To steal a bit of description from auctioneer, Florence Theriault, "Extraordinary and arresting beauty is the keynote of this extremely rare doll. Her enigmatic, yet compelling presence is achieved by masterful sculpting, the eyes, and the artful painting of facial features and complexion tones."

The auction was well underway when Number 24, a Gibson girl, was auctioned and taken away. There was a movement of chairs and the sound of low voices. The 3-H-doll was picked up and the room was suddenly without sound, hushed completely in anticipation. The H-doll herself counseled, persuaded, and instructed the enchanted bidders. Her message was, "You must have me for your very own—to admire and love. My presence will fill the heart and soul like the delicate beauty of spring violets under the birches."

At least these 12 bidders were confident they would take the H home to fill that choice spot in their cabinet. They had put aside seventy to eighty thousand dollars, knowing full well that the Theriaults must be wrong in their estimate of $90,000 to $120,000. In less than a minute, the doll was sold for $100,000—a record price for a French doll and a U.S. record for any doll sale at that time.

Something none of us had expected also happened. For the many years I have collected dolls, the historical background

Comfort, the Bru from the bag lady of Albany, New York.

of the H-doll has been a complete mystery. The Theriaults, with the aid of François Theimer, found in the Paris National Archives, the maker of the H-doll. he was Artistide Marcellin Halopeau, successor to the firm of Eugene Barrois. Halopeau purchased the plant about 1875 and introduced the H-bé-bé in 1882. His plant produced dolls until 1888. The doll heads were made by Frayon, a film in Montreuil. Doll crafters around the country are reproducing 3-H, 4-H, and 5-H dolls from molds made originally by Vernon using the dolls from

our collection. There are few other dolls so precious.

Bru Comfort

On the poorer side of many cities there are the street people. This was some 40 or 50 years ago, as it is now, around New York State's capital city, Albany. The Bag Lady, as she was known, was seen for years going through the garbage and the throw-outs from the city's well-to-do. With her bent figure, her black coat, and her grizzled gray hair, she was a familiar sight. She carried her battered shopping bag from one of Albany's finest stores.

When she died, the police found she was not exactly a street person, but had a single basement room where she lived. Upon entering the room, they found it completely filled with dolls—dolls of all kinds, of every shape and size.

The room had to be cleaned out. They threw the dolls into large bags and delivered them to Lillian Sproul who had a doll museum called "Yesteryears." She did not want them as her husband was sick. The dolls were put in her garage anyway.

Lillian decided the dolls must be checked over before sending the lot off to the city dump. She took an hour or so each day to sort them, between looking after her husband. She was on the very last bag of dolls when, to her great surprise, she pulled out a blue-eyed Bru. A BRU. A marked BRU! She couldn't believe her eyes and took the doll in to show her husband. She put the doll on the dresser. "That doll will be some comfort to you for all your work," he said. Lillian named the doll "Comfort" and the doll gave her enjoyment every time she looked at it.

Lillian made Comfort's costume using material from a very lovely old French silk gown. She copied the costume from a photo of another Bru. The underclothing looks all original: the shoes are marked, wig is original. Comfort was sold to me after Lillian's doll museum closed. I am sure the price received for the Bru was a comfort.

I used Comfort as a porcelain plate design on my first plate in "The Doll Collection," and the plate originally sold for $39.00. The edition sold out quickly and the plate is being resold for over $200. This has been a comfort to many plate collectors, especially those who bought two. I used Comfort as a cover for my book *Dollmakers Workbook French Children Dolls*, and that cover is one of my favorites. Comfort is now world-known.

Comfort now stands with the other Bru dolls in my doll cabinet. Her appealing blue eyes charm all doll collectors. I cannot pass her without getting a bit of comfort for possessing her.

So Comfort, from the time she belonged to some little rich girl in Albany, through her years with the Bag Lady, her museum time, and now having been shared with the world, has lived up to her name.

Beloved

Jennie Mable Hastings received an incised Jumeau doll when she was six years old. The doll was purchased by her father, Thomas E. Hastings, in 1886. He had a friend bring the doll from New York City. After Jennie's mother died, the child was so unhappy and her father hoped the doll would help. It did—it became her constant companion. The doll shows signs of tender love. Jennie Hastings gave the doll to me in 1959.

The Hastings family lived in the mountainous area of Bovina, New York, just over the mountains from New Kingston.

These side-hill, poor dairy farms are not exactly the place you would expect to find an elegantly dressed Jumeau doll. Yet she still has her original beads, undies, wig and shoes.

Bru Jne 4

I was called to go to a town nearby to look at a doll that Adeline Jones wanted to sell. The lady's shaking hands handed me the doll. It was a small Bru, dressed in cranberry red. I checked the doll for cracks and offered the going retail price for Brus. The woman was astounded. Then she told me she was 89 and had kept the doll in her dresser drawer ever since she was married. She went on to tell me, "I didn't much like the doll, probably because my grandmother had given it to me to stop sucking my thumb. I didn't stop, so I never really got to play with the doll until I was too big for dolls.

Needed, One Steiner Head

"Please don't use my name. My cousin might hear about it. He's still around," the collector confided in me as she began her story. "I cried for weeks after my brother was born because I wanted a sister to play with. I cried and cried and cried. I had boy cousins and I wanted no more of boys. It was the 15th of December when brother was born. I must have been still crying by Christmas. Under the tree on Christmas morning was a beautiful girl doll. It was my mother's doll that had been purchased in Paris. I loved the doll and for years I partied with her, wheeled her in my carriage, talked to her. I must have been 11 or 12 when my cousins ran over the doll's head with a wagon. They buried the doll in the garden, but I found her." She brought out the body of the doll wrapped in an old piece of linen. "Do you know where I can get a head just like the one that was on there?"

A. T. Silver

The Tabor residence was the most pretentious on Capitol Hill of Denver, Colorado. It was on Thirteenth Avenue and its grounds ran through Sherman to Grant Avenue. A brownstone wall ran around the lower end of the velvety lawn where the ground sloped to two driveways, leading to the stables. Tabor engaged five gardeners and housemen, two coachmen and two footmen. He had three carriages and six horses.

Two pairs of horses were jet black. One carriage was brown trimmed in red, another dark blue trimmed in gold. The inside was upholstered in light blue satin. A third carriage was black, trimmed in white with white satin upholstery. Baby Doe Tabor chose the carriage that best suited the costume she was wearing that day.

Into this world was born, July 13, 1884, Elisabeth Bonduel Lillie Tabor. Her christening dress was hand-embroidered lace with diamond and gold pins and a tiny necklace with a diamond-studded locket. The outfit supposedly cost $15,000.

Adeline's Bru Jne 4.

A.T. Silver from the last belongings of Baby Doe Tabor's daughter of Leadville, Colorado.

This was just the place one would expect to find the child holding a fine French doll. Lillie cuddled a small but beautiful A. T. doll (an Andre Jean Thuillier doll)—nothing but the finest would do.

Many doll collectors are familiar with the story of Baby Doe and Horace Tabor and the silver mines of Leadville, Colorado. This little A 3 T and a few old books were the last and only belongings of their daughter Lillie. She was living with the McCourt family, her grandparents, when she died. The doll and books were sold after the McCourts died. The doll is in fine condition. The head, shoulder-plate and bisque hands are on a kid body. The doll was completely without clothing. We call her Silver.

French All-Bisque

As a child I had three German bisque dolls and was very happy with them. Whether dolls were German or French, I'm sure I didn't know or care. At seven, I was invited to visit my aunt and uncle on Staten Island. It was just before Thanksgiving and my folks agreed to take me down as they would be buying some Christmas goods for our small store. Aunt Lillian and Uncle Morris wanted me there for Saturday, when there would be a big charity bazaar for which they were working.

The bazaar had imported a huge French doll to raffle off. This was the first time I remembered hearing a doll called "French." Aunt Lillian used "French" so many times in talking about the doll that it was impressed forever on me. My aunt and uncle were so hoping I would win the huge doll that they could hardly stand it. They stood me up beside the doll. It seemed to me it was as big as I was. I remember clearly, I never thought for a minute I would get the doll, nor did I want it, particularly. It just seemed too big. *But* for each chance that anyone bought on the large doll, they got a five inch all-bisque French doll. These dolls were dressed in silk by the church ladies. I remember that chances were 35 cents. They kept giving me another one of these little dolls until I had four. I carried the little dolls home on the train. I couldn't have been happier. These dolls were like a family, they played school, took baths, and had cooking sessions. I shared them with my only girlfriend.

Auction Googlies

The Withington auction at the Highway Hotel in Concord, New Hampshire, was about half over. This was where we attended our first doll auctions when we lived in Oneonta, New York, about 30 years ago when Brus were selling for $500-$600, not $20,000. At that time, dolls were scarce, only a very few good dolls came to the auctions.

We had only had the hobby of dollmaking underway for a few short years. To give it a test we took to the auction a couple of J.D.K. reproduction googlies that I had made.

Group of dolls with googlie.

K*R googlie 131.

Hertel and Schwab 165 googlie.

Heubachs from Germany.

As they came up, the auctioneer said, "Now I want to call your attention to the fact that these are reproduction dolls."

The bidding started at $40, $100, $150. "I need to remind you that this googly is a reproduction," the auctioneer put this in no uncertain terms between his auctioneer jargon. On it went "$200, $250, $300, do I hear $350? Sold for $300 to Gladys Hillsdorf." The second doll went for the same amount. Gladys bought both.

We couldn't believe our reproduction dolls sold so high. We were just delighted. Gladys Hillsdorf was a doll dealer. She sold antique dolls. We talked to her after the auction.

She said, "Googlies are almost impossible to find, and I am sure a couple of my customers will be just delighted with these." She had paid almost as high for the reproduction googlies as she would have had to pay for antique ones—if she could find them.

I wasn't certain whether Gladys wanted the googlies or just ran them up to help us. Gladys was known for helping doll people. When she ordered another googly for another customer, then we knew for certain that she liked and wanted our googlies.

Atlanta

We were returning to Oneonta with a load of dolls. They were from the White Doll Museum in Florida that we had bought out. We had some domes and cases, as well as dolls.

It was mid-morning coffee time, and we stopped at an antique place. We bought Jay a wind-up clown. As we were departing, Vernon asked the owner if he knew of any dolls for sale.

"As a matter of fact, I do. There are three sisters—school teachers—in Atlanta who are cleaning out their family home and want to sell their dolls." He gave us a telephone number. Vernon ended up calling the teacher out of her classroom.

The huge white house with giant pillars was surrounded with azaleas and dogwood. It appeared to have fallen from the pages of *Gone With the Wind*. The house had been empty of people for a long time and was in great need of repair.

The woman took us to the play room. Dolls, played-with dolls, broken dolls, and doll furniture were everywhere. The dolls were German children, toddlers, babies, all-bisques and dollhouse dolls. She showed us a set of lovely dollhouse dolls that were still rolled in their original cloth pocket wrapper. These she said she had given to a friend.

All the time we looked, the teacher reminisced in her Atlanta accent about the play-room and dolls. Her grand-mother had bought dolls for every occasion for each of the three sisters and had spent days making clothes for the dolls. "Never a holiday passed with-out a new doll for each of us," the teacher told us.

To visit this mansion's play-room with the little girls who had played there, who rock-ed the babies, dressed and undressed the girl dolls, and danced with the bears, was like an interlude. She turned on an old music box. Here we were in our pinafores and long curls playing dolls. I was transplanted to a time some 60 years earlier.

I said doll collecting is a gentle, loving hobby. She want-ed me to have the dolls, really wanted to give me the dolls. Then she picked up a shoe box. We looked inside. Here was a Simon Halbig toddler in her Easter dress, bonnet, shoes and socks. Her head was unattach-ed, legs hanging loose.

She had to tell me the story. "It was Easter morning and all three of us girls had new dolls. We ran to the neighbors to show them to a friend. I fell, the doll came apart, a small piece broke from her neck and released the elastic. I went cry-ing back to Grandma. She took the doll, put it in this box, and miraculously produced another new doll from her supply. She saved my Easter. I never saw the broken doll again until a week ago when we were cleaning the attic. It all came back to me."

I hated to leave. I wanted to stay and play dolls. I gave the teacher a generous check and we piled the dolls in the car. It was so full, I even had them around me in the front seat. One doll, a large composition walking doll with screen on the upper legs, had to be left be-hind. No more room anywhere.

When we were getting ready to move from Oneonta to Green Valley, Arizona—to a smaller home—I decided I must sell some of my dolls. I picked out 467 German dolls that I must part with. I called a well-known doll dealer and she bought them all. A doll shop in Vermont bought all of my reproductions.

There have been many times when I wished I had never sold them, but then I was still in the business of making molds. I know now that all the charm-ing German character dolls should have been hoarded as an investment.

Milvex

It was just a year since we had developed and started advertis-ing our Milvex composition doll bodies. Our business was going great.

We had driven 60 miles for a dinner party with good friends and customers. "Have another drink," Bill suggested, pouring the fifth or sixth for himself, "Have another drink, Ed."

Vernon looked at his watch. It was already 7:15 p.m. It was a big dinner party. We knew everyone there. Dinner was scheduled at six. The hostess peeked in from the kitchen where she was preparing an exotic dinner all by herself. "It will be a few minutes yet," she disappeared back into the kitchen. "Let's have another round," Bill was pouring every one another.

Vernon looked at his watch —just ten minutes past eight. At that very moment, the door to the dining room was opened and our hostess seated us at the magnificently set formal table.

Being the female guest-of-honor I was seated to the right of the host.

"Now that I have you right where I want you, I need some information," Bill began. "About this Milvex you are using for doll bodies. I sent some in to the H.R.D. Lab and had it analyzed. I then purchased the ingredients to make it. It doesn't work. It cost me about $80. I almost killed my family with the fumes trying to melt the stuff in the oven. Where did you buy the Milvex?"

"Milvex," I said, "is just our trade name for the doll body formula. I named it. Mil is for me, V is for Vernon, and the X is for the unknown." Well, his over-consumption of alcohol threw him. His face turned crimson. He was so mad, he jumped up and hit the table, rocking the goblets of water. "You mean that this is just your concoction?"

His wife was so embarrassed. In fact I think all the guests, good doll people, were embarrassed. We quietly consumed the exquisite exotic dishes our hostess had spent so much time preparing. Bill heeded his wife's signaling and finally calmed down.

This man and his wife were excellent dollmakers. Here he was telling me he was attempting to steal my doll body formula. He had already taken our JDK Googly mold from our expensive doll and reduced it down to a mini. They were producing the googly to sell. They shrunk others of our doll molds to produce their own line of tiny dolls.

Lyric

We were at a Rock Club meeting. One of our friends said a friend of hers had a small doll collection that she wished to sell. She had told the lady she would give us her number.

Most of these things turn out to be wild goose chases, but we do always chase them down, even today. Then too, this was only 60 miles away.

The next morning I called the number. Yes, she had some dolls. I would have to come and look. Vernon took off work early, and we hurried on our way. She was a youngish lady. She took us to a bedroom where she had dolls laid out on the bed.

I'm sure my disappointment showed in my face, there was nothing there but battered composition and plastics. I lifted one after another. Down in the bottom layer I found a Schoenhut boy with molded hair. He was well, very well, played with. I should say battered. I said that I would buy this one. Vernon said, "You don't want that thing."

I like the all-wood Schoenhut dolls and had accumulated about a dozen of these. I kept them, and eight years ago I sold the collection. I never displayed the Schoenhuts. They were always in a box. This tells the story of how much you like anything. If they are not out where you can see them, they should be sold to someone who likes them better. While I was collecting them, they went from less than $100 to a $1,000 for one with molded hair.

I asked the woman how much she wanted for the Schoenhut. "Is $15 too much," she asked? I told her these dolls had gone up, and that I must pay her a fair price. I started to get out my money. "I have another one you might like to see, but I want to keep him." She brought out a large bisque baby doll. I was working on the *Dollmaker's Work Book, Baby Dolls Volume I* book at the time. He was a rare Heubach Koppelsdorf. I hadn't seen one, but I knew what he was. I said, "That doll would be worth $500 to me to use in my book." She looked at me and said you can have him. We later used him for the cover. Vernon called him, "Moose Face," because of his unusual fat baby face.

We picked up the two dolls and were about to leave. "I do have one more you might want to look at." She left us and returned with a doll all wrapped in a white towel. I sat back down and unwrapped the doll. I couldn't believe my eyes.

There in my hands was a Jumeau with the perfection of a flower dressed in a fragile shade of cream and pink with honey-colored hair. Unwrapping her was like raising the curtain on a stage, her beauty dramatically unfolding. There in my hands was a 15" Tete Jumeau in all-original clothes, and except for a few moth holes, perfect down to her marked shoes. I loved her. It was the first time I had ever seen a French doll in this remarkable condition. I studied her face, her deep azure paperweight eyes. I looked at the woman. "Will you sell her?" I said, "I can give you a check for $3,000." The woman almost choked. She already had her hand out for the check.

She had absolutely no idea of the value of the doll. Then too, I had offered more than the going rate at that time, because the doll was so perfect. I wondered where this woman had gotten these dolls without knowing anything about them. I asked.

The three dolls that we had purchased came from a great aunt and the composition dolls had been her daughters. "I don't really care for dolls—they make such a clutter. But after meeting you people I like them better," she commented.

We named the Jumeau, "Lyric." We used her over and over again. She stands in my cabinet today with her Jumeau sisters, as much loved as the day we bought her.

A.T. Stephanie

In an old *Dimples and Sawdust* book there was a black-and-white picture of an A.T. The book had a poor binding that did nothing to hold the pages together. The page with the A.T. was loose. It kept falling out. Each time, before I put the page back in, I studied the gentle face. The doll had captured my very being with her elegant true beauty. She belonged to the author, Marlowe Cooper.

Andre Jean Thuillier's (A.T.) *Stephanie*. The doll I dreamed of owning.

At that time I didn't have an A.T., or any doll that beautiful. This fascination with the black-and-white photograph went on for some years. An A.T. doll or dolls in that category are neither easy to find or pay for.

Vernon and I were in Arizona for a few winter months. We had some California doll guests. I happened to mention that I would like an A.T. and could pay for one, if I could find it. Our guest returned and apparently told just the right person about my wants. I had a phone call.

Lyric, a special Jumeau Tete in all-original clothes.

If I would come to the doll show in Santa Monica she would bring an A.T. I could look at it and pay for the doll —in the parking lot. This was not exactly the way I like to do business, but it was her doll and she could sell it any way she pleased.

We drove into the parking lot and saw a woman who looked like she might be waiting for us. She unpacked the doll that had been in the trunk.

I could not believe my eyes. It was an A.T. all right. It was the A.T. from *Dimples and Sawdust* that I already loved. Even in the morning's brassy sunlight she, the doll, was a bit of poetry. The quality of her artistry was beyond words. It was like roses had suddenly come up all around me.

I was so nervous and excited I could barely check the doll for cracks. If the whole back of her head was smashed, I am sure I would not have noticed.

There was my black-and-white *Dimples and Sawdust* A.T. now like a watercolor in pastel shades. She was luxuriously dressed in her original soft pale aqua dress, her lace-trimmed bonnet matched. She even had old shoes.

Her dreamy, big sapphire eyes, dimpled chin, perfect painting—all went together under her blond wig. Everything came up roses. I had acquired another century's bounty. This was another doll adventure, a magical adventure.

The doll stands with her A.T. sisters. We now know she was made by Andre Jean Thuillier during the 1880s. Can you believe she is still perfect?

Stories

I stopped making dolls when I no longer was steady enough to do good lashes and brows. I felt it was better to stop than to go on winging my way thru poor dolls. I get just as much satisfaction collecting and working with antique dolls.

When it gets right down to it—is it the dolls I love, or is it the wonderful doll people who have become my friends? I go places where people greet me, hug me, bring me little things, and tell me how dolls have changed their lives—how happy dolls have made them.

I love their stories. "I discovered dolls thru your books." "I got a blue ribbon because of your criticism." "I made the Marque look like a Marque after I saw yours." "I learned from your judging seminars not to be picky, but to see the good first." "I learned to share from you. Before I was afraid dollmakers would learn my technique and make dolls as good as me, but now I tell everyone everything I know. It makes me so happy—this sharing."

Then there was the woman who waited until after the lecture and everyone was gone to talk to me. She said, "You are the best thing that has ever happened to me. My husband was killed in an accident. I lost my son. I was a wreck. The only thing I wanted to do was go from bar to bar.

"A doctor suggested I go to a doll studio or ceramic studio and make something. I did. I found many of your books. I started making dolls. I have not been in a bar since or had a drink. I have found something I enjoy doing. You are my wonder woman."

Through letters and word-of-mouth, I kept hearing that a person was copying my patterns. My patterns were not that great, but I decided to check it out. Sure enough, these were my patterns in envelopes with a picture of her doll wearing the dress on the outside.

I looked the situation over and thought: this woman needs something to make money. Then I gave her permission to copy my dolls' dresses and say "with Mil Seeley's permission" on the patterns. I did what I could to help her. She is a very talented doll painter and shoemaker as well as dressmaker.

A company in California that produces school supplies decided to go into dolls as decorations for stationery, stickers, cards, pads and folders. She commissioned an artist to produce original artwork for the items. One morning the company's owner and her husband were watching the *Today Show* which was showing our series of doll plates.

The woman said to me when she called, "It was at that moment I knew I was in trouble." Her artist had copied our Marque, Steiner and others. Her new pieces had gone on sale all around the country. I had already been trying to locate her and her company.

The next day she flew to Tucson. I picked her up at the airport and we went to Green Valley for a visit—a strained visit.

I liked the woman immediately. We discussed the situation. She said she was in the wrong, but she had thousands of dollars worth of doll pads, cards, stationery, etcetera tied up. Could she give us a percentage of the sales? It all worked out great. The next time we were in California, she and her husband took us to dinner. Since then, she has kept me in Marque doll desk pads.

The world has gotten smaller because of dolls. Last year the girls from Australia wanted Vernon and me to come over, all expenses paid, for their convention. Health-wise, I wasn't up to it, but we talked back and forth to those wonderful girls like it was across the street. I sent them books and plates for prizes, and they sent me all the things from the convention. I was at their convention in spirit.

Recently, for another convention of Australian dollmakers, they asked me to send a greeting to be read. I did, along with some books from Scott Publications. I also sent imaginary star-studded golden halos for all the teachers—my way of giving the teachers the credit they deserve. I had given these halos out once before at the Doll Artisan Guild Convention, and they were a big hit.

Character Dolls

Doll collecting and dollmaking are gentle hobbies embraced with breathtaking moments, intriguing interplay, and off-and-on subtle magic. Yet there are those who infiltrate the hobby for business and dollar signs. I guess any hobby must have its business partners.

The wonderful Jumeau character dolls sculpted by Carrier Belleuse.

Many, many years ago we met Gladys Hillsdorf. She was New York State's most aggressive collector, that is, after the death of Margaret Strong. This was the Mrs. Strong of the now-famous Margaret Woodbery Strong Museum. Mrs. Strong bought up everything, good or bad, in the eastern states. Gladys knew dolls, she knew dolls from first-hand study. She had a memory for dolls. She helped other people with dolls. Gladys helped Ralph Griffith as well as other dealers get started. I believe she taught him from scratch, everything.

Ralph happened on a source for Jumeau character dolls in France. Under Gladys's watchful eye, he bought these character dolls and hoarded them. Every time he went to France he hunted for more of these characters. Now don't get the idea that these were plentiful. These were really very rare and only a few were ever made. Ralph planned and hoped to get them all. He pretty well succeeded except for the few Gladys had bought.

Ralph said to me numerous times, "These are my security, my money in the bank, anytime I need money for some-

These dolls show the different emotions of children. Laughing Jumeau.

Contemplative character in plaid.

thing big, I will sell one. Oftentimes I buy it back later. The more screwed up the character faces are the better I like them.''

I felt that the character dolls would add a new dimension to my collection. I like the more pleasant characters. Celena Carol had two of Ralph's character dolls on her sales table. Ralph came around and convinced me I should buy them. Vernon wasn't very enthusiastic, he likes beautiful dolls as I do.

Their prices were high, sky

high. Ralph put another in a Cohen auction. I bid on it, and Ralph sat ahead of me and bid me up. He was building a new house. In the years that followed he tried to talk me into two more. I bought them by mail, but they weren't being delivered.

Ralph was sick, very sick. He and his partner, Elmer Bell, decided to bring them to Green Valley on their way to Kansas City. They wanted to see my collection. Elmer called and said Ralph was worse, and they

were going to fly him to Kansas. (I was a little more than worried that I might not ever get the dolls, but I did. After Ralph died and Elmer came back to Scottsdale, he made sure I got the dolls.)

Now I have six of these Jumeau character dolls that I am sure were designed for mechanicals originally, only a few were put on regular doll bodies. I have since found these were sculpted by Carrier Belleuse, the sculptor who created the Long Face Jumeau.

162

Premier Jumeau.

Gaynell's Long Face Jumeau. I bought dolls from Gaynell over a period of 16 years or so.

These character dolls stand in my case. Each face shows a different emotion. They are a little like toads amongst my pressed meadow flowers, but they are fun.

The Allisons

There is no way I can convey the fun and friends of dolls, and the joy doll activities have added to life—everyday life, our life.

We were in San Antonio, Texas, at Jill Johnson's International Doll Makers Association first convention. This was a one-lady project. She had put on the convention all by herself. I had exhibited dolls and had blue ribbons and rosettes all over the place. So many that I was embarrassed.

It was here that we met the Allisons. We were friends from the first. Over the years we worked on numerous projects with the Allisons. She even loaned me her beautiful Hilda for our plate picture and a little Jumeau for the Milette project.

She made dolls for Nieman Marcus and other fine stores. They drove a well-equipped van to the shows.

We were in Florida at a show and they invited us to come down and have breakfast with them. They were parked in the parking lot of the exhibit hall.

They set up a card table with tablecloth and portable chairs beside the van on the asphalt. Everyone going by carrying their doll stuff laughed. It really was funny—but what a good, hearty breakfast of bacon and eggs Carl prepared for us. He had been a short-order cook in his earlier days. They were a neat couple to work with, and their friendship thru many years was a delight.

Dolls Are For Everyone

From the time that I conceived of dollmaking as a hobby, I believed dolls were for everyone—for the rich, the poor, the young and the old. I really believed it and stressed it in my books and articles.

The first big doll auction was held in one of the huge, elaborate, for-the-rich only hotels in Scottsdale, Arizona. It was at the height of the winter season.

Vernon and I sat toward the back. We watched the people pour in. You would have thought it was an Arabian horse auction with $100 tickets to get in. People were dressed, over-dressed, and strutting like peacocks. Not having much interest in showing off elaborate clothing, I found their antics more than amusing.

It was obvious that these were would-be doll people, or new doll people not yet settled in. These were not the doll people I was used to. Just as the auction started, a large man in a cowboy hat, boots and outback clothing stepped lively down to the front row. He had flown in from Australia to purchase a Bru. People had flown in from all over the U.S. also.

Part way thru the auction I got up and went to the ladies' room. A maid was scrubbing the wash basin. She glanced in the mirror in front of her. She

swung around, cleanser in one hand, cloth in the other, and put her arms around my neck. "Mil Seeley, I'd know you anywhere. I make dolls Tuesday and Friday nights and study your books. You have changed my life from misery to a happy one. I can't wait for doll nights."

So many times I've had proof of how dolls have changed peoples lives, how dolls have made people happy, all kinds of people, in all walks of life.

Upgrading the Collection

Today we returned from a Theriault's auction in Burbank, California. Many of our good dolls have come from these doll auctions. This time we have $49,500 worth—just two dolls—a Bru and an E.J.A. Forty years ago we could have purchased these same dolls for $400 or $500. Then, we didn't have the money to do that.

I expect both these dolls to work for us. They will let us make two new molds and perhaps an article or two for magazines.

Here, too, I must explain about upgrading a collection—my collection. Collectors should upgrade their collections all the time. I already have an E.J.A. All E.J.A.'s are the same size, I believe. I bought my first E.J.A. about 17 years ago.

One of the chefs from New York City's Stork Club called me. He said he had a doll he would like to sell. He said he would bring it up to Oneonta on Sunday afternoon. He was more interested in the money

than the doll. As I talked to him on the phone, I imagined the Stork Club's chef in his white coat and tall white hat playing with a doll.

The chef was late in arriving, it was nearly dark. We met in the poor light of the butterfly and mineral museum. He had the doll folded up in a paper sack. He handled the doll like a piece of warm French pastry. He was in a terrible hurry.

He stood over me like a large mother hen. Don't take off the dress, don't mess the hair. I wanted to unglue the wig to see inside. As I looked up, I again put the white apron and chef's cap on the huge, unbendable French chef standing over me. He kept saying, "I have to leave, do you want the doll or not." I didn't feel I had half-inspected the doll, I gave him a check for $4,500 ($500 down from his original price). He invited us down for a free dinner at the Stork Club.

I later used this doll and her imperfections in one of my books. This E.J.A. did have some big problems.

Now, many, many years later, I will put the perfect new E.J.A. doll in her place in my cabinet and send the old doll to the auction. I will subtract what I get for her, from what I paid for the new one. Then the price won't seem so high. I will have upgraded my collection.

Seven years ago I sold my cracked P.D. (Petit and Dumontier). I got $6,000 for her. She looked okay, but her head was badly cracked. The P.D. is rare, and I bought her hoping to find a better one. It took me six years. The P.D. I got last year was smaller, but absolutely perfect, and, of course, three times the value I got for the old doll.

I do not like cracked dolls in my collection, but rare dolls, difficult to find dolls, I feel are better purchased when you find them, and then, in time, up-graded!

Columbian Exposition Dolls

You can have the two for $19,000. Dear Grace Dyer was offering us a bargain—a real bargain. We were at a small doll show in New England about 29 years ago. On the side of the box and the souvenir booklet was marked World's Colum-bian Exposition Chicago. The year of the exposition was 1893. These were two dolls in their original marked boxes. In the boxes were Brus, two number nines, 19'' Brus. They had been dressed especially for the Co-lumbian exposition in court presentation costumes.

The boy doll was dressed in a red collapsible high opera hat and a red cut away jacket. His white shirt had pearl buttons. His black trousers were tied with ribbons at the knees. His pointed Bru shoes had black ribbon bows. His gold watch chain looped to a Paris mark-ed gold watch. His white silk handkerchief was edged in red and tucked into his red jacket.

He had white gloves with black stitching. These went over his very unusual wood hands.

E.J.A., a super rare Jumeau in all-original clothing.

The girl Bru was dressed in satin brocade with lace around her neck, at the elbow, and down the front. The dress train was of the same fabric. She wore an exquisite solid gold bracelet that appeared to be tied in a loose knot. She had long white kid gloves and car-ried a bouquet. Her Bru shoes were pointed and had rosettes.

Her elaborately designed coiffure was encircled with a wreath of tiny blossoms. Her eyes were blue. His hair was reddish brown and sort of tou-sled. I can't remember the color of his eyes.

The bodies on these dolls were a bit unusual. They were kid-over-wood bodies and wooden legs and feet. She had bisque hands.

These dolls were the kind a collector dreams about finding. They were magnificent. We would have gone without eating for a week, consider giving a left hand each, giving up our car—well almost anything—for those dolls. There was no way we could come up with $19,000, no way. Our ceramic and doll business was not that good.

We felt this and talked about the dolls for months. I had better correct that last sentence —you can see we're still thinking and talking about them. The dolls were originally from the wonderful collection of Raymond and Hazel Knapp. (They were the people who had five A Marque dolls at one time.)

We saw Grace Dyer once in a while at shows. The Brus were sold to a California couple. Grace had told them, that at anytime, if they didn't want the dolls, they were to sell them back to her. I believe it was 1988 when they came back to Grace. At the United Federation of Doll Clubs Anaheim Convention, Richard Wright had the dolls on exhibit and had already sold them. I am sure they were many, many times $19,000 now. The dolls didn't quite look the same. This pair of exquisite roses were not meant to be ours.

Corning

Doll lovers everywhere become intrigued with the intrinsic beauty of the antique French doll's eyes. How could there be such depth, such rich shades of blue, of brown, and the soft, simple appeal of grey. The eyes of these dolls, these Brus, these Jumeaus, are like small things that touch us and remain life friends.

I was more than intrigued. I saw the yawning holes in our reproduction heads and longed to fill them with glass—glass paperweight eyes like the antique ones. The eyes are the personality of the doll.

I was at that stage where I must find a solution to the eye problem. Vernon and I decided to go to Corning, New York, the glassmakers. We sat as close as possible to the art glassmakers. They blew in tubes and red hot glass flowed like melting butter. We watched them shape and turn and heat again. We were so star struck by the whole process, we sat for hours frozen in one position.

I told earlier about Schoepfer in New York City who had started making eyes at a very early age. This was the same process, the same hot, molten fragile affair, right before our eyes.

As the men turned down their furnaces, laid down their blowers, and inspected their morning's masterpieces, we coaxed our hungry stomachs to leave.

Vernon, always on top of our doll project, asked the office girl if she knew anyone in the area with dolls. She did. The woman's husband had worked his lifetime for Corning, but he had died a few months ago. She gave us a phone number.

We found a place to eat our carried lunch. (We were always economizing. Then too, we both loved picnics.) At lunch we decided we couldn't come up with glass eyes for dolls since the process was too complicated and these glass blowers weren't in a position to make eyes for us.

Early afternoon we hunted up Margaret Knowlton whose number the office girl had given us. She had dolls. She lived in a new house built after the big flood hit Corning and central New York State. She had big glass cases across one end of her living room filled with dolls, stuffed with dolls. Her home was filled with priceless antiques, a grandfather clock, a huge cherry table—everything was older than her 83 years.

It turned out that we already knew her, she had been in ceramics and had been a customer of ours. She was a collector. She collected buttons. There were frames and frames of military, of glass, of cloisonne', every type, and age of button. There were large paperweight buttons used on show horse halters. She collected toys, tiny silver pieces, tiny and large old carriages, doll stoves. The house was a museum.

At this point in time with things not yet settled from her husband's death, she explained that she needed money and would like to sell us some dolls.

She had a complete set of dollhouse dolls. She had some big baby dolls. There was a K*R 114. We bought, more or less, what she offered us and what we had enough money for. I fell in love with an iron stove and a tiny old telephone. She said both were a salesman's sample. This little old telephone with a hanging receiver was mailed to me a year later.

Jay has the iron stove now and is wishing for the telephone.

We used up all our time and money and decided to stay all night in Corning. We took Mrs. Knowlton out to dinner. She had not been out to dinner in many years. It did me more good than her to see her enjoy it so much. We became good friends, talking back and forth on the phone.

Several times we went to Corning to buy a few more of her dolls. She sold me the big Corning globe that holds my 29" Long Face Jumeau. She died a few years later when we were in Arizona. We could never find out what happened to the rest of her dolls and her wonderful antiques.

It is doll people like Mrs. Margaret Knowlton who keep this doll world such a happy place.

Dr. Iob

I was standing in line for the banquet at a United Federation of Doll Clubs convention in Florida. We were discussing places for retirement. We mentioned Green Valley, Arizona. A woman just ahead of us turned around and said she was retiring to Green Valley too. This was Dr. Vivian Iob. She got to Green Valley a year or so before we did. She had bought a house with her brother and his wife. We became great doll friends. She dressed old dolls for me, and I fired dolls for her. We took her with us to

auctions, seminars and conventions. She had been a medical researcher working under grants at Michigan State University.

Her researching mind was great in the doll world. She often criticized my books for lack of research and would come up with some little bit of vital information. She was an admirer of doll underclothing. She appreciated every hand stitch. She made underclothing for several of my dolls, copying the old split drawers and even making tatting to put around the arm holes and neck. Cancer got her.

I was sad when the bank called me to go appraise her doll collection. She made sure I had her little wax doll with the inset hair. She had never had it out of its original box—Hamley's, 612 Oxford St. 1881—it was still tied in. I also got her china fortune teller and her little Jumeau. I look at them and think of Vivian.

Gaynell's Museum

From the time I bought the boy Marque doll, I had an ongoing thing with Gaynell Densen from North Carolina. She built her house and bought dolls as she graduated from college in the '30s. She purchased dolls directly from France.

I liked her collection and bought her French children dolls one after another, whenever I could afford one. Her prices were high, but the dolls were good. Most of the dolls were in their original clothing

K*R 114, Margaret Knowlton's pride and joy.

The wood Kubelka's from Gaynell's museum.

and had never been touched since she put them in her little museum. I also bought her mechanicals and Vernon bought some.

This year (1991) she decided to sell her home and move. She had a sizable collection of French Fashions she wanted to sell. Vernon and I bought them. These dolls had not been cleaned, or messed with, since the '30s. Their hair fashions and hats were untouched. Their gowns, here and there, had gotten wet from a leaking roof, but the dolls were great.

My wonderful doll friend Gaynell died of a heart attack in December 1992. She left me a huge box of old silks, lace and other materials for dressing dolls.

Country Kitchen

Not all collecting trips turn out roses. The one I want to tell you about did not turn out roses, not jewels, but more like mud clods or grey rocks. Only an amateur collector, a naive collector, a collector who had not studied, could have gotten involved in this one. It was me. I was just starting.

I said before that we tracked down every doll that we heard about. Vernon had to take a day off from work for us to make the trip. The lady who had some dolls was an unknown doll dealer on the far edge of the Adirondacks.

We got lost twice. We finally located the dirt road and the little old house, not much more than a shack. Vernon and I had the same idea, we looked at each other. This certainly wasn't the place to find dolls, certainly not Brus.

The darling little woodsy blend of a woman swung open the door to her kitchen and made us welcome. There was a fire in the old wood stove. Breakfast dishes, perhaps even breakfast dishes from the day before, were stacked on the edge of the iron sink. The oil cloth covered kitchen table stood nearly covered with a disorderly pile of papers and magazines. The broom and dust pan partly filled with dirt leaned against the table leg. The tri-colored mamma cat was nursing two kittens on a piece of rug.

She was expecting us. I had sent her a note.

"The dolls are in the little bedroom." She led us to the other side of the house. Inside the living room door, on a well-marred drop leaf cherry table stood a globe.

I couldn't believe my eyes. Here was a 16" Bru in what appeared to be mint condition. I wanted to wipe the dust off, so I could see better. "I would like to buy this one." "Oh, that one is not for sale. This is my special doll, and I intend to keep her until I die. No amount of money could buy her."

We went into a tiny bedroom with a cot against the wall. The bed was covered with dolls. They were all for sale and had price tags on them. These were all small fashion dolls. This is what we came to see. We had hoped to buy our first French Fashion.

We studied the dolls over in the half-light from the small curtained window. They were marked F.G. mostly, and one marked Bru. We were not overly impressed, even in this tender shadow, with the dolls. But we decided to take the Bru and two F.G.s.

The price was very reasonable. She assured us they were good dolls. The price was low, because she had to sell them. At this date, good Brus were selling at auction for $400 to $600. These were only $200 to $250, which is like $2,000-$3,000 in today's money.

We took the dolls home. Their leather bodies were well made and in excellent condition. They looked almost too good. The wigs were horrible and glued on ever so tightly. I had a feeling these dolls had a problem.

Several months later I was at a doll show. Gladys Hillsdorf, a well-known collector and dealer of New York State had a table full of dolls, which I was studying over. Here on the table was a Bru lady doll exactly like the one I had purchased from the Adirondacks lady. There were more, several more, similar dolls.

Gladys was a friend. She knew everything there was to know about dolls. Gladys said "Come here and sit down. I'll tell you all about these dolls."

"The New York City Doll Hospital had purchased a large shipment of these dolls from France. They called me and asked me how many I would like. I bought 40 from them. I

thought they would make a less expensive doll I could sell along with my good dolls. I was told that they were reproductions made by a woman and her son in France. I always tell everyone when they buy them that they are reproductions. Just like I do when I sell one of your reproduction googlies." (She had bought a few reproduction dolls from me.) "But how did I get three from the little old lady in the Adirondacks," I asked.

"That's easy, I sold them to her, and she knew the story just as I have told you. She promised to sell them as reproductions. That little old lady has been selling dolls for 30 years. She knows all about dolls, she just saw how green you were and took advantage of you."

This was a good lesson for me, but a hard and expensive one. I still have one of these dolls in a box of other doll junk in the closet. I only look at it when I clean the closet as a reminder. Some things I learn the hard way.

I have gotten this doll out and shown many a new collector, so they will not make the mistake I did. These French reproductions dolls are still around and still sold from one stupid collector to another for the real thing.

Upon close inspection you can tell that fine leather bodies had been antiqued with a little tea. Under the awful wig was not a cork pate but some cardboard. Inside the head was a piece of French newspaper dated 1940. The bisque itself was not the smooth pale, rose tint. It was more of a cream. The painting was good. On the back where it should say F5G, it would only say F.G. as the number would tell the size it should be. On the Bru, it was marked Bru with no size number.

Hawaiian Jumeau

I was busy autographing books at the Anaheim Convention Center. I had several people waiting. I glanced up after signing a book, "For the Love of Dolls" as I usually do. There was a young beautiful woman with long blond hair standing off to the side. She had a large paper shopping bag. I noted that she stepped back and let two other women go in front of her.

It was late in the afternoon and people were pretty well cleared out. The blond lady came to my table and cautiously set the bag down beside her. "I have a doll that I would like to have you look at," she said. "A lady at the entrance said you would be the one who knows all about old dolls."

I asked her to come around and sit in the chair next to me so I could look at what she had. I looked into the shopping bag. Here was a doll, on its head, her feet sticking up, with no wrapping—no packing of any kind.

I lifted the doll out—it's a Jumeau I told her. The doll measured about 24". It had its original almond-colored wig. The doll's beauty dramatically unfolded as I pushed back her hair and straightened her yel-low silk dress. "This is a good French doll," I told her.

"I am not interested in dolls, or doll collecting. I just want to sell this doll for all I can get. My husband has financial problems in Hawaii. I am selling what I can and going back to Hawaii. No, I did not know it was a French doll or what it was. I really wasn't interested. How much can I get for the doll? Will you buy it?"

I liked the doll, love at first sight. I asked her about the doll shoes. "She had shoes, but I don't know where they went," she said. I examined the doll to see the condition. It was an unplayed-with doll in original dress, underclothing and wig. My mind was dancing. Then I turned the doll over and looked at the back of the head. There was a single crack from the top of the crown down.

I showed the young lady. "I probably did that when I was taking her out of the trunk of the car. I was in a hurry and whammed it against the lock. You can't imagine the trouble I had bringing this doll into the convention hall."

My rose-colored afternoon faded to a dull grey. I looked into the girl's face. I could see her urgency and almost dislike for the doll. I said I will buy the doll and offered more dollars than the cracked doll was worth. I thought I could make a mold of it, even if it was cracked. I wrote her a check for $2,000. The girl's expression changed. It was obvious that I offered her much more than she had expected.

Then I asked her where she got the doll.

"This doll was given to my great-great grandmother for her tenth Christmas. She gave the doll to my great grandmother. My mother had it last and she gave the doll to me when I was 18. I never had an interest in the doll. I'm sure my mother never knew what the doll was or how much it was worth. I didn't; I had expected $50 or $60."

It is part of me to urge people to keep heirlooms, to keep family dolls, and I started to "preach" to her. She didn't look at me. She was digging down into her purse. She brought out a picture, "Here's a family picture taken at my wedding. Here is the original owner of the doll, the next owner, all the way down to me. Here, you can have the picture. I don't want it."

I feel bad when I look at the doll, at the picture. I like to see people hold onto their heritage. Once in a while I tell people about the Hawaiian Jumeau. She stands in my case with the picture of her family behind her.

Makeovers

We were at a United Federation of Doll Clubs convention. I spied a doll that was different—that would make a great mold. Vernon looked, he liked her. The price was way too high, as it often is at conventions. The doll was an 18" Tynie Babe with red hair on a toddler-type body.

The more we looked at this

doll, the more we wanted it for a mold. We bought it. When we got home from the convention, we soaked off the tightly glued on hair—here was a baby head —Tynie Babe. Tynie Babe in this large size is indeed rare, but we felt for a while we had been taken. (Usually I name the dealer when something like this happens.) We did like the doll so well with her red hair and toddler body, we put her back the same way. We made a mold and sold her as "Little Grump." We loved her as "Little Grump." Jay has her now. She had always been on his list.

Things of this sort sometimes happen with over-anxious buyers of dolls, like us. We had really just gotten underway with our mold business when we found the head of a doll baby in an antique shop. It resembled the Bye-Lo baby except the corners of the mouth were turned down and there were tears on the cheeks. The eyes were a little wider than the usual Bye-Lo also. We studied the doll. There was no identification or markings. We could not find the doll in any book. There was never any mention of a crying Bye-Lo, but we had one. We made a mold of this doll. It has been a best seller since the '60s. Yet no one knows from where or from whom she came.

Baby Stuart

Vernon and I had a system for making the first mold from the antique doll. I would study the undercuts, fill in around the

Above: Tynie Babe with wig and without (below).

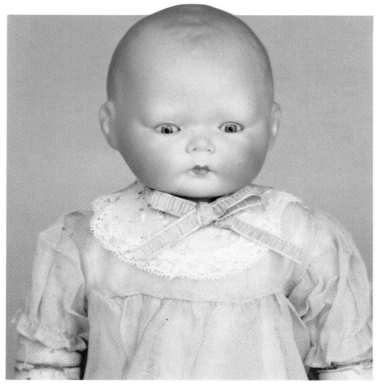

171

The Baby Hilda whose photo we used on a plate.

eyes, and mark the mold lines. I marked Baby Stuart much the same as I had been doing.

We had bought the doll for the purpose of making a mold. Vernon set the doll and poured the plaster. We couldn't get it out. We saw our money going down the drain as we pried, and it came out in pieces.

Being the kind of person I am, I studied all the little pieces. It should have been a three-piece mold. I had missed the line going down the back. Some things I learn the hard way. This was the first doll mold I had ever seen with more than two pieces to the mold. Later, when we did the mold of the Marque doll, we found that we had a five-piece mold.

The biggest problem with doll mold making is what we have labelled "delayed cracking."

We have a few dolls that this has happened to. There is both stress and heat put on the doll with the plaster. It sometimes takes months (one doll it was a year later) before we found a crack.

This cracking was from the mold making, but was not apparent until sometime later. Now we know and when we make a mold of these great old French dolls, we have to think about it. We have to take a chance or make a choice not to make a mold. Nothing in the doll world comes easy or without risk.

Hilda Baby

About 18 years ago, when we first had a home in Arizona, I

met Elsie Ray at an antique show. She said she had dolls for sale and that we should come and see her.

We didn't go to Elsie's but one day she called us and wanted us to come to see a Hilda she had.

We searched the back streets of Tucson for her address. If you know Tucson with its hundreds of tiny four-room houses, you know what we were looking for.

Elsie greeted us. She was in a large flowery nightgown and slippers. She always wore slippers. Her weight and age made it difficult to get anything else on. Her beloved beagle greeted us too. He was also in his nightshirt. He wore a dirty T-shirt, dragging it under his too-fat tummy. Elsie remarked that his shirt was dirty, but he just couldn't be without it. He had worn the shirt since he was a puppy.

She brought out the Hilda Baby. It was a large beautiful one with molded hair. We told her yes, we would buy it. Did she have any other dolls for sale? She said Ralph Griffith had pretty well gone thru all the other dolls and culled out the good ones.

She had just gotten the Hilda. She opened the door to what could have been a small bedroom. It was packed and stuffed with boxes. The floor was covered with boxes and clothes baskets full of newish plastic dolls, partly dressed and undressed dolls with hair standing on end.

Each box she pulled off an-

Boots Tyner presents me with her *Mil Seeley* doll. Boots produced a mold from this doll and people all over the world make her.

other was worse than the one before. "All filled with junk and stuff," she said. "I got more in the kitchen." There was no order anywhere, just stuff piled. There were dishes in the sink but otherwise there was nothing that looked like food preparation.

"I don't like cooking anymore," she said, "I go down to the restaurant. I love pancakes at Carrows." It was obvious she loved pancakes and maple syrup.

We visited Elsie several times over the years. The last time we were back, Elsie wasn't in very good health. Her beloved beagle had died and she had gotten a pair of puppies. This was more than the house could stand, everything seemed to be in shreds. Everything was covered with shredded paper and toys—everything. They had

completely taken over. I feel they were more than the elderly Elsie had planned on.

Several years after Elsie died all her dolls were brought to me to appraise. This always makes me sad. I still feel we should be allowed to take the dolls with us when we go.

Boots Tyner's Mil Seeley

Boots gave me a call. We were living in Green Valley on Vista del Rio then.

When she came she had a portrait doll of me at the age of five to five-and-a-half. She did not just have a portrait, she had the whole of me, the hair-do, the shoes, even the dress my mother had made for me—all were perfect copies.

The following morning my sister came in. The doll was sitting on the table. "Someone made a portrait of you—the

Above: Me at 5 wearing a dress my mother had made for me. Right: Boot's portrait doll of me wearing a copy of the dress.

doll even stands like you." This was her comment without even knowing it was supposed to be me.

This was one of the wonderful little dolls in Boots Tyner's series of small children dolls done from real children. I gave her permission to sell the mold, which she did. People all over the world use the mold of Mil Seeley.

The doll is a favorite of mine. It does look very much as I did at that age. Darlene Lane reproduced one for Colleen. When she opened it at work, her friends said how much it looked like her.

The Milettes

I was always coming up with projects for selling doll molds, even after we no longer owned the business. For a couple of years I had the idea to offer molds of dolls that were all the same size. Each would fit the same body, take the same size clothes, wigs, etc. It would make a great studio project and a great home dollmaker project. I couldn't convince Rolf Ericson.

The Milettes—small French dolls used for the book *Project-Milettes*.

PAN doll made by Henri Delcroix.

I hunted for small French dolls all about the same size. These are not easy to come up with, especially when you live in the Arizona desert.

I finally convinced Rolf it would be a good money-making project. I would write the whole project up for him and write a book to go along with the project.

I got the work underway—the molds, body molds, the writing of the book was started. I still needed more dolls. I had contacted a few dealers.

One evening when I returned, there was a message on a pad by the telephone, "Tell Mil I've found another Milette." The dealer had named my next book—*Project Milettes*. I had been searching for a title that could work. Now dollmakers use the word Milettes, as though it were in the dictionary, to mean small French dolls.

The project and the book were a tremendous success for the Ericsons. Both the book and the Milette molds are still selling. *Project Milettes* now has been reprinted by Scott Publications.

These little French dolls stand in my cabinet. I still love these little ones. I could make a whole collection of French dolls under 12" if I could find them.

The PAN

Again, after we were in our exquisite doll house, Shandele,' I had an occasion to purchase a rare, extremely expensive doll—The PAN. Vera Kramer had brought her doll museum from England to Florida. She had not counted on the damp, moldy Florida weather, and the lack of people interested in nursery rhyme set ups.

She wanted to sell out the dolls. She said I could buy the PAN for $44,000. She guaranteed it to be the only one in existence. She owned it since 1929 and had never seen another. We had never seen one!

Now I knew I was becoming senile. Why did I even consider purchasing this doll? Anyway, she would not ship it. We would have to come to Florida to pick it up. I knew I could sell a mold of the head. I knew I could use it in a book, but would it ever come up to that value in an auction if I had to sell it?

We decided yes. I was never a gambler. The only thing I ever gambled on was dolls. Vernon and I went to get it. The doll was given the publicity to sell the mold. Within two years, the dolls by Henri Delcroix were coming out of the woodwork. Other PANs showed up at auctions. We now have five of his dolls in our collection. We like the PAN, she is great in my collection.

Portrait Jumeau

One day there was an auction book from Christie's in New York City. They had two Jumeaus in original clothing. I wanted them so badly I placed a bid much higher than they were worth. I was mad when I didn't get them.

Less than two weeks later, two Jumeaus (about the same size) came my way. These Jumeaus were portraits; Christie's dolls had been just Tetes. I realized then it was the not the Jumeaus, but the costumes I wanted so badly.

The next month, the cover of *Dolls* magazine had the two Christie Jumeaus. I took the cover and my two portrait Jumeaus to my dressmaker Jacke Jones. She copied the dresses for me. She made the most perfectly copied hats out of old straw you could imagine.

I just love the antique clothing on dolls. It thrills me to get a doll in antique clothing. I even love the old underwear and especially the shoes.

Auction Fever

The psychiatrist and her husband were coming out of the hotel at the same time we were. They were standing, looking, trying to decide if they could get a cab. We picked them up. We had never met either of them but had seen them at numerous doll auctions.

We didn't know them any better after we let them out at the auction door. I do believe they said they were horse collectors rather than doll collectors.

I was studying thru the dolls to be auctioned. To my right was the psychiatrist and her husband checking out one of the little French dolls I wanted to look at. I couldn't help overhearing their conversation.

"She is just perfect. I just love her. This is the only doll I want. She is in Coleman's first book."

"Don't pay more than

$3,000," her husband said, "I mean it, no more than $3,000. I don't really like the doll."

"But I work hard for our money, and this is something I really want. I won't be happy unless I get her," the psychiatrist mumbled.

I passed around the couple still looking at the doll, intending to come back later to inspect her.

The doll came up. "Perfect little French doll in original clothes, catalog number 26," the auctioneer said. Hands and number cards were in the air, everyone wanted her, bids started low. My card was up too. I wanted her.

In only seconds the auctioneer said, "Sold. $3,500 to number 201." The psychiatrist's husband got up, slammed his auction book down, and in a temper tantrum, left the auction room—red faced and angry.

No one paid any attention. Just a bit later the psychiatrist got up and left. Half-an-hour or so later, Vernon went out to get us some coffee. She was sitting in the hallway, crying her eyes out. Vernon, wanting to help, went and talked to her.

"My husband is so mad; he has left me. He may have gone home to California and left me here. He is mad because I went $500 over the $3,000 he said I could bid on the doll. He is so mad," she sobbed. "It was the only doll in the whole auction I liked. I really loved that little doll. I really wanted it," she daubed her eyes with a wet Kleenex. "I wanted the doll no matter the cost."

Vernon said, "The auctioneer will probably take the doll back and resell it. I am sure they will. Ask them."

"I don't really want to, but I will", she said. Sometime later we saw her back at the recording table. No. It was against their policy to take back a doll unless there was something seriously wrong with it. No. They couldn't take it back.

The woman went weeping out into the hall again. Two hours or so later when Vernon went out in the hall, there was the woman still crying.

"My wife likes the doll. She will pay whatever you bid for the doll. She was bidding on it. Will that make you feel better?" Vernon asked.

"Maybe I can get the doll from your wife some time later?" she asked, still clinging to the doll. Vernon assured her she could.

Vernon came in and told me what he had done. I did like the doll, but I had only planned on paying $3,000 for it. My enthusiasm for the doll sort of flickered and went out. I didn't want to get Vernon into trouble, so I said I would take it.

At lunch time the psychiatrist was still crying. It was as if she had given up her only child.

Late in the afternoon, just before the auction's end, the red-eyed lady and her husband came back into the auction together. He was smiling.

I explained to the recorder, paid the bill, and picked up the little French doll in all-original clothing. I closely looked at the doll's face for the first time. Both eyes turned in.

It was at that moment I realized why the very cross-eyed psychiatrist had fallen in love with that particular doll —why it was the only doll in the auction she really liked or wanted.

Lost Concentration

The auctioneer, in his loud, monotonous sing song chant, said, "32-5, 32-5. Do I hear 32-5? Going once, going twice." The gavel came down. "Sold to Mil Seeley for $32,000."

Richard stood up immediately, "I was not done bidding," he said. He then went down the narrow aisle thru the anxious crowd to the podium.

The auction room was jammed. People stood in the back and the hall. This was the doll, the prize of the day. Everyone wanted it or wanted to see what it would go for. "But," Richard started.

Theriault, not wanting to break up the auction, quickly thought of a way out. "Go buy it from Mil," he said.

Richard, leaning over the shoulders of several irritated people from three rows in front, tried to explain to me that he needed that doll.

I had carefully chosen the doll and really wanted her. I had planned on getting her. I had saved for her. It was a beautiful 16" A.T. made by Andre Jean Thuillier in the early 1880s. It had bisque hands, a leather body and wore her original clothes.

Tiffany, the A.T. from Iowa. She is on a leather body with bisque hands—just 14''. Her dress came from her trunk of clothes and I made the mohair wig.

I said to Richard, "I'll think about it." He went back to his seat. Later, as the auction was breaking up, he asked again.

Sometime after the auction I went looking for Richard and found him in the bar. He was still feeling bad. "I had already sold that doll," Richard said. I could see that people as pleasant as Richard sometimes get upset with the way things go.

"What were you going to bid the doll up to?" he asked. I opened my catalog and showed him that I had marked it for $40,000. "I would have gone the same amount," Richard added.

I could see Richard's predicament. Richard is a world-known reliable doll dealer. I had bought dolls from him and also from his mother some 30 years earlier.

"You can have the doll, as you need it worse than I do," I said crying inside at my loss. "Go pay Theriaults and give me a check for another bid."

The next morning's auction was underway. Vernon and I were only going to stay an hour or so, then catch our plane for home. Richard came in and sat in the row ahead of us.

"Did you get the doll?" I asked. "Yes," he said. "She is gorgeous, absolutely gorgeous."

"I have to leave to catch my plane and you haven't given me a check," I said. Richard dug out his checkbook, "Here. Put whatever you want on the check," and he handed me his checkbook. Vernon said, "Don't do it. Make him write the check."

I handed him back the checkbook. He wrote me a check, a check for $8,000! I could have dropped dead. I had expected $500 to $1,000, which would have been the next bid. Instead, he gave me my maximum bid!

Little Treasure in a Trunk

The way these doll things unfold is more exciting than a mystery novel. Even though this same type of thing has been going on for 40 years, the thrill of acquiring something sends me with happiness. This time it is something very special, an unmarked A.T. (maybe).

Today is Thursday, October 24, 1991. It was Wednesday that I had a phone call from Dorothy Buyers in Iowa. She had written Seeley's in Oneonta, New York, for our phone number. They had written us, and Vernon had sent out a note.

She had recently completed a doll appraisal for Agnes Parcell of Fairfield, Iowa. Agnes had taken her to the bank to check out a little doll that she had kept there for many years. Agnes had had the doll for 40 years.

She wanted to know if I was interested in buying the doll. Well, I just got back from Theriault's auction and spent all my money on an E.J.A. (This is what happens when you have no money—dolls appear like magic, always the best dolls.)

She described the doll as 16" and with a trunk. The price was very high. I called the owner, Agnes Parcell, who had a bro-

ken leg. I had gone thru the broken leg thing myself not too long ago.

She told me how she and her husband had a neighborhood store that carried everything, just like Dad's store. She said, "Even black stove polish." She had a few dolls on exhibit in the store and an elderly woman came in and said that she had one since childhood. Did she want it? Now Agnes was young and put this doll on exhibit too.

The two women, Agnes and Dorothy, compared the face to pictures in my books and decided it must be an A.T.

Agnes borrowed a new *Blue Book* and gave me the top price listed for an A.T. She wouldn't budge an inch. I finally said I would buy the doll, thinking it would take almost all of my big certificate of deposit that was due tomorrow. The next question was how could I get the doll? There is no way of insuring a doll that valuable by any form of delivery. How would she get the doll to me and get her money?

Dorothy Byers has a son in Tucson, so she said she would fly the doll and the trunk out. How this will all work out, we will see tomorrow. I have a cashiers check for $45,000 waiting. Dorothy will come in at 1:30 tomorrow with the doll and trunk. I will wear my light blue dress that is splashed with roses.

I filled the house with roses in jubilant anticipation. The woman came with the doll and trunk. She stayed all night and left the next morning.

Vernon was more let down than I was. There were numerous things on the doll that did not agree with the telephone description. It was the highest price I had ever paid for a doll. The trunk that was supposed to be so great is just a metal trunk. The doll's wig had been replaced. Her old satin dress was rayon and made in the 1930s. The doll was 14" not 16". The body was rough and discolored. Almost all roses have a few thorns.

I looked at the doll. I knew in a moment she was a very early A.T. Her angelic face, her blue, blue eyes melted me. She was as warm as a holiday hug. Her played-with leather body was heart warming. Her head and shoulder-plate with the glue and leather removed read A.T. 4. She looked a lot like Silver, our Baby Doe Taber A.T. We will call her Tiffany.

Tiffany is part of my collection and a part of me. This gentle doll goes beyond the painter or the poet. She colors my whole collection roses. She throws a tender shadow over the other French dolls.

The doll has a story. She came in the trunk and was given to Edith Synder in 1882. Edith was five years old at that time. The doll was given to her by her Aunt Ester (Harland). (The card that came with her is still in the trunk.) United States Senator Harland had been to Paris numerous times. He was co-owner of the Washington D.C. *Post*. After his senate term, he became the president of Iowa's Wesleyan College.

Me at home in my rose garden.

Abe Lincoln's son Robert married Harland's daughter and lived in Mt. Pleasant, Iowa, for some time. There was a Synder jewelry store in Fairfield, Iowa, for more than 60 years. Henry Synder, brother of Edith Synder, ran the store after his father died. Oscar Synder was Edith Synder's father. He was the first child born in the town precinct at Mt. Pleasant in 1839. Edith Synder, the owner of the doll, never married.

Now, Leonard and Agnes Parcell owned a neighborhood store in the same vicinity as the home of Edith Synder. She did her grocery shopping in their store. She was a frail little woman in her mid 80s. Leonard Parcell always helped her with her groceries and took special pains to see that she got everything she needed.

Agnes had some of her doll collection on exhibit in the store. One day, Edith asked Agnes if she would like to have her doll. Shortly after, Edith came back with the trunk that I now have. The doll was in it. Edith liked the doll and put it on exhibit in the store with the other dolls. But first she had a dress made for it of blue rayon. At the same time, the dresser put on a new blond wig.

Mrs. Agnes Parcell had the collection photographed and written up in the Fairfield paper in 1968. At that time, she still thought the doll must be a Jumeau. They wrote it up as being her most valuable doll.

Some years later, a dealer told her that it was a valuable doll. After they had a break-in she decided to put the doll in the bank vault. (It turned out she was very valuable. She was like a certificate of deposit earning 20 percent interest for 40 years.) Agnes never really had a chance to enjoy the doll.

Not until I got the doll and called her was she absolutely sure the doll was an A.T. She had never turned down the leather on her shoulder or unglued the wig on the back of the neck.

End
February 1992

My book ends. I have written enough. Anyone who has read this far can see dolls, doll people, roses, flower gardens, and a loving husband and children were the components of a satisfying life—even with its hardships, accidents and illnesses.

I was crossing the parking lot at Anaheim, California. The doll convention was opening the next morning. A very child-like voice somewhere behind me was calling, "Mommy, Mommy, Mommy." I turned with the thought of rescuing a child.

Here comes Pam Lembo from Connecticut, full of fun as usual, calling, "I want my Doll Mommy." Pam is one of my lifetime doll children.

This book is the story of the joys and stumbles of the "Doll Mommy." Any book is a wonderful or worthless thing, depending on whether the reader learns something, enjoys an hour, gets a few duck bumps, or has a hearty laugh or two.

For the love of dolls and roses.

Dedication to Vernon, My Love

Vernon died of lymphoma, cancer of the lymph nodes, on September 24, 1992.

They speak of "bonding" between a mother and newborn, but bonding between a husband and wife—Vern and me—was much stronger. Having loved and admired each other for over 50 years, we were bonded—one body, one soul.

We counted on each other for everything. We depended on each other for moral and physical support. He took care of my big problems and my little ones. He was my consultant, my protector. We lived in a hermetically sealed world. I had no need of anything he couldn't provide. Our 50-year romance was still as fresh and loved-packed as our honeymoon years.

Through these years came new vistas, new ideas, new horizons. Our views and hopes focused on the same star with one mind, one heart.

He was the children's hero. He offered love, patience, wisdom, strength and teaching. They were always proud to say, "My Dad."

Disillusioned that the golden years were cut short and from the abyss of despair, I try to yank myself around and shine as he would wish. Other times, as pain slices through me, I cannot repress the bitter taste of

Vernon, my love.

tears. What seemed like a permanent, healthy graft had been killed by the storm of cancer; only one branch, lame and broken, is left twisting in the wind.

This book, encouraged and typed by Vernon, was completed about February, 1992.